UNIVERSITY OF SOUTHAMPTON DEPARTMENT OF ARCHAEOL

CW00631354

SIGATOKA

The Shifting Sands of Fijian Prehistory

Yvonne Marshall, Andrew Crosby,
Sepeti Matararaba and Shannon Wood

Oxbow Books
2000

Southampton University Department of Archaeology Monographs are published by
Oxbow Books, Park End Place, Oxford OX1 1HN

ISBN 1 84217 011 2

A CIP record for this book is available from The British Library.

This book is available direct from

Oxbow Books, Park End Place, Oxford OX1 1HN
(Phone: 01865–241249; Fax: 01865–794449)

and

The David Brown Book Company
PO Box 511, Oakville, CT 06779, USA
(Phone: 860–945–9329; Fax: 860–945–9468)

or from our website

www.oxbowbooks.com

Cover photo: Simon Best during excavations of Burial Ground 1, 1988. Best is shown photographing Burial B16, a young woman in her early 20s who was buried with a large pot over her head. In the background is Burial B15, a child 4–5 years of age, and rising in the foreground are the leg bones of Burial B17a, a young woman in her late 20s.

Printed in Great Britain at
The Short Run Press
Exeter

Contents

Acknowledgements

The fieldwork reported here has been conducted by the authors over several periods between 1991 and 1997 and was achieved with the co-operation and support of a large number of organisations and individuals. Principal among these are the Fiji Museum, the New Zealand High Commission (Suva), the National Trust of Fiji, the University of Auckland and the University of Southampton.

We are grateful to Rishi Ram and Kiti Makasiale (Permanent Secretary and First Assistant Secretary of the Ministry for Women and Culture) for their enthusiastic efforts in raising the public profile of the Sigatoka Dunes and for actively supporting the various archaeological projects. We also thank Ratu Inoke Kedralevu (Roko Tui Nadroga) for graciously blessing the archaeology and providing an invaluable liaison with the local Nadroga community. Birandra Singh (National Trust of Fiji), Chris Work (Kulukulu Village), John Kobbe and Marcus Oliver (both of Club Masa) all kindly allowed access onto the various land holdings on which the sand dunes lie.

Many organisations have provided funding for the work reported here. The 1991 excavation of burials on the dunes was funded by the Fiji Museum. The 1992 survey was funded by a grant from the New Zealand High Commission, Suva. Further field assistance was provided by the Fiji Museum. Marshall's 1993 survey and test excavations behind the dunes were supported by grants from the Green Foundation and the University of Auckland Research Committee. Crosby's walkover survey in August 1993 was partly funded by Auckland Uniservices. Crosby and Marshall's walkover survey in November 1997 was supported by a grant from the Faculty of Arts, University of Southampton. The preparation of this report has been funded in part by the Department of Archaeology, University of Southampton and in part by a grant from the School of Research and Graduate Studies, University of Southampton.

This volume owes a great debt to the contributions of other archaeological researchers at the Sigatoka Sand Dunes. We are particularly grateful to Simon Best (Auckland), Elizabeth Pascell (University of Auckland), Christine Burke (Fiji Museum) and David Burley (Simon Fraser University) for providing copies of their reports and field notes and for sharing their insights and expertise on Fijian archaeology. We are also grateful to Patrick Nunn (University of the South Pacific), Alf Simpson (Department of Lands) and Michael Shepherd (Massey University) for their expert advice on Fijian geomorphology.

Finally, we are greatly indebted to the services and support of the many individuals who gave freely of their time, advice and encouragement to ensure the success of the various field projects. Joji Chongsu (Kulukulu), Farhaz Khan and Vicky Luker (Suva), Vasiti Ritova (Drauniivi), Sue Loughlin (Wellington) and Patrick Hunkler helped with the fieldwork. Stefan Cabaniuk (Native Land Trust Board) has resolutely supported all of our archaeological efforts, assisted us in the field and has been an effective advocate for the preservation of the Sigatoka Dunes. Antoine de Biran (formerly National Trust of Fiji) generously contributed valuable aerial photographs and historical documents and has kept us informed of his own work on the dunes. Richard Shutler kindly provided copies of photographs taken during the Birks excavations. Roger Green provided copies of further photographs and he and Doug Sutton (both of the University of Auckland) have provided constant support. This support was instrumental in helping to raise money for work at the dunes. Dilys Johns (University of Auckland) advised on the conservation and removal of bone materials.

Kathryn Knowles and Penny Coupland (University of Southampton) drafted the illustrations apart from the survey maps and Figure 3.1 which were drafted by Shannon Wood. We also thank Andy Vowles (University of Southampton) for his advice on photographs and the care with which he processed both photographs and figure reproductions.

For their generous comments on our earlier report, (Wood, Marshall and Crosby 1998), and on drafts of this book, we thank Atholl Anderson, Simon Best, David Burley, Bill Dickinson, Roger Green and Chris Gosden.

Chapter 1
The power of a picture

Introduction

Fiji is a tiny nation of islands surrounded by the vast waters of the western Pacific Ocean (Fig. 1.1). Significance in this maritime location is not measured by landmass. Rather it is a question of strategic position. Fiji marks the traditional divide between Melanesian and Polynesian cultures and is understood to be the route by which Polynesia was originally colonised from the west, some three thousand years ago. Although people from the west subsequently reached Fiji's shores on several more occasions, these newcomers never ventured further east. Thus Fiji is thought to have formed, first, a portal for Polynesia's colonisation, and then a frontier across which Polynesia was never again colonised until European settlers arrived in the 19th century. Fiji's location at the doorstep to Polynesia has given it a curious inbetween-ness. Physically, culturally and linguistically Fijians have always been characterised as half Polynesian, half Melanesian: an early offshoot from the ancestral Polynesian community that was then "Melanesianised" by new migrants from the west (Hale 1846; Howells 1973; Pawley 1972; Clark 1979; Serjeantson and Hill 1989:288–9).

Because of this shift in Fiji's strategic role, from portal to frontier, Polynesia has famously earned a reputation as a unique 'laboratory' for the study of evolutionary radiation from a single ancestral stock (Linton 1955:183; Vayda and Rappaport 1963; Sahlins 1958; Kirch 1984; Kirch and Green 1987). It has been seen as providing the ideal conditions for the comparative study of societies evolving in isolation. The conventional view is that following first colonisation Fiji and Western Polynesia formed a sort of community of cultures for up to one thousand years, then separated into culturally distinct entities by the end of the first millennium BC (Davidson 1977; Kirch 1978; Green 1981). After that date, despite periodic contact, the narrow sea gap to the northeast and east of Fiji formed a divide and no significant influences subsequently flowed from Fiji into Polynesia (Davidson 1977). The early prehistory of Fiji, then, is intimately bound up with and sets the parameters for the entire development of Polynesian society.

Recently, this conventional view has cracked under the strain of a growing scepticism generated by an expanding archaeological record and a raft of new biogeographical and voyaging models. These models challenge the isolation of Oceanic cultures and cultural regions (Irwin 1992,1993; Terrell 1997; Terrell et al. 1997; Graves and Green 1993; Weisler 1997). Geoff Irwin's voyaging studies in particular suggest that Polynesian peoples had an extraordinary capacity to span massive oceanic separations and to maintain sustained connections across these divides. They could and often did transport themselves and their materials over long distances with apparent ease. These new ideas and data call into question all models based on assumptions of isolation punctuated by periodic migrations. They demand a review of the role of distance and isolation in shaping Fijian and Polynesian prehistory and have initiated a search for alternative models for explaining cultural change and resistance to it (Terrell et al. 1997; Kirch 1997; Spriggs 1997). Such models must consider how the selective absorption and impact of some cultural influences can occur simultaneously with resistance to others.

There is, however, a difference between rejigging the interpretative overviews for the prehistory of a region, and redoing the archaeology from the ground up. It took, for example, a complete re-examination of evidence from the Hane Dune site in the Marquesas Islands before Pat Kirch was famously able to 'rethink' the prehistory of East Polynesia (Kirch 1986). This volume attempts a similar revision of an equally famous site situated at the nub of the Melanesia/Polynesia divide: the

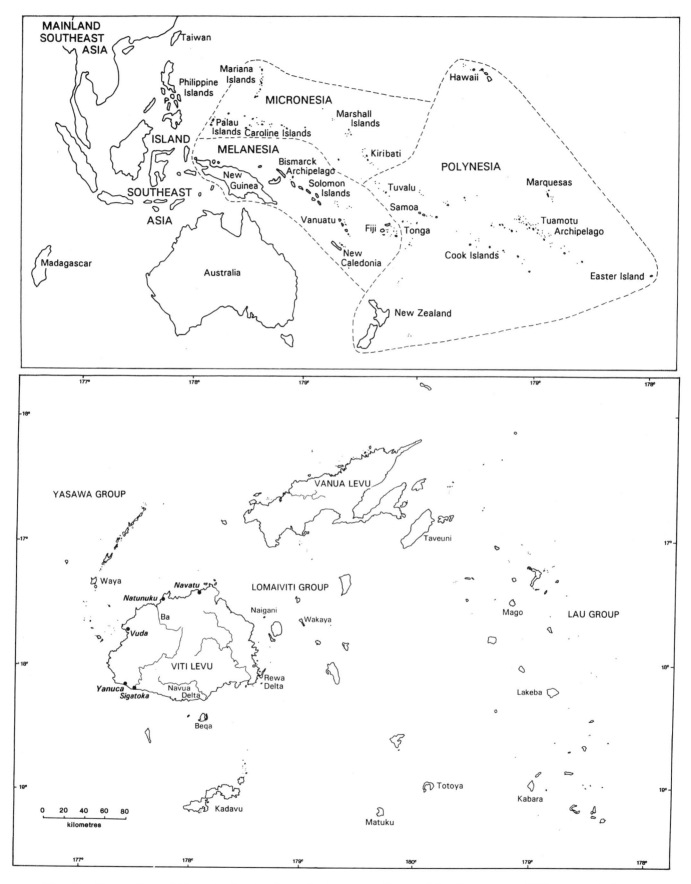

Fig. 1.1 Above: Map of Oceania showing key island groups discussed in the text and Fiji's strategic location on the Polynesia/Melanesia border. Below: Map of Fiji identifying key island groups and locations of major archaeological projects.

Sigatoka sand dunes, located on the south-western shore of Fiji's largest island, Viti Levu (see Plate 1). This site, perhaps more than any other, has shaped our thinking about Fijian and Polynesian prehistory. It lies at the very root of the geographical separation between the two regions and its archaeology stands as an icon to the migrationist and evolutionist approaches that have dominated Oceanic archaeology. This iconic quality arises from the unique stratigraphic layering of the site and the way in which these layers convey an image of cultural stability or stasis punctuated by events of rapid change. The aim of this volume is to strip away the layers of interpretation that have built Sigatoka into an icon for migration and isolation models of Fijian and Polynesian prehistory. To do this we reanalyse the archaeological evidence from the Sigatoka site, placing it within the context of a surface map rather than just a stratigraphic sequence.

In this process the culture history sequence of Fiji and the way in which it was constructed is shown in a new light. Throughout the volume an attempt is made to shift attention away from discontinuities between stratigraphic layers and cultural phases and to focus instead on the Sigatoka dunes as a lived-upon surface; a surface on and around which human occupation took place in a nearly continuous mosaic of shifting settlement. Previous interpretations have been modelled on small slices through this mosaic. They captured only a part of the broader picture, exaggerating differences between the sequential occupations and freezing them into a simplified culture history sequence. To avoid these reductions new interpretations will need to find ways to take account of far greater complexity. They will need to acknowledge the multiplicity of different sorts of occupations on and around the dunes and the growing evidence for much greater ceramic diversity than was previously suspected. The complexity of the archaeological evidence recovered from Sigatoka suggests that Fijian prehistory has been so consistently dynamic that the presumption must be that Fijians were in constant contact with their neighbours to both the west and east. Such a presumption demands a new kind of model based on interaction, communication and exchange.

The archaeological evidence reported in this book comes from a single, if very significant, site in Fiji. But the implications of our rethinking of Sigatoka extend beyond the prehistory of Fiji and Polynesia. They concern the very way in which archaeologists study and model continuity and change and challenge archaeologists wherever they work to value and understand the complexities of human behaviour, not just its generalities.

The four-phase model of Fijian culture history

Because Fiji is so central to our understanding of both the colonisation of Polynesia and the subsequent development of Polynesian societies, there has been great interest in establishing its culture history sequence. Excavations by E.W. Gifford in 1947 provided the first indications that Fiji's prehistory had sufficient depth and complexity to allow that Polynesians might have "come via Fiji." His excavations, particularly at the two sites of Vuda and Navatu located on Viti Levu's western and northern coasts (Fig. 1.1), revealed a late horizon characterised by incised ceramics and an early horizon characterised by "relief wares", or vessels decorated with the impressions of carved paddles (Gifford 1949, 1951). Subsequently, evidence of an even earlier style of pottery was found at Sigatoka (Green 1963b). In 1963, Roger Green revised Gifford's sequence by incorporating into it the new Sigatoka ceramics and dividing the late horizon into two phases. The result was a four-phase model of Fijian culture history based on changes in pottery styles (Green 1963a).

1) Sigatoka phase (dentate stamped and plainware ceramics), 1200–100 BC;
2) Navatu phase (paddle impressed ceramics), 100 BC to AD 1100;
3) Vuda phase (plain and simple incised/shell impressed ceramics), AD 1100–c.1800;
4) Ra phase (elaborately incised/impressed/appliqué/modelled ceramics), c.AD 1800–1900.

Similarities between the Sigatoka phase pottery from Fiji, and Lapita pottery with its characteristic dentate-stamped decoration were quickly recognised. Lapita pottery had been found to the west, from the Bismarck Archipelago to New Caledonia, and to the east, in Tonga and Samoa. This distinctive distribution pattern led Green to posit initial Lapita colonisation of Fiji, and to suggest that Fiji did indeed form the most likely route by which people first entered Polynesia (Green 1967). The subsequent ceramic changes that defined the four phases of Fiji's culture history were very poorly understood, but the most commonly accepted view was one of multiple migrations or cultural replacements. This explanation was particularly appealing because it seemed to explain the common perception of Fijians as physically and culturally heterogeneous, or even as hybrid "Melanesianised Polynesians" (Howells 1973:96; Hunt 1986; Spriggs 1997:99–100). Everett Frost's 1979 review of Fijian prehistory reflects this sense of an "interweaving of influences" resulting from "the ebb and flow of Oceanic migrants who sailed to and sometimes through Fiji during the eastward populating of the Pacific islands" (Frost 1979:62). Crucially, this ebb and flow, as indicated by the four Fijian ceramic traditions, did not extend to Western Polynesia, where, following Lapita colonisation, pottery gradually declined then disappeared. Thus Green's four-phase model appears to demonstrate that following Lapita, and with the onset of the Navatu phase around 200 BC, Fiji and Western Polynesia were, if not isolated from one another, at least separated by a cultural "frontier" (Davidson 1977).

Green's model has been tinkered with and refined over the years (Green and Palmer 1964; Shaw 1967; Frost 1974, 1979; Hunt 1986) but it survives with only minor alterations. The Sigatoka or Lapita phase has been subdivided into early and late periods denoted by a simplification in vessel forms and a reduction in decoration. These changes occurred throughout the entire eastern Lapita region of Fiji, Tonga, Samoa, 'Uvea and Futuna and are taken to indicate a gradual loss of contact between this eastern Lapita region and the area further west where complex Lapita wares continued to be made for longer (Green 1974, 1979:42; Kirch 1997:157–159). The Sigatoka phase in Fiji has been further subdivided to include a still simpler, terminal plainware phase, comparable to the Lapitoid or Polynesian Plain Ware of Samoa and Tonga (Green 1974:245–253; Kirch 1978, 1988). Kirch has recently argued that the plainware phase signifies the "end" of Lapita and the "beginning" of Polynesian culture (Kirch 1997: 68). Thus, within the first ceramic phase of Fiji's culture history the region was colonised from the west, subsequently became isolated, and perhaps saw the consequent development of a new ancestral Polynesian culture after 500 BC.

The later three phases of Fiji's culture history have received less attention. Most interest has centred on a debate over the transition from Sigatoka phase Lapita pottery to the paddle impressed Navatu wares. Was this change in pottery styles an internal Fijian development or was it brought about by a second wave of colonisers from the west, who reached Fiji in sufficient numbers to effect a rapid, radical replacement of the existing ceramic tradition, but did not move east into Tonga or Samoa? Such a radical replacement would suggest a real break had occurred between Fiji and Western Polynesia by 200 BC (Green 1981:150). On the basis of detailed evidence from a small number of well stratified sites on Lakeba in the Lau group (Fig. 1.1), Best has argued for a radical transition. He identifies abrupt changes in a wide variety of ceramic attributes, which affect almost all aspects of pottery manufacture and decoration (Best 1984: 635, 654). New Caledonia provides a suitable

source for most of the new traits (Garanger 1971; Galipaud 1990; Spriggs 1997:144–145). Hunt, however, takes issue with the migrationist implications of the radical break scenario and argues there is evidence of transitional pot forms among ceramic assemblages excavated from the Yanuca Rockshelter, on the southern coast of Viti Levu, that suggests internal development from the Sigatoka to Navatu pottery traditions (Hunt 1980:126–136; 1986). Although the Yanuca stratigraphy is mixed, Hunt argues that there is sufficient sharing of Lapita Plainware and Navatu paddle impressed form and style elements on individual pots to demonstrate a transitional technology. Ceramic evidence from the islands of Beqa and Ugaga reported by Crosby (1988:215), and reinterpretations of the Sigatoka evidence reported in this volume, both indicate that the Sigatoka-Navatu transition may actually be more complex than either of the above scenarios allow. In particular, they suggest that the transition may have proceeded differently in different regions.

The migrationist theme is reiterated throughout the later phases of the Fijian culture history sequence. Best has noted the widespread appearance throughout Fiji, at around AD 200, of a suite of new ceramic traits, mostly decorative, accompanied by the simultaneous appearance on Lakeba of obsidian from northern Vanuatu (Fig. 1.1). These new artefacts demonstrate an event of external contact within the Navatu phase (Best 1989:59–62). Similarly, Frost has employed migration to account for the Navatu-Vuda transition. He combined several sources of evidence including oral historical accounts of westward migrations to Fiji, a congruency between the appearance of incised wares and fortifications on the island of Taveuni at about AD 1100, and the disappearance of similarly incised pottery in Vanuatu, to argue that the Navatu-Vuda transition is also due to external contact (Frost 1974:119–122). In contrast, Best has established that the emergence of fortifications and other significant changes in settlement pattern appeared 1–200 years earlier on Lakeba than on Taveuni, and are associated with a relatively gradual ceramic change. On Lakeba there is a slow diminution of paddle impression and a gradual introduction of the new incised elements characteristic of the Vuda phase (Best 1984:644).

Lakeba also provides evidence of a different kind of external contact during the Vuda phase. Basaltic adzes from Samoa appear and a dramatic increase in pottery exchange within Fiji occurs. Best (1984: 658) suggests these changes on Lakeba could indicate the first imposition of Tongan political influence in eastern parts of Fiji after AD 900. By the time of European contact some 750 years later, this influence was indisputable. By then, veritable colonies of Tongans and other Western Polynesians lived throughout the Lau group and on Taveuni (Best 1984:657). Their presence seems to be associated with the proliferation of the new stylistic and form elements that characterise the final Ra phase of ceramics. In short, Best's work on Lakeba confirmed what had long been suspected on oral historical grounds; that contact between Fiji and Polynesia was firmly re-established by 1000 AD, if it had ever been abandoned, and the resumption of this contact is associated with major social and cultural change in Fiji ranging from the development of fortifications to the emergence of status and hierarchy markers within Fijian settlement patterns.

The four-phase model has been a robust and useful interpretative tool. However, it has now become the victim of too many explanatory migrations and too much evidential complexity. It is now inadequate for dealing with the increasingly fine detail of cultural change which archaeologists are identifying in Fiji. Simon Best cautioned long ago that the four chronological phases have no inherent meaning and that the nature and exact timing of cultural change is likely to have been different within different parts of Fiji (Best 1984). He argued that archaeologists need to think of Fiji's prehistory in terms of the cumulative effects of individual events, each marked by discrete and possibly minor archaeological traits, the appearance of which may have little relationship with broad changes in ceramic styles. Already archaeological evidence points to significant subdivisions within phases, and contact events that occur during phases rather than at the transitions between them. There is suspicion that some very minor ceramic changes may have had wider cultural impact than the major phase transitions. In expressing caution, Best prefigured the current shift in Oceanic prehistory away from culture historical models to models based on assumptions of complexity, diversity, and, above all, sustained inter-island connectivity (Irwin 1992; Weisler 1997; Terrell et al. 1997).

Growing disagreements over the nature of the Sigatoka-Navatu transition, over the appearance of fortifications, and even over minor details of ceramic and settlement pattern change as noted for example by Crosby between Lakeba and Beqa (1988: 233–237), highlight some of the specific weaknesses of the four-phase model. Some broad changes appear to have occurred simultaneously and in the same fashion throughout all Fiji. Even some very precise events such as the introduction at AD 200, within the Navatu phase, of new ceramic elements, seem to have happened almost instantly over a wide area. But many changes and events appear to have occurred differently, at different times, or at different rates. Best has argued, for example, that the early Lapita deposits on Lakeba are more similar to those of Tonga and Samoa than those of the rest of Fiji (Best 1984:654). This argument for an early cultural division or difference within Fiji has linguistic support. A similar division existed at European contact and indeed can be seen today in the many Tongan influences found in the Lau group. Fiji today is a highly diverse cultural mosaic. Some of this diversity can be attributed to its wide geographical range and major environmental differences between the interior and the coasts on the larger islands (Hunt 1987). Other differences can be attributed to historically recent migrations of people from Tonga, Samoa, 'Uvea, the Solomon Islands and many other places. The impact of both geography and migrations is often significant at a local level but barely visible on a national scale. A phase-based model is incapable of seeing these internal differences and is not therefore a useful analytical tool for topics such as internal colonialism, regional nationalism and inter-regional conflict. Indeed, such models obscure these important issues.

Unfortunately, however, even recent writings in Fijian prehistory remain entrenched within the four-phase model (Dickinson et al. 1998; Burley and Shortland 1999). This is in part due to the lack of a current synthesis of Fijian archaeology. The only general reference remains Everett Frost's 1979 overview (Frost 1979). A new review that pulls together the wide-ranging body of research that has been completed over the past two decades is badly overdue. In the meantime, this volume sets as its goal the more fundamental task of interrogating the roots of the four-phase model. Much of the allure and enduring power of this model is its simplicity: its capacity to order the rising sea of complexity in Fijian archaeology in a straight forward, accessible way. This power goes back to the archaeological circumstances of its creation and the stratigraphic integrity of the sites from which it was formed. Archaeologists respect stratigraphy above all else, and the four-phase model has powerful stratigraphic credentials that derive largely from the Sigatoka sand dunes.

Sigatoka and the four-phase model

The continued survival of the four-phase orthodoxy is due in no small part to the role that the Sigatoka dunes have played in its creation. Indeed, no site has played a more central role in constructing the culture history of any region in Oceania. This is partly because of its eponymous

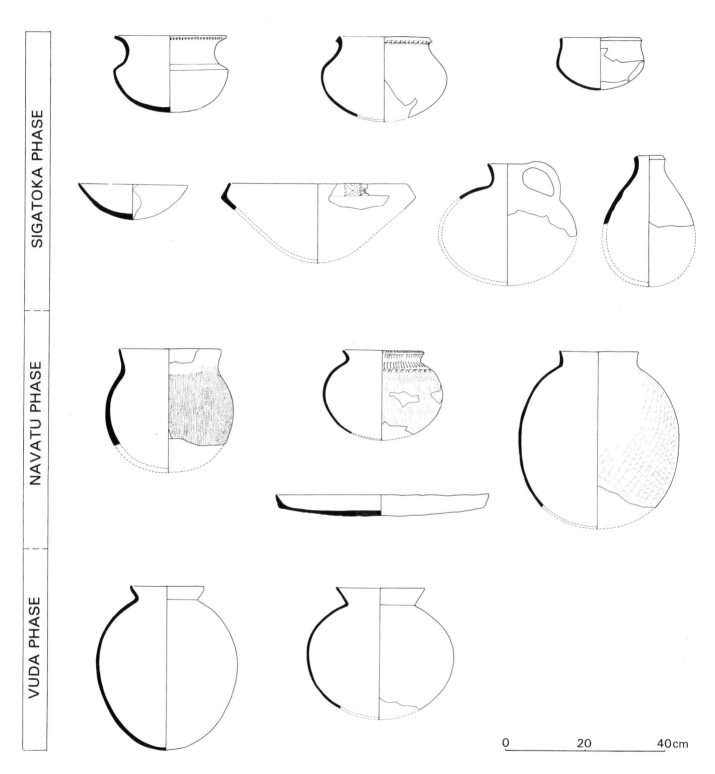

SIGATOKA PHASE

NAVATU PHASE

VUDA PHASE

0   20   40cm

Fig. 1.2 Type pottery from Sigatoka for the Sigatoka, Navatu and Vuda Phases. The three cooking pots reproduced at the top for the Sigatoka (Lapita) phase are ordered from early on the left to late on the right. Change can be seen in vessel form, decorative style and in the gradual reduction in the variety of vessel forms. All examples are drawn from Winifred Munfords' illustrations of vessels recovered by the Birks in 1965–6 and published in Birks 1973.

association with the earliest period of occupation of Fiji. Although Sigatoka is not the oldest site in Fiji, it was the first to demonstrate the presence of Lapita pottery and to signal its significance for the human colonisation of Polynesia. But, more dramatically, Sigatoka's breathtaking sweep of dune face appears to provide a visually striking endorsement of Green's model. Three of the four phases are represented by pottery bearing soil layers which thrust outwards from the dune face like three layers of chocolate cream in a sponge cake of deep, sterile sand; a visual analogy of stunning eloquence (see Plates 2, 5 and 14).

This analogy was fashioned in the report on the first ever excavations conducted on the dunes, by Lawrence and Helen Birks in 1965 and 1966 (Birks 1973). Their excavations were restricted to the three soil layers, which they labelled Levels 1, 2 and 3. Throughout the report, Lawrence Birks refers to these Levels as "separate cultural horizons" (1973: 9) and assigns to them archaeological materials broadly comparable to Green's Sigatoka, Navatu and Vuda phases (Fig. 1.2; Plate 9). The horizon-like nature of the Levels is strikingly represented in a simple profile diagram that depicts them as three dark, horizontal bands separated by white space (Fig. 1.3). This illustration does not in fact represent a profile that occurs anywhere on the dunes. It is a composite of two spatially discrete trenches. They were excavated at Roger Green's suggestion in an unsuccessful attempt to determine the precise stratigraphic relationship and degree of separation between all three Levels (Birks 1973: 9). Nevertheless, the profile diagram conveys the lasting impression that Levels 1, 2 and 3 at Sigatoka are synonymous with Green's first three ceramic phases; that they extend as more or less horizontal planes into and along the dunes; and that they are completely separate both chronologically and stylistically. With the publication of the Birks' profile diagram, the three physically separate soil layers on the dunes and the three apparently discrete cultural phases constructed by Green came together and were established as the central orthodoxy of Fijian prehistory.

Archaeologists routinely use pictures and diagrams like the Birks' stratigraphy profile to represent their findings because illustrations convey information that it is difficult to explain in words. Illustrations construct and express ideas about the past and are therefore an important part of the process of creating it. While all archaeological illustrations contribute to this process, some images convey ideas so powerfully that they are used over and over again until they become what is known as visual icons (Moser 1998:19–20). Such images acquire meanings that transcend their original context and become so definitive of an idea or theory that theory and image become synonymous.

Perhaps the best known example of a visual icon in archaeology is the striding man image so frequently used as shorthand for the modern scientific theory of human evolution (Fig. 1.4). This image has become so pervasive and so well known it no longer requires a caption or explanation. Its meaning is international, crossing language barriers and cultural boundaries (Gould 1989:30–1). The striding man is the theory of human evolution. He has the power to shape expectation by directing in advance the way we will receive each new idea or piece of evidence about evolution. Yet, as Gould (1989) points out, this image has ancient roots reaching

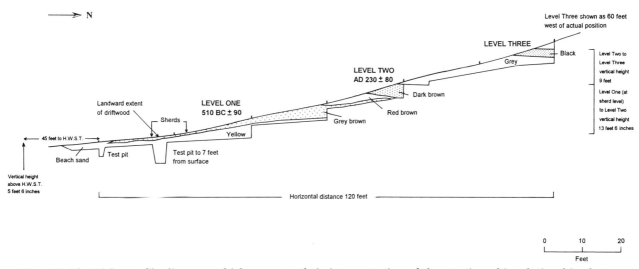

Fig. 1.3 The Birks profile diagram which presents their interpretation of the stratigraphic relationships between the three palaeosol Levels at Sigatoka. After Birks 1973:10, Fig.4.

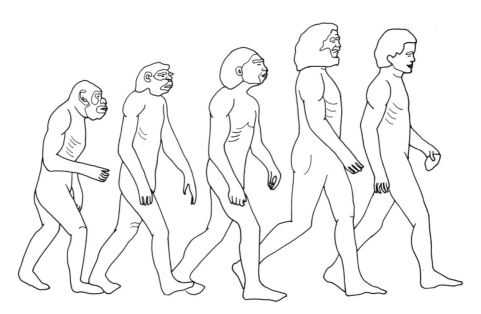

Fig. 1.4 Striding man icon of human evolution.

back into the eighteenth century and theories of a great chain of being – theories now regarded as antithetical to modern evolution. From this ancient heritage the striding man carries with him ideational baggage about notions such as progress and western cultural superiority which insinuate themselves into theories of human evolution. As with textual representations, such illustrations develop histories and in the process their meanings come to exceed those originally intended.

The simple line drawing that Lawrence Birks used to reconstruct the stratigraphic layering of sands and soils at the Sigatoka sand dunes has become a visual icon within Fijian prehistory (Fig. 1.3). In contrast to the striding man icon, whose impact is dramatic and assertive, it is the unassuming quality of this image that has given it its power to direct our thinking. Published at a time when Fijian archaeology was in its infancy and little was known of the history of human occupation anywhere in Oceania, this diagram made the link between the visually compelling layercake of soils and sands at the Sigatoka dunes and Green's ceramic phases. Because images convey information in different ways than text they can make "theories for which evidence is limited seem credible" (Moser 1998:16). In other words, they can turn fragments of data into coherent, plausible stories. In 1973 archaeologists needed to do that in order to get started in Fiji. They needed a framework for organising the scattered pieces of evidence then available to them. In bringing together soil layers and ceramic sequences, Lawrence Birks' simple stratigraphy diagram became that framework.

We now know a great deal more about Fijian prehistory. But we continue to labour under the power of the Birks' diagram because archaeologists have come to think Fijian prehistory in the simplified, layercake way it is represented in their drawing. The most recently published interpretative revision of the dunes stratigraphy and human occupation by Dickinson et al. (1998) reproduces the Birks diagram in a form even more simplified and reduced than the original (Fig. 1.5). Just as the striding man became visual shorthand for the theory of human evolution, the Birks' stratigraphy diagram has become entrenched as a visual icon for Fijian prehistory. Although originally created to advance our understanding of Fijian prehistory, the power of this image to define in advance the manner and terms by which we will make sense of each new idea or piece of information has become a barrier to understanding. As Moser (1998:20) puts it, the icon comes "to restrict or limit knowledge" rather than expand it.

Moving beyond the orthodoxy

In an effort to move beyond the layercake model of the Sigatoka dunes, and of Fijian prehistory generally, this volume proposes a shift in perception from the vertical to the horizontal, from one of geological epochs to one of anthropological complexity. The heart of this book, then, is not an argument about stratigraphy or changes in cultural styles, but a map. This volume pulls together the results of all previous archaeological work on the dunes and for the first time maps the dune surface over 1.2km at the eastern

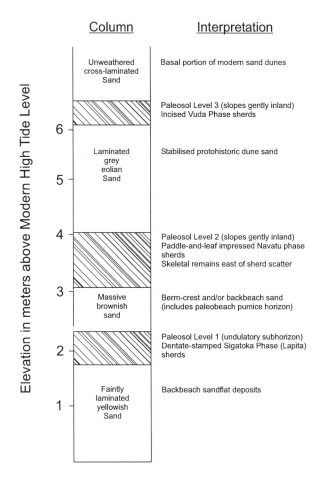

Elevation in meters above Modern High Tide Level

Column — Interpretation

Column	Interpretation
Unweathered cross-laminated Sand	Basal portion of modern sand dunes
	Paleosol Level 3 (slopes gently inland) Incised Vuda Phase sherds
Laminated grey eolian Sand	Stabilised protohistoric dune sand
	Paleosol Level 2 (slopes gently inland) Paddle-and-leaf impressed Navatu phase sherds Skeletal remains east of sherd scatter
Massive brownish sand	Berm-crest and/or backbeach sand (includes paleobeach pumice horizon)
	Paleosol Level 1 (undulatory subhorizon) Dentate-stamped Sigatoka Phase (Lapita) sherds
Faintly laminated yellowish Sand	Backbeach sandflat deposits

Fig. 1.5 The Birks' stratigraphic profile as reproduced and simplified in Dickinson et al. 1998:6, Fig. 4.

end, where the bulk of the currently known archaeological deposits lie. As a result of reviewing all of the archaeological knowledge of the dunes within this framework, an overwhelming body of evidence has emerged that the dunes were not as previously thought: the three soil layers do not form discrete horizontal planes, they are not always separated by sterile sand, they were not the only venue for occupation on the dunes, and the occupation debris contained within, and between, each soil layer is much more varied than previously thought. The archaeology of the dunes is no longer analogous of a culture history sequence of discrete stylistic phases. Rather, the indication is of a complex array of often subtle but significant archaeological traits, which simultaneously split and bridge the geological strata, and of a series of lived-upon surfaces that vary in their form and the nature of their occupation across the dunes environment. The value of the dunes lies not in the broad-brush separation of ceramic phases but in understanding how and why different parts of the dunes were used for different purposes, at different times.

The objective of this book, then, is to rethink the archaeology of the dunes. This requires a reconsideration of the archaeological evidence collected from the Sigatoka Sand Dunes over the last three and a half decades. In the past this information has been organised and interpreted around the stratigraphic argument set up by the Birks. We have chosen, instead, to reorganise and reinterpret this large body of data around a surface – the surface of the dunes as they were mapped in 1992. This surface is a much more complex representation of the dunes than the Birks' stratigraphy diagram. Using it as a basis for interpretation is challenging because it demands that we acknowledge and work with the complexity of both the sand dunes and Fijian prehistory, rather than reducing and simplifying them. It demands that we view the dunes not as a generalised vertical profile but as a series of intercutting and overlapping surfaces. The relationships within and between these surfaces are highly specific in both their vertical and horizontal dimensions.

The book has three purposes. Firstly, it presents the information contained in the map and associated test excavations. Secondly, it collates and compiles all of the archaeology conducted on the dunes prior to and after the completion of the map. Thirdly, it discusses and interprets the results. Chapters 1–3 discuss the significance of the dunes, the need for the map and the mechanics of its creation. Chapter 4 presents the results of the 1992 mapping project in a summarised form. Further details are provided in Appendices A–D. Chapters 5 and 6 collate the results of previous and subsequent research conducted on the dunes up to 1998. This information is located within the framework of the 1992 map. Chapters 7 and 8 rethink the archaeology of the dunes and present it in two forms; firstly a reconstruction of the dune surface as a constantly changing landform, and secondly a reconstruction of the nature of human occupations on that changing surface. In Chapter 9 we consider some of the specific implications of our rethinking of the dunes on our knowledge of Fijian prehistory. Finally, in Chapter 10 we examine the wider implications for Fijian prehistory by constructing a new model which values regional complexity and cultural continuity above the obvious discontinuities of the ceramic sequence.

One thing is abundantly clear. The continued filtering of archaeological data through the orthodox four-phase culture historical model, so eloquently represented by the Birks' stratigraphy diagram, is defeating attempts to theorise Fijian prehistory in a more sophisticated way. This book is a step toward the deconstruction of the four-phase model and the presentation of archaeological data in a new light.

The preliminary results of the reanalysis indicate not only that the archaeological phases are a fudge, but that the geological strata with which they are associated are also different than is believed, even in the most recent publications (Dickinson et al. 1998). For these reasons we are aware of the need for the data to be persuasive, as we ourselves have struggled to comprehend the results of the mapping exercise. It is only after repeated excursions over the dunes spanning a decade and half, years spent relocating previous archaeologists' datums, triangulating their sketches and plans from surviving landmarks and aerial photographs, and for the first time collating all this data together with the results of a new series of test excavations, that we feel confident to present our findings.

As we write, archaeological projects on and around the dunes are proliferating. New materials are recovered all the time and a major project on reconstructing the ancient geomorphology of the wider environment is underway. Results from this work will add further to our understanding of Sigatoka. We hope that our rethinking of the dunes and Fijian prehistory, as presented in this book, will provide a stimulating context for the interpretation of results from this subsequent work – a context which helps to draw from Sigatoka the exciting insights it has to offer.

Chapter 2
The Sigatoka Sand Dunes

Introduction

The Sigatoka Sand Dunes are located at the mouth of the Sigatoka River (Figs. 1.1 and 2.1). They extend west of the river mouth for a distance of 4.8 km, forming a teardrop shaped, 240 hectare expanse of sand which is about 200m wide at the river mouth and about 1 km wide at the broad western end (Plate 1). The dunes rise steadily from east to west and at their highest points reach elevations of around 50 metres above sea level. The southern face of the dunes which rises from the sea to the dune crest, although steep in parts, slopes gently compared to the very steep northern face which drops precipitously down to farmland behind. This farmland comprises a relatively flat area of fertile, deltaic and beach sands, marked by a series of low beach ridges that run parallel to the dunes (see Plates 16–18).

Findings from two major archaeological investigations conducted on the dunes prior to 1992 by Lawrence and Helen Birks in 1965/66 and Simon Best in 1987/88 have identified them as a site of pivotal importance in Fijian and wider Oceanic prehistory. These investigations, conducted at the eastern end of the dunes in the area known as site VL 16/1, established the existence of at least 3 phases of dune stabilisation of sufficient duration to sustain the development of vegetation and the formation of deep palaeosols (Birks 1973; Dickinson 1968). During each of these periods of stabilisation people occupied the dunes and left behind them extensive archaeological deposits. These include a type series of Fijian pottery which has been used to identify initial Lapita colonisation and to help construct the Fijian culture history sequence (Fig. 1.2), and a cemetery of at least 61 human skeletons which have helped identify what sort of people the early Fijians were (Best 1987a,b, 1989; Visser 1994).

Cultural materials from the two lowest palaeosols, Levels 1 and 2, have been radiocarbon dated to around 2500 BP (Birks 1973:57; Petchey 1995:94) and 1720 BP respectively (Birks 1973:57; Best 1989:48). Pottery recovered from the third and most recent palaeosol, Level 3, suggests a date of around AD 1000–1500, which is tentatively supported by radiocarbon dates from associated features (Burley 1997:9). Despite the wealth of ceramic, skeletal and dating evidence recovered by the Birks and Best the nature of human occupation on the dunes remained largely unknown.

Since their excavations, subsequent wind and wave erosion along the seaward edge of the dunes has exposed more of the three palaeosols and has progressively revealed massive concentrations of archaeological materials which spill onto the sloping dune surface along almost their entire 4.8km length (Plate 2). At various times archaeologists have returned to the dunes in attempts to recover and record this material before it is lost. Such is the breadth of the archaeological deposits, however, that the scale and extent of the human occupation on the dunes and the precise nature and form of each of the palaeosols has never been accurately delimited. It is within this context of the inherent instability of the dunes environment, and the lack of any wider framework for delimiting and reconstructing the nature of the human occupation at such a significant archaeological site, that the 1992 mapping project was initiated.

The significance of the Sigatoka Sand Dunes

No archaeological site in the southwestern Pacific is as visually spectacular or potentially informative as the Sigatoka Sand Dunes. They are known both locally and internationally for their unique natural vegetation, unusual and dramatic landforms and extensive archaeological sites. As a scientific, cultural, ecological and potential eco-

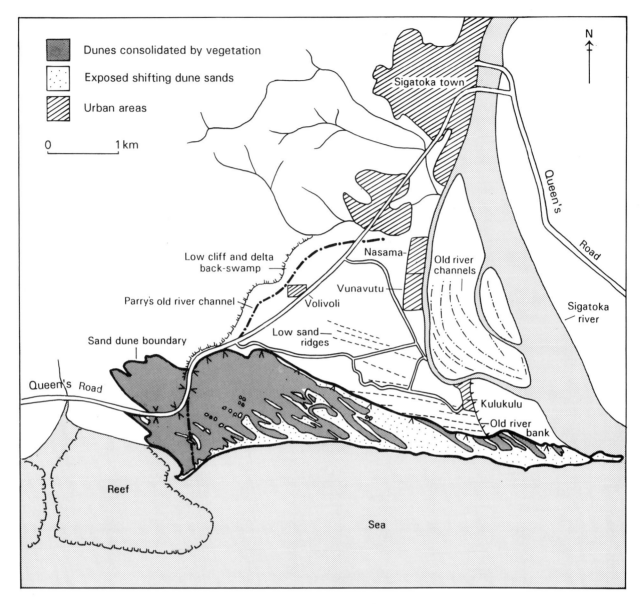

Fig. 2.1 General morphology and environs of the Sigatoka Sand Dunes.

nomic resource, the Sigatoka Sand Dunes are exceptional.

The general importance of the dunes was officially recognised in 1988 when the Fiji Cabinet declared the dunes a National Park. Since then, the particular environmental, scientific and tourism value of the Sigatoka Sand Dunes has been recognised in a series of government initiatives at both national and international levels. In 1991 they were included on the Pacific and Antarctic areas World Heritage List by the World Heritage Working Group Task Force Meeting on a Global Inventory of Geological and Fossil Sites. In 1992 they were included on a Preliminary List of Sites of National Significance in the National State of the Environment Report and the National Environment Strategy Draft Report. In 1997 a visitor

centre was opened at the western end of dunes and a full-time ranger was appointed to monitor the number of visitors coming to the National Park and the impact they are having on its ecology and archaeology.

Since the dunes were declared a National Park, and particularly since the opening of the Visitor Centre in 1997, the dunes have gained increasing prominence in Fijian tourist literature and have become a major asset in promoting the tourism industry along the Coral Coast and in Fiji generally. The Sigatoka Sand Dunes are, then, an extremely important resource for a small island nation heavily dependent upon tourism. They also hold unique clues to the prehistory of Fiji and the Pacific region generally. Appropriate protection and development of the dunes is therefore of critical importance to Fiji's economy and to Fijian people's understanding of their more distant past.

Present condition and conservation problems

Given the significance of the dunes, the monitoring of their condition and conservation is vitally important. Over the past five decades archaeologists and other concerned observers have at increasingly regular intervals recorded the changes taking place in the structure of the dunes themselves. These records indicate that the western part of the sand dunes, most of which is well vegetated, is fairly stable (Cabaniuk et al. 1986). In contrast, there is considerable concern over the rapidly eroding eastern portion of the dunes.

The accumulated evidence of aerial photographs and the last four decades of archaeological monitoring make it clear that since the 1960s the eastern dunes, particularly in the area of site VL 16/1, have been in a destructive phase. In general, the sand has been stripped away by the wind faster than it has been replaced and has been redeposited to the northwest. As a result, the depth of loose sand on the front, seaward slopes of the dunes has been reduced while the dunes have become wider. This erosion and redeposition is causing the dunes to migrate northward and to encroach onto the farmland behind at a rate of approximately 5 metres a year (Cabaniuk et al.1986:8). The degree of northward progradation has been most extreme in the east, between Kulukulu and the river mouth. This process started to accelerate rapidly after 1988.

Sea erosion is also accelerating. The gradual intrusion of the sea along the seaward edge of VL 16/1 accelerated catastrophically after 1990. Following cyclone Sina, which passed directly over the Sigatoka area in November 1990, the sand bar which cut off much of the mouth of the Sigatoka River was substantially altered and abnormally large surge waves were reported at the dunes by local residents. Over time these surge waves almost completely removed all remnants of the beach ridge or foredune which ran along the front of the site and acted as a buffer to sea encroachment (compare Plate 11 with Plates 6, 7 and 14). When cyclone Kina also passed directly over the Sigatoka area in January 1993 it caused such severe flooding of the Sigatoka River that part of the Sigatoka Bridge was destroyed and the entire sand bar at the mouth of the river was washed away. Initially, these changes to the river had little effect. However, from 1994 to 1996 the wave erosion advanced in a westerly direction along the full seaward edge of VL 16/1 removing most of the archaeological deposits mapped during the 1992

survey. Since then the situation has begun to stabilise.

This weakening of the dune structure by cyclones is an important factor. However, as Shepherd (1988:2) points out, hurricane waves "are unlikely to influence significantly the long-term evolution of higher energy sandy embayments," of which Sigatoka is an example. What they may do is set in motion a short-term cycle of change, for instance through the deposition or removal of large amounts of fluvial materials at the river mouth. Thus, although cyclones will probably not be a major determinant of long term cycles of construction and destruction on the dunes, and while direct damage to the dunes immediately following a cyclone is often minimal, the processes set in motion by changes brought about by cyclones, such as the removal of the sand bar at the mouth of the Sigatoka River, can be extremely destructive in the short term.

Several other factors also play a part in the present phase of erosion. One is the progressive decline of vegetation, especially colonising ground creepers, on the eastern part of the dunes. A reason for this is that the volume of wind blown sand is at present too great even for well-adapted dune grasses to avoid being buried. Another factor is the trampling and grazing of the dunes by stock and regular disturbance by increasing numbers of day visitors, destroying fragile vegetation, thus exacerbating erosion and dune destruction. A further contributing factor is sand mining, which has resulted in the removal of large volumes of sand from the steep, backslope of the dunes (Plates 16 and 18). This destroys the fragile vegetation along these slopes and undermines the stability of the surrounding dune structure.

No single cause, such as a cyclone, then, is responsible for the current instability at the eastern end of the dunes. Rather the multiple and joint effects of different agencies must be taken into account. The specific threats posed by this instability to the archaeological deposits and its contribution to the overall erosion effect are, however, well appreciated.

Dune formation and human occupation

The Sigatoka Sand Dunes are composed of elongate parabolic dunes orientated parallel to the prevailing southeast trade winds so that they lie at angles between 25 and 45 degrees to the shore (Dickinson et al. 1998). Their distinctive morphology is the product of the natural forces that are constantly forming and re-shaping them. Most of the southern coast of Viti Levu is protected and sheltered by fringing and barrier reefs. As a result this coast is generally characterised as low-energy (Shepherd 1988) with little build up of sandy beaches. However, there are "a number of gaps in the reefs where coral growth has been inhibited by the presence of major river mouths" (Shepherd 1990:547) and where the coastline is directly influenced by high energy southerly swell waves and waves generated by southeasterly trade winds. In these higher-energy locations long, relatively wide sandy beaches consisting of "non-calcareous sediment derived from nearby rivers" typically form (Shepherd 1988:1).

The Sigatoka River mouth is an example of a moderate-energy coastline formation developing at a gap in the protecting reef. Sediments carried down the Sigatoka River are deposited at the river mouth and offshore as sand bars, spits and shoals. This material constitutes a sand reservoir, which according to fluctuating wind and wave conditions, may either accumulate or erode. At times of erosion material from the offshore sand reservoir is carried westward and washed to shore by waves driven by the prevailing southeasterly winds. This process forms the wide sandy beach. Sediments from both the river mouth and beach are also picked up, carried, sorted and re-deposited by the southeasterly winds, thus building up the dunes and extending them inland in a northwesterly direction.

It is widely agreed that in general the dunes formed first as low foredunes close to the river mouth and built up progressively, in a northwesterly direction. The oldest sands are, therefore, expected to be located at the eastern end and at the lowest elevations along the current dune system. However, because both the beach and dunes are subject to the vagaries of fluctuating wind and wave action, they form an ever-changing landscape caught in the constant flux of a natural erosion–construction cycle. At different times, and in different parts of the dunes at any one time, sand can be accumulating, stable or eroding. Actual dune formation is therefore an uneven process of successive and irregular phases of construction, stabilisation and destruction.

As a result the age of the dunes and the more precise details of their formation are subjects of considerable debate. Nunn (1990) and Shepherd (1990) point out that dune formation at Sigatoka could have begun as early as 4–5,000 years ago following the stabilisation of sea levels around Fiji at their present levels (Nunn 1990; Shepherd 1990). We argue that the dunes probably began to form soon after this date and were well developed by the time of initial human occupation around 3000 BP. The general consensus, however, recently reiterated in Dickinson et al. (1998) is that the dunes did not form until considerably later, following an extended period of human occupation in the dunes area.

The excavations of the Birks and Best have suggested that the three palaeosols identified on the eastern dunes are horizontal or gently undulating surfaces separated by sterile deposits of wind blown dune sands – an interpretation iconographically represented in Lawrence Birks stratigraphy diagram as discussed in Chapter 1. The Birks evidence indicated that the rate of accumulation of dune sands had been accelerating over time. As a general rule they found there was approximately one metre of sand between Levels 1 and 2, two metres of sand between Levels 2 and 3, and considerably deeper deposits of sand overlying Level 3 (Birks 1973; Parry 1987:13). These indications have led most researchers to assume that the palaeosols, particularly Levels 1 and 2, formed on quite flat land prior to any significant dune formation, and that the current high parabolic dune forms are relatively recent, probably post-dating the deposition of Level 3.

Birks (1973), for example, suggested that expanding settlement up the Sigatoka Valley led to deforestation, which in turn caused increased erosion, sediment discharge and ultimately accelerated dune formation. This implies that the primary cause of the dune formation was human induced environmental change and that this change occurred slowly through the gradual growth and inland movement of human populations. Birks' model has an attractive logic in explaining how the volume of sand available as a reservoir for dune formation could have built up over time at the river mouth as a result of human agency. However, it does not explain why at some times throughout the geological history of the dunes conditions prevailed which allowed the formation of consolidated organic palaeosols that were suitable for human occupation while at other times the dunes comprised an apparently unliveable environment during which deep deposits of drift sand accumulated.

Parry (1987:14–16) and Shepherd (1988, 1990) point out that the positioning and nature of the offshore sand reservoir is a crucial factor. Erosion and sediment discharge generate the materials, but conditions that retain the sediments at the river mouth must also prevail before dune build up is possible. Parry argues that these conditions were only present when the river exited on the eastern side of the delta, as it does at present. If the river exited further west a sand reservoir could not accumulate. Parry therefore argues that periods of dune stability and human occupation occurred when the river exited well to the west of its present position along an old river channel that he has identified at Naivolivoli (shown here on Fig. 2.1).

More recent archaeological work on the dunes has refuted this suggestion. Dickinson et al. (1998) have established that if a western river channel did ever exist in the location identified by Parry, it would have been completely cut off from the sea by beach ridges at least 5000 years ago, well before the formation of the oldest identified palaeosol.

The 1992 survey has established a wider range of problems with the Birks and Parry models. Firstly, the survey results demonstrate that significant dune formation occurred prior to the deposition of the Level 2 palaeosol and probably also prior to Level 1. Secondly, the survey has shown that, except at the very eastern end of the dunes, none of the palaeosols form uniformly horizontal or even gently undulating surfaces but include slopes of dune-like proportions. Thirdly, by the time of the formation of the Level 1 palaeosol the build up of sand at the eastern end of the dunes was already sufficient to divert the river mouth to the east of an old river channel that runs beside Kulukulu village, approximately 600m west of the present river bank (Fig. 2.1). And fourthly, the 1992 survey defined a well

marked eastern margin of the dunes that remained unchanged between the Level 2 and Level 3 palaeosols indicating little or no alteration in the positioning and nature of the river mouth in the interim.

While many of these findings agree with interpretations put forward by Dickinson et al. (1998) on the basis of their 1996 investigations, we disagree on a number of key points:

- the date at which dune formation began
- the degree of sand build up at the time of occupation on each palaeosol
- the origin point of the dunes
- that the dunes grew only in a westerly direction from their origin point
- that the sequence of palaeosol formation identified at the eastern end of the dunes is typical of the dunes as a whole

These points of debate are taken up in Chapters 7 and 8. In the following four chapters the evidence recovered from the Sigatoka Sand Dunes is collated and summarised beginning with the 1992 survey.

Chapter 3
The 1992 mapping project: aims and methods

Introduction

The 1992 survey project was a response to two very different kinds of crisis. One was the growing concern over the conservation and management of the dunes in the face of accelerating dune erosion and destruction of archaeological evidence. The other was an impasse in the debate over how the dunes formed and the extent to which human occupation of the area directed this process. Previous responses to both problems had focused on compiling a more and more detailed understanding of the dunes stratigraphy. The 1992 survey took what was in this context a novel approach. Its aim was to define a dune surface at one point in time and to thereby establish horizontal relationships between palaeosols, sands and cultural remains rather than just their stratigraphic positions. This would enable us to construct a more fully three-dimensional understanding of the changing form of the dunes over time.

Description of the project

The immediate objective of the survey as laid out in the initiating proposal was "to provide a basis for calculating the extent of the archaeological deposit remaining on the site and of gauging its significance in the face of recent increased threats to the stability of the sand dunes" (Crosby 1991a: 1). It was recommended that the entire area contained within the Sigatoka National Park designation and the area of sand dunes contained within the two private land holdings at the eastern end of the sand dunes be surveyed, giving particular attention to the area known as archaeological site VL 16/1. To these ends four survey requirements were outlined:

- To locate and accurately map all currently observable surface archaeological materials within the area of the sand dunes.
- To conduct limited test excavations in order to test for the presence of subsurface archaeological materials where no surface deposits are visible and in order to confirm the extent and significance of surface deposits.
- To identify features on the sand dunes – natural and cultural – that are likely to effect the preservation of archaeological deposits, including evidence of recent erosion or disturbance, built structures, areas of dense vegetation etc.
- To provide recommendations on the placement of signs, walkways, fences and access points for visitors onto the site and to identify areas where access should be restricted.

The proposal was submitted by the Fiji Museum to the New Zealand Government, who in August 1992 agreed to provide funding. The survey fieldwork was carried out between 18th August and 9th September 1992 under the auspices of, and with the assistance of the Fiji Museum. Most of the work recommended in Crosby's proposal, and several additional tasks, were completed:

- A simple walk over survey was conducted along the full length of the dunes and the locations of exposed archaeological materials noted.
- A kilometre long stretch at the eastern end of the dunes which includes VL 16/1 was mapped in detail, precisely locating all surface evidence of eroding pottery, rock, human bone and palaeosols.
- A series of 17 testpit transects and 4 probe transects were excavated in order to identify the eroding palaeosols.
- One large mound of eroding pottery was completely excavated and the pottery removed to the Fiji Museum.
- One large pottery and rock scatter was partially

excavated; a small hearth feature was cross-sectioned; and the partial remains of at least 8 eroding pots were collected and removed to the Fiji Museum.

- Two human burials were fully excavated and a third human bone scatter was surface collected. All three sets of remains were removed to the Fiji Museum.
- A new area of archaeological importance was identified in the undulating ground between the dunes and Kulukulu Village. Pottery was found eroding from the bank cut by the field road.

A seven-person field crew conducted the survey. Andrew Crosby (University of Chicago), Vasiti Ritova (Fiji Museum), Yvonne Marshall (University of Southampton, formerly Simon Fraser University) and Shannon Wood (Simon Fraser University) carried out the Sigatoka Sand Dunes survey. Sepeti Matararaba joined the field crew in his capacity as Field Officer for the Fiji Museum. Sue Loughlin and Patrick Hunkler volunteered their labour to the project. Shannon Wood and Yvonne Marshall assisted by Sepeti Matararaba and Vasiti Ritova carried out the mapping of the dunes. Andrew Crosby, Sue Loughlin and Sepeti Matararaba excavated the burials. Andrew Crosby assisted by Patrick Hunkler conducted the testpits and feature excavations.

After the completion of mapping in 1992 several pieces of follow up work were undertaken. In 1993 the dunes were briefly surveyed to monitor changes, and mapping and test excavations were carried out behind the dunes. In 1994 and 1997 the dunes were again surveyed to monitor further changes.

Mapping methods

The map was made using a Nikon Optical Theodolite. The survey method employed was based on establishing a grid using two parallel baselines, 50 metres apart, running approximately parallel to the shoreline. The grid method was adopted due to its efficiency in recording and plotting procedures and because it built into the survey the numerous checks necessary to maintain accuracy when mapping a constantly shifting surface.

A site datum point (SD) was established at the eastern end of the dunes utilising an existing steel pipe that protruded from the dune for approximately 1 metre. This point was located well to the east of any exposed archaeological remains (Fig. 3.1). The highest identified tide line was selected as the elevation of 0.00 metres. High tide was identified as the maximum vertical extent of the surge line, which has resulted in parts of the mapped site area appearing as if they are under water.

An upper baseline (Baseline 2) was established from a point (Station 0) situated 9.13 metres from the datum at a direction of 317° 33′ 00″ (magnetic), running approximately east to west for 1200 metres at 266° (magnetic). This baseline traversed the steep side slope of the dune for its entire length (Plate 3). A parallel lower baseline (Baseline 1) was established 50 metres to the south of Baseline 2. It ran along the less steep shoreline near the high tide line. It was established by turning 90° south from a point 100 metres west along Baseline 2.

The original intention was to maintain the 50 metres parallel separation of the two baselines for their full length. However, irregularities in the dune surface and in the surge line had to be adjusted for resulting in both baselines having a parallel offset. Baseline 1 (Lower Baseline) was offset 10 metres north from a point 300 metres west of Station 0 and Baseline 2 (Upper Baseline) was offset 10 metres north from a point 550 metres west of Station 0. Both baselines maintained their 10 metre offsets until they terminated (see Fig. 3.1). Stations were set up along the length of each baseline at 100m intervals using large steel pegs. Sub-stations were set up at 20 metre intervals between each station using smaller steel spikes. Each station and sub-station along the two baselines was labelled with the distance from the baseline start point (0 + 000) so that comparisons between the two baselines could easily be made and the integrity of the grid maintained.

Transects were run perpendicular to the baselines at 20 metre intervals. Each began at the sea, passed through the relevant station or substation on each baseline, and continued to the crest of the dunes. Transects were kept perpendicular by lining up the corresponding stations and sub-stations on the two baselines.

The following points were recorded for each transect:

- Contour points at 5 metre intervals.
- Every change in slope.
- The boundaries of all natural features.
- The boundaries of surface cultural debris.
- All surface exposures of palaeosols.
- The locations and boundaries of subsurface archaeological investigations.

In general, instrument set-up was carried out on each of the 100 metre stations on both baselines. Occasional irregularities or shifting sands required that a nearby sub-station be used instead. Additional points were taken in order to accurately locate and define the boundaries, contouring and arrangement of natural and cultural features.

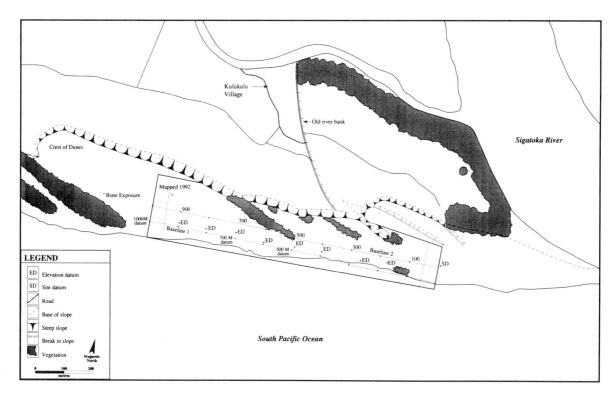

Fig. 3.1 The eastern section of the Sigatoka Dunes showing the area mapped and the layout of baselines and datums used during the 1992 survey.

Transects were carried out from Station 0 + 000 to 0 + 1025 metres west. A number of additional points up to approximately 0 + 1150 metres west were needed to encompass additional Level 2 exposures and human remains located high on the dunes in this area. An additional station was set above Baseline 2 between Station 0 + 900 and 0 + 1000 to survey right to the crest of the dunes in this area.

In the mapped area the dune surface was in perpetual motion. The sand was constantly moving, eroding from one part and building up in another area. Even overnight, a strong wind could create sand drifts or valleys over a metre deep. As a result, no part of the dune surface had a constant elevation from one day to the next. To control for these circumstances, a series of elevation datums (ED) were set up between the two baselines and readings were taken from these at each station set-up.

Difficulties encountered in keeping the instrument level on the shifting and often steep dune surface were controlled by using a plywood base. This consisted of a sheet of plywood with three holes cut just large enough for the ends of the tripod legs to penetrate. A further central hole allowed the instrument to be centred over the

station or sub-station peg (Plate 3). This arrangement stopped the legs from sinking or shifting in the soft sand after the initial set-up.

Further difficulties were encountered when pegs marking stations and sub-stations either shifted in the sand or were removed by visitors to the dunes. This was controlled for by taking appropriate backsights, and whenever necessary re-chaining distances between station and sub-station points.

The accuracy of the baseline placement was checked by using Baseline 1 as a control. Right angles were turned from the stations on Baseline 1 north to Baseline 2 at each station (i.e. every 100 metres). The distances between the stations on Baseline 2 were chained (Plate 4). Errors in distance over 100 metres along Baseline 2 ranged from 0.02 to 0.05 metres. The total accumulated error over 900 metres was 0.14 metres (0.16%). Distances between Baselines 1 and 2 were more difficult to chain due to the extreme steepness of the slope in some places. In the worst case the error was 0.21 metres over 50 metres (0.420%). In areas of more gentle slope the error ranged from +0.05 metres to -0.02 metres (0.100 to 0.040%). The occasional large errors in the distance between the baselines can therefore be attributed to difficulties in chaining and plumbing in multiple steps down steep slopes.

Elevation datums established near Stations 0 + 100, 200, 300, 400, 600 and 800 and were left in place on the dunes. Three permanent datums, in addition to the site datum, were established on Baseline 1 at Stations 0 + 500, 0 + 700 and 0 + 1000. These datums consisted of metal rods approximately 1.5 metres long, driven into the sand until they protruded about 50 cm above the surface of the sand.

To describe the locations of features and cultural remains, mapped distances west of the 0 + 000 datum we use the following convention: a feature located at 0 + 200 metres west of the datum will be described as located at 200M.

Excavation methods

Excavations were of three kinds:

- A testpit and probe survey was conducted in order to collect more detailed information on how the various layers exposed on the surface were related to each other stratigraphically.
- Limited excavations were carried out to record and/or remove cultural features and human remains exposed by recent dune erosion and in danger of being destroyed.
- Testpits were excavated in an area of undulating ground behind the dunes and in front of Kulukulu Village to establish the extent and composition of cultural deposits initially identified from eroding sections along the Club Masa access road.

The testpit and probe survey was conducted unsystematically over the site. Testpit and probe transects were excavated where necessary to identify exposed palaeosols; to determine the stratigraphic and areal relationships between palaeosols; and to provenance pottery scatters and other artefacts found exposed on the surface. Testpits were excavated by spade to a maximum depth of one metre. Deeper spade excavation was impossible in the dune sands. In two locations, where confirmation of the presence or absence of palaeosols beneath deep surface sand was required, the sand was probed to a maximum depth of 1.6 metres. The probe used consisted of a stainless steel shaft cut along its length to give a 0.5 cm channel. When twisted in the ground the probe collected a sample approximating the subsurface profile.

A total of seventeen testpit transects and four probe transects were excavated. These consisted of testpits or probes put down at 1–2 metre intervals along a transect line. A typology of soil and sand types was created based on macroscopically observed characteristics of colour, soil/sand density,

moisture content and angle of striation of wind blown deposits. This typology enabled field identifications of the palaeosols labelled Levels 1, 2 and 3 by the Birks during their excavations as well as several other wind and marine deposited sands.

Individual testpit and probe profiles were recorded as depths below the surface. Transect profiles were then constructed based on surface height measurements recorded during the theodolite survey. Minimally, height readings were recorded at each end of a transect, heights for the intermediate testpits being extrapolated from the grid survey readings. Given the overall accuracy of the grid survey, the resulting profiles afford a good indication of the subsurface angles of slope of all three palaeosols and provide the basis for a three dimensional reconstruction of the dune surfaces at the time each palaeosol was occupied.

Excavations to record and/or remove cultural features and human remains were only conducted where the material was in danger of immediate destruction. All excavated materials were marked and incorporated into the survey and, following excavation, were deposited in the Fiji Museum. The majority of features excavated were in-situ ceramic vessels or surface scatters of sherds. In each case the excavated area was irregular and defined by the size of the feature to be removed. An area just large enough and deep enough to recover the identified artefact or feature was opened. Because these excavations only encompassed a single artefact or feature they did not recover a great deal of stratigraphic information.

Human remains were excavated only where significant sections of articulated skeletal material existed and were in immediate danger of destruction. Surface scatters of severely eroded fragments of human bone and teeth, which were common on the site, were recorded on the survey but were not collected. These surface scatters indicated likely subsurface concentrations of uneroded burials, particularly in the area of Burial Ground 2. No effort was made, however, to identify or excavate unexposed burials.

Two relatively intact burials were excavated during the 1992 survey. In addition six burials excavated by Crosby and Matararaba in 1991 are also reported here. In all cases large numbers of loose and severely eroded fragments of bone, particularly of crania, teeth and lower limbs were found in the upper 5cm of loose surface sand. These bones were collected and bagged without conservation treatment. They represent the upper extremities of the skeletons damaged during exposure prior to excavation. The remainder of the skeletons was excavated using the methods developed during Best's 1987/8 excavations. They involved scraping down each bone with delicate bamboo tools then spraying each bone with three treatments of 20% solution of Rhoplex consolidant and water shortly after they were exposed. Individual long bones were allowed to dry in situ, then disarticulated, lifted and treated and dried on the undersides before being packed in foam. Crania, rib cages, pelves, vertebrae and hands and feet were exposed for photography and then lifted in blocks. As much excess sand as possible was removed from the undersides of the blocks to allow consolidation treatment before they were packed in foam. Once lifted and packed, the bone was deposited in the Fiji Museum.

Excavations carried out in 1993 on the undulating ground behind the dunes consisted of four one by one metre square testpits located along the crests of three ridges. The aim of the test excavations was simply to establish whether intact cultural layers were present on these ridges, and to collect sufficiently large samples of pottery to establish their approximate age.

Chapter 4
The 1992 mapping project: summary of results

Introduction

This chapter describes the dune surface mapped in August 1992. It begins with a description of the basic dune stratigraphy then goes on to describe the cultural remains and palaeosol exposures mapped on the surface. These descriptions are only a summary of the results. Precise details of the excavated features, excavated burials, testpits and probe transects and the 1993 excavations behind the dunes can be found in Appendices A–D. Relationships between the palaeosols and cultural remains are interpreted using both survey and excavation results.

Basic dune stratigraphy

During the survey the following deposits were recognised on the dunes surface and within the testpit and probe transects. The general classification of sands developed by Birks (1973) and Dickinson (1968) has been maintained. They represent three consolidated soil layers or palaeosols and a series of sterile wind-deposited (eolian) sands over a base of beach and/or eolian sands. The deposits are ordered below from the lowest to the highest, although any of the loose eolian sands may be found in any position above Level 1. In general these sands are differentiated by colour, organic content and texture. The complete sequence was not encountered in any single testpit or probe transect. For simplicity, minor variations in the deposits have been ignored.

The green-brown moist sand proved a universal base found beneath Level 1 and occasionally beneath Level 2. It was never found between Levels 1 and 2. The deposit dries to a yellow-brown colour and becomes increasingly yellow and dry at greater elevations above sea level. In general, the deposit is moist and dense, occasionally having a soil-like consistency. No significant laminating, banding or

striations were visible. This deposit is the same as that described by Birks as a "Yellow beach sand ... extending north under the dunes and of an unknown depth" (Birks 1973:9; see also Hirst and Kennedy 1962:1). Its description as beach sand is questionable, however, given its presence on the dunes at heights well above 5 metres elevation. The coloured appearance and soil-like nature of the deposit may be partly due to leaching of materials from the paleosols above. Significantly, on some areas of the site Level 2 was found resting directly on this deposit. In these places Level 1 may never have been present, it may have eroded prior to the formation of Level 2, or Levels 1 and 2 may comprise a single soil with no intervening sterile sand deposit.

The brown sandy soil ranges in colour from dark brown to dark tan and comprises a densely compacted organic soil-sand matrix. It contains little in the way of charcoal or organic staining indicative of cultural occupation but on some parts of the site could be directly associated with Level 1 type pottery. The deposit is consistent with that described by Birks as "Grey-brown sand, (Level 1)" (Birks 1973:9). Birks records the depth of the deposit as 24 inches over the site. The 1992 testpits

Deposit	Nature of deposit	Name
Green-brown moist sand	?Beach sand	
Brown sandy soil	Palaeosol	Level 1
Loose grey sand	Unsorted eolian sand	
Loose striated sand	Eolian sand with angled laminations	
Loose banded sand	Eolian sand with horizontal laminations	
Dense brown-grey sand	Compacted eolian sand	
Black-brown sandy soil	Palaeosol	Level 2
Dense grey-black sand	Iron sand/?palaeosol	
Black-brown sandy soil	Palaeosol	Level 3

Table 1: Basic stratigraphy identified on the dunes during the 1992 survey.

revealed the deposit ranged in thickness from 22 cm in the west (Testpit Transect 8) to 82 cm in the east (Testpit Transect 4).

The loose grey, striated and horizontally banded sands are loose deposits of wind blown sands found between and above all palaeosols (Plate 1). In general, the laminated sands occur high on the dunes in deep drift deposits or lower on the dunes where older sands have been scoured by erosion and recent banded or striated deposits have filled the resulting hollow. The unsorted loose grey sands form more even, layer-like and sometimes semi-consolidated deposits. Along the seaward margin of the dunes, they tend to become thicker at higher elevations on the dunes. Deposits up to 1m thick separate Levels 1 and 2, up to 2m thick separate Levels 2 and 3, and thicker deposits overlie Level 3. Further north at higher elevations on the dunes, this situation is reversed. Deep deposits of loose sand underlie Level 2 and only relatively shallow deposits separate and/or overlie Levels 2 and 3. The significance of this build up of loose dune sands beneath Level 2 is discussed in Chapter 7.

The dense brown-grey sand ranges in colour from dark grey to reddish brown and corresponds to Birks' "Red-brown sand." It underlies Level 2 over much of the surveyed dune surface. It is a friable matrix indicative of a wind-deposited sand, compacted and stained by the leaching of organic material from above (see Dickinson 1968:117; Birks 1973:10).

Level 2 comprises a black-brown, densely compacted organic soil-sand matrix, described by Birks as a "dark brown sand" (1973:9). It is generally 30–40 cm thick and forms the most uniform and extensive palaeosol on the dune surface (Plate 11). It appears to contain more organic material than either Level 1 or 3 and contains the widest variety of cultural debris including shell, animal bone, worked and unworked stone, rich deposits of pottery, burnt and unburned wood and fully articulated human burials.

Dense grey-black sand was occasionally found extending as a palaeosol-like deposit of moisture retentive black iron-sands above Level 2 in the central and western parts of the surveyed area. It has an oily, moist consistency but contains little or no organic matter and does not hold together like the other palaeosols. It was not possible to gauge its depth accurately and surface exposures were not mapped. There is evidence, however, to suggest that some scatters of plain pottery and eroded human bone on the dune surface may be associated with this deposit. It may represent a heavily leached continuation of Level 3 on the western part of the site, or it may represent a different sort of

partially compacted surface that was sought out for sporadic human occuapation.

Level 3 comprises a black-brown, densely compacted organic soil-sand matrix, present only over the eastern half of the surveyed area (Plate 5). Its depth was not reliably gauged but appeared similar to Level 2, at about 30–40 cm. It also contains concentrations of cultural debris including worked and unworked stone, charcoal and burnt wood but contains less pottery than Level 2. Many of the unprovenanced bone scatters found over the upper dune surface may derive from this deposit, but no human bone was found within the Level 3 palaeosol during the survey or excavations.

Surveyed cultural remains

The cultural remains identified during the 1992 survey are described below by Level. They were assigned to one of the three soil layers on the basis of pottery styles and their proximity to an eroding palaeosol. It should be noted, however, that not all cultural remains could be positively associated with one of the three palaeosols. Indeed, it is one of the findings of this project that some cultural remains, particularly human burials, were originally deposited in loose sand. The significance of this finding is discussed briefly in Chapters 6 and 8.

Each Level is described from east to west. Locations of cultural materials are described in the text using metres (M) west from the 0 datum and elevation in metres above the 1992 high tide line. Fig. 4.1 shows the general distribution of cultural remains and exposed palaeosols across the surveyed area. The details of all surface cultural remains are illustrated in Figs. 4.2a–d.

The locations of all testpit and probe transects are summarised in Fig. A1 and details of the results of those excavations can be found in Appendix A. Of the many features exposed on the surface of the dunes, eleven (F1–11) were considered to be of special interest and were still sufficiently intact to be worth excavating. Their locations are summarised in Fig. B1 and the details of their excavation can be found in Appendix B. F3, F5, and F10 were Level 1 features; F8 and F9 included both Level 1 and 2 pottery; F1, F2, F4, and F11 were Level 2 features; and F6 and F7 were Level 3 features. All recovered materials were removed to the Fiji Museum.

The survey identified and partially recovered a large number of human skeletons of widely varying degrees of preservation. These are discussed in greater detail in Chapter 6 and Appendix C. One major concentration of human remains (B1–6), now referred to as Burial Ground 2, was mapped and

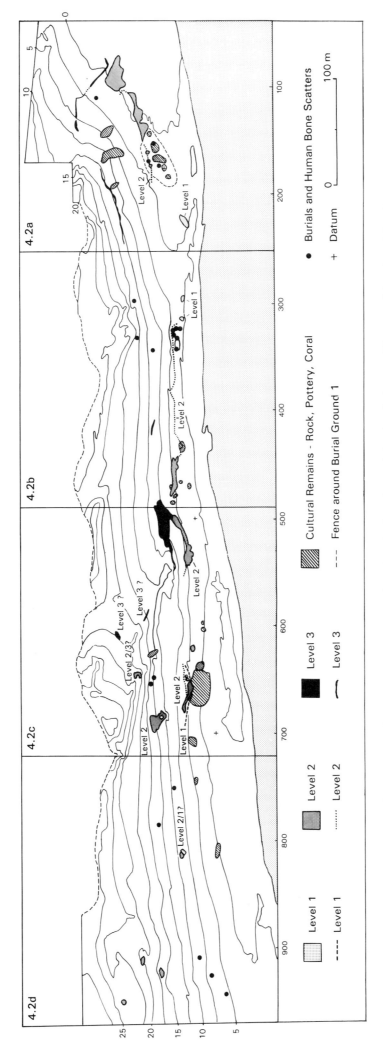

Fig. 4.1 Simplified version of the 1992 survey map showing the locations of the detailed maps illustrated in Figs. 4.2a–d

Cultural Remains - Rock, Pottery, Coral

Burials and Human Bone Scatters

Fence around Burial Ground 1

Datum

Level 1

Level 2

Level 3

Level 1

Level 2

Level 3

100 m

4.2a

4.2b

4.2c

4.2d

two partially complete skeletons, B92/A and B92/B, were excavated at the far eastern end of the surveyed area. In addition the locations of a further 10 scatters of human bone (HB1–10) were recorded and a scatter of human teeth located high on the dunes at 330M was collected as B92/C. Again, all materials were removed to the Fiji Museum.

Level 1

Exposures of the Level 1 palaeosol and of cultural remains associated with this palaeosol occurred intermittently over a distance of 650 metres, between 150M and 800M. The elevation of exposures rose gradually from east to west. At 200M, Level 1 was exposed at 2 metres elevation, rising to 3 metres by 300M, 5 metres at 700M, and 9 metres at the possible Level 1 exposure at around 800M. Within this 650 metre span exposures of Level 1 were concentrated in two areas. The first occurred between 200M and 300M and the second occurred between 600M and 700M. All cultural remains identified as belonging to Level 1 consisted of pottery.

The first definite appearance of the Level 1 palaeosol on the surface occurred at 210M. From this point the line of exposed soil continued west below a relatively shallow deposit of loose sand until re-emerging in two exposures around 300M. No cultural remains were found directly associated with these soil exposures although scattered sherds of Level 1 pottery were identified just to the east, on a badly eroded area around the eastern end of Burial Ground 1 (150M– 200M).

Testpit Transect 15 revealed that between 210M and 300M Level 1 dips slightly into a shallow depression. This may represent the formation of Level 1 over a depression formed by a continuation of an old riverbank identified at the back of the dunes directly north of this point (see Chapter 7). To the east of this depression, at 210M, probing indicated that the palaeosol formed a more or less level surface sloping down slightly into the dune face to the north. This suggests that the occupation took place on a low-lying flat or shallow back slope of a beach ridge, prior to the formation of any significant dunes close to the old river course. By 330M, which is west of the old river course, Testpit Transects 1 and 4 indicated that Level 1 rises to the north at a gradient of c.1:9 and continues rising into the dunes until it is truncated by or conflated with Level 2 at c.4m elevation.

Just past 300M the Level 1 palaeosol disappeared, both on and beneath the surface, and did not reappear until 640M. Testpit Transects 5–7 suggest the Level 1 and 2 surfaces were conflated in the area of 400–500M at c.4–5m elevation. Two Level 1 features, F3 and F5, were excavated in this area. Both features consisted of partially intact Late Eastern Lapita plainware pots. They were resting on green-brown basal sands suggesting the Level 1 palaeosol had eroded, deflating the pottery onto the basal sand. Weathered, redeposited Level 1 sherds were also present in this area among the storm tossed debris close to the high tide line.

At 640M the Level 1 palaeosol reappeared on the surface where it was exposed continuously for a distance of at least 60 metres (Plate 2). The eastern end of this exposure is marked by F10 where two Late Eastern Lapita plainware pots were recovered from the interface of Level 1 with the green-brown basal sand. Two further features, F8 and F9, were also associated with this palaeosol at the western end of the exposure. Both features included late Lapita plainware sherds and Level 2 pottery. F8 consisted of scattered sherds recovered from loose grey sand. Some of the Level 1 pottery from F9 included in situ sherds recovered from a mixed black to brown soil matrix resting on green-brown basal sand. The sherds were up to 30cm below the surface and pottery was found throughout this depth.

Testpit Transect 8 revealed the reason for this mixing to be the near conflation of Levels 1 and 2 in this area. It revealed that at c.650M Level 1 formed a sloping surface, rising into the dunes to the north at a gradient of c.1:10. Just a few centimetres above it, separated by a thin compacted grey-brown sand, Level 2 was found rising north into the dunes at a steeper gradient of c.1:6. In the now eroded section of dune just to the south (seaward) of where these palaeosol exposures occurred, the two cultural Levels would therefore have been conflated, accounting for the mixed pottery types scattered on the surface. Further north, into the dune face, the two Levels increase their separation and the pristine survival of the Level 1 surface can be expected.

The final occurrence of Level 1 on the surface was a possible palaeosol exposure at 800M. This exposure appeared to consist of two superimposed soils suggesting Level 1 and 2 were both present. However, no definite identification was possible on the basis of such a small, isolated exposure. Level 1 was not encountered in any of the testpits west of 650M.

Level 2

Exposures of the Level 2 palaeosol and of associated cultural remains occurred along the full length of the mapped area beginning at 80M and continuing west beyond 960M. Like Level 1, the elevations at which these exposures occurred gradually increased from east to west. At 80M they

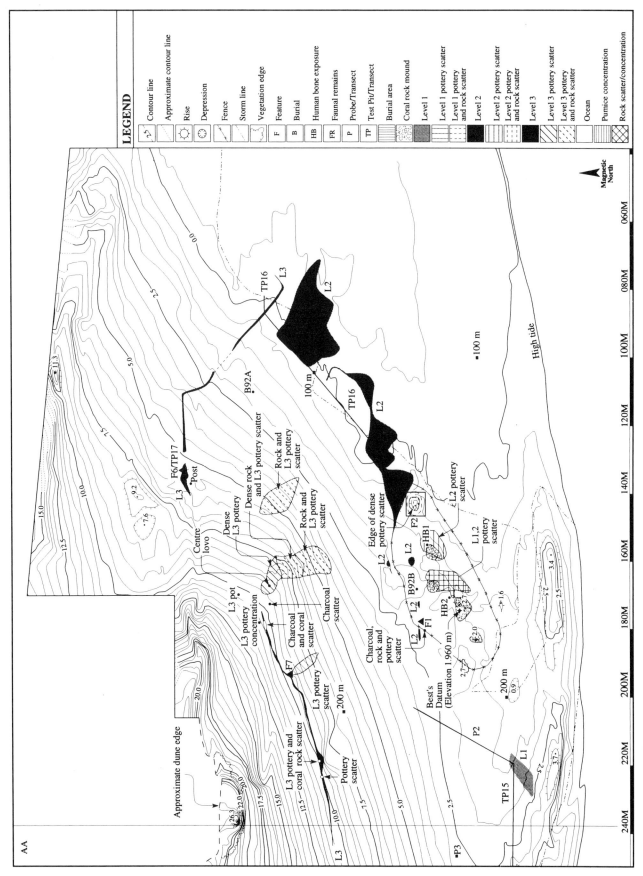

Fig. 4.2a Detail of the 1992 survey map, showing the far eastern section, M40 – M250

were at, and even below, 0 metres elevation – in other words below the 1992 high tide line. By 500M most exposures were around 5 metres in elevation. West of 600M exposures up to and above 20 metres elevation occurred. Although these exposures are intermittent on the surface, it would be reasonable to describe Level 2 as virtually continuous across the mapped area and beyond.

Unlike Level 1, the visible Level 2 cultural remains were extremely varied. They included many kinds of pottery from extremely fine, thin walled, paddle impressed wares to thick, crudely made trays (Plate 9). Other cultural materials included the following: exposures of concentrated rock and/or coral; numerous burials; occasional scatters of faunal remains; occasional fragments of worked stone; burnt posts; *lovo* (oven) features; and in one case a possible pottery firing or salt-making hearth. Although pottery, rock and coral dominate the cultural debris, this should not be allowed to obscure the fact that a wide variety of cultural materials have now been identified from Level 2.

The first exposure of the Level 2 palaeosol occurred at 80M and continued on the surface for a distance of about 120 metres until it disappeared at the western end of Burial Ground 1, the cemetery excavated by Best in 1987 and 1988. Pottery was eroding from the face of the palaeosol along this length but was not uniformly distributed – rather it occurred in just a few concentrations separated by areas of sparse, scattered sherds. This distribution pattern was especially evident in deflated areas along the seaward side of the eroding soil line where several mounds of pottery were left like islands raised above the soft beach sand. The largest example, F2, which also contained the densest concentration of pottery identified during the survey, was excavated and around a tonne of pottery was recovered. The pottery from these mounds, especially F2, included many examples of very fine, thin-walled, paddle-impressed pottery and few, if any, of the crude trays so common further west. Apart from the pottery several other forms of cultural remains were present. They included the following: several concentrations of rock; considerable amounts of charcoal, mostly scattered but including one burnt post or tree stump (F1); human bone including the excavated burial B92/B and a possible intact coral mound burial; and a scatter of fishbone associated with the knoll on which Simon Best's datum is located.

In 1988 Best found that Level 2 formed a slight mound or rise in the area of Burial Ground 1. Beyond this he found Level 2 extended level into the dunes to the north, but dropped slightly to the east and probably to the south (Best 1989). Best's interpretations were confirmed by Testpit Transect 16 and by the excavation of a new burial on the north side of the burial ground (B92/B). These excavations indicated that, as for Level 1, in this location Level 2 probably formed on a largely flat surface prior to any significant dune formation this far east. Testpit Transect 16 revealed that at c.80M the Level 2 surface drops sharply to the east at a gradient of c.1:3, indicating a clear edge to the occupation surface, apparently the edge of the beach flat and the western bank of an old river channel.

No Level 2 exposures were present in the area between Burial Grounds 1 and 2 although probing indicated the presence of Level 2 beneath c.1m of recent drift sand, a situation similar to that mapped by Best in 1988 (1989: Fig. 2). The Level 2 palaeosol reappeared on the surface at the eastern end of the area now designated as Burial Ground 2, at around 310M. At this point there were a few surface scatters of Level 2 pottery and trays and concentrated scatters of badly eroded human bone. Testpit Transects 1–4 were excavated in the area. They demonstrated that to the west of the area of bone Level 2 formed a flat surface, possibly dipping slightly into the dune face. In contrast, where the surface bone was concentrated the palaeosol rose slightly to the north. It seems likely that, as for Burial Ground 1, a slight rise or mound had been utilised for the deposition of human remains.

From Burial Ground 2 west, Level 2 was exposed as a continuous line though to 560M, a distance of 250 metres. Just above F5 there was a small break in the surface exposure of Level 2 but it continued just below the surface. Along this exposure pottery was eroding out of the Level 2 palaeosol and spilling downslope. Testpit Transects 6 and 7, excavated between 450–500M, indicated that in this area Level 2 still formed a more or less flat surface extending into the dunes. At 500M the testpits indicated that Level 3 had conflated onto it and Level 2 had itself conflated onto Level 1 below. At a point around 500M, all three palaeosols, therefore, were virtually juxtaposed. This location is within 100m of the Birks' extrapolated stratigraphy profile. It is the only area on the dunes where all three levels approach each other.

Although pottery was present throughout the full 250 metre length of exposure of Level 2 in this area, its density varied greatly and, in general, increased to the west. In some places there were just a few scattered sherds, and in other places the pottery was so dense it formed a continuous carpet. Trays and coarse plainwares were particularly common but fine wares and decorated sherds with paddle-impressed designs were also present. A particularly dense concentration occurred at the

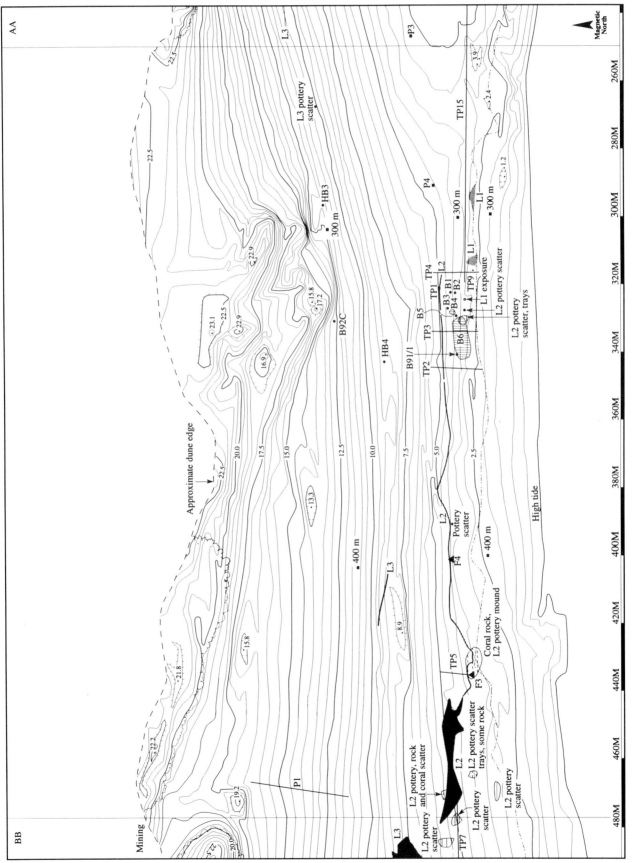

Fig. 4.2b Detail of the 1992 survey map, showing the eastern central section, M240 – M490

western end, between 520M and 540M. At this point the palaeosol formed a 50cm high eroded scarp, from which an exceptionally dense carpet of pottery spilled down the slope. Among the sherds were trays, coarse wares and many examples of the very fine, thin-walled, paddle-impressed pottery which had also been recovered from F2.

In this area, weathered, redeposited pottery was also found scattered between the Level 2 palaeosol and the high tide line. Mounded concentrations of deflated cultural remains occurred at intervals just downslope of the soil line. The composition of these concentrations varied. Almost all concentrations contained pottery. Some also contained dense concentrations of broken rock, coral, or both while others included just a few pieces of rock or coral amongst dense piles of pottery. One unique example, F4, consisted of a small fireplace lined with baked clay, which may have been used to fire pottery or to evaporate brine to produce salt (see Appendix B).

Between 560M and 620M the Level 2 palaeosol disappeared from the surface although scattered sherds and deflated concentrations of Level 2 pottery continued in the interval. Between 600M and 700M the Level 2 palaeosol reappeared at two, possibly three different elevations. The most extensive exposure occurred below 5 metres elevation.

At 640M both Level 1 and 2 appeared at around 5 metres elevation (Plate 2). The Level 2 palaeosol was exposed for a distance of 50 metres parallel to and just upslope of Level 1. Testpit Transect 8 showed both palaeosols rising into the dune face at this point, separated by a thin layer of compacted grey-brown sand. Directly below the Level 2 palaeosol exposure was the most extensive concentration of eroded pottery identified during the 1992 survey. It measured approximately 40 metres east–west and 25 metres north–south. Both Level 1 and 2 sherds were present but the vast majority came from Level 2 pots, and to a lesser extent, trays.

At 690M a large exposure of Level 2 occurred between 10 and 15 metres elevation. Some characteristic Level 2 pottery was scattered on the palaeosol surface and pottery excavated from F11 located at the uppermost extent of the exposure included cross-hatch paddle impressed sherds from a single very fine walled *kuro* (cooking pot). Testpit Transects 8–10 confirmed that this exposure was Level 2 and demonstrated that Level 2 rises to the north from the lower exposure at a gradient of c.1:6. Pottery recovered from the palaeosol in the upper extent of Transect 8 included neck sherds from a thin walled *kuro* decorated with asymmetric incision, considered highly characteristic of the Level 2 occupation. It could not be determined by testing whether this Level 2 exposure continued rising into the dune

face because at c.15m elevation it was overlaid and possibly truncated by a deposit of densely compacted iron sand. Some unprovenanced surface bone scatters to the east loosely associated with this iron sand deposit suggested it may represent the heavily leached remains of Level 3 (see Appendix A for details).

At 640M another Level 2 exposure occurred high on the dunes in an exposed profile located at the base of a steep crest at 20–21 metres elevation. Numerous scatters of potsherds were present around and downslope of this exposure. Significantly they included Level 2 trays and pots alongside undiagnostic plain *kuro* sherds. The largest scatter was located downslope from the palaeosol exposure, at 620M and 12–15 metres elevation. It included rock and Level 2 pottery and trays. In situ sherds could be seen in the face of the exposed palaeosol, but none could be confidently assigned to a particular pottery type. On balance this soil exposure is almost certainly Level 2 but there remains some possibility that it represents the westernmost extent of Level 3 yet found on the dunes.

Although, at low elevations, the Level 2 palaeosol disappears on the surface at around 690M, exposures of deflated Level 2 type pottery mixed with rock and coral continue to occur below 5 metres elevation until 810M. Further exposures of this pottery, characterised by paddle impressed pots and large trays, also occurred at low elevations beyond the mapped area. In April 1993 when Marshall surveyed the dunes for cyclone damage an exposed *lovo* feature was recorded 15–20 metres from the high tide line and very close to the base of the large ridge that begins at 1220M. The *lovo* consisted mainly of burnt white stone and dense charcoal. Some red stone, coral, small bone fragments and weathered sherds of Level 2 type pottery were also present. This *lovo* is almost certainly the same feature as that reported in Burley (1997:14) as Feature 2, and in Burley and Shortland (1999:9) as Feature 10. In both reports it is mistakenly assumed to be a Level 3 feature.

Thus, at low elevations Level 2 is present beyond 690M only as deflated cultural debris, but at higher elevations the Level 2 palaeosol continues to appear at sporadic intervals. These exposures commonly include only small amounts of pottery, but sufficient sherds were found embedded in the exposed soils to confidently assign them to Level 2. At c.920M Testpit Transect 14 revealed the presence of Level 2 at c.10m elevation. It lay beneath a thin layer of surface sand and climbed steeply north into the dune face at a gradient of c.1:4.5. This indicates that on this section of the dunes the Level 2 surface approximated the current steeply sloping dune

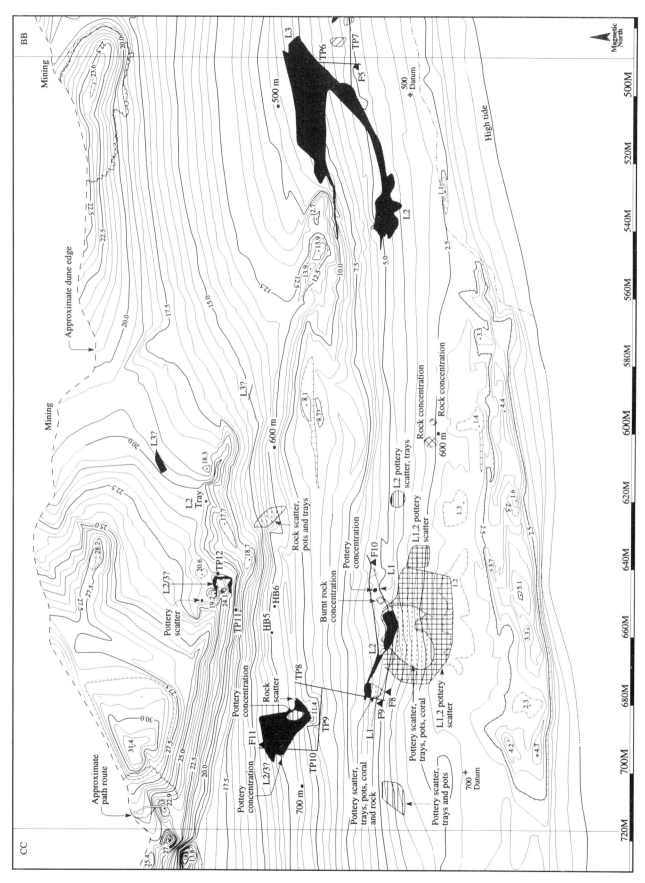

Fig. 4.2c Detail of the 1992 survey map, showing the western central section, M480 – M730

surface but has been eroded below c.10m elevation such that all that remains low on the dunes are deflated scatters of pottery, bone and other cultural debris.

Within the mapped area the last exposure of Level 2 occurred at 940M and 24 metres elevation where a Level 2 tray sherd was found imbedded in the exposed palaeosol. An intermediate station had to be surveyed in, in order to record this exposure (see Figs. 3.1, 4.2d). Further palaeosol exposures, presumably also of Level 2, occurred considerably further west at even higher elevations. These occurred up to and beyond the outlying bone exposure shown on Fig. 3.1. This bone exposure occurred at approximately 1150M and 31m elevation. A large palaeosol exposure occurred 10–20 metres above it (Plate 1). All palaeosol exposures this far west occurred around or above the elevation of the bone exposure.

Level 3

Level 3 was identified over a distance of approximately 500 metres. The Level 3 palaeosol occurred on the surface between 80M and 550M at very consistent elevations of between 8 and 12 metres. Four further soil exposures, which may be Level 3, occurred between 550M and 700M at elevations between 10 and 20 metres. In addition a number of unmapped compacted grey or black iron sand deposits which may represent the leached remains of Level 3 were identified on steeply sloping sections of the dune face.

Level 3 first appeared around 80M, just inland of Level 2, at or below the high tide mark. From this point it could be followed as a dark line in the sand sweeping in a north-westerly arc up the dune to F6 where it spread out into a large palaeosol exposure approximately 10 metres in diameter (see Plate 5). This feature appeared to be a deflated living surface and included pottery, broken river stones, coral, small chert cores, burnt clay, charcoal and 5 possible posts or burnt tree stumps (see Appendix B). Each type of material was concentrated in a particular area within the feature suggesting a structured deposit, possibly resulting from a working area, rather than oven or midden discard.

Testpit Transects 16 and 17 revealed that this arcing exposed edge of Level 3 represents the steeply sloping back (northern) and eastern faces of the dune at the time of its occupation. At 80M it drops sharply to the east at a gradient of c.1:2.5 immediately above the similar drop off in Level 2, indicating that the eastern margin of the dunes was well defined at this point during both occupations. Excavations along this section of the Level 3 exposure were conducted by the Fiji Museum in

1995. They reached a similar conclusion (Burke 1995b). In the vicinity of F6, Level 3 slopes down equally steeply to the north, indicating that this feature may represent the spill of cultural debris down the back of the dune slope, probably at a point where the dune begins to drop away from a relatively level surface.

Between 140M and 180M the palaeosol briefly disappeared from the surface leaving two large scatters of deflated rock and pottery. The larger and more westerly of the two scatters is located on top of the remains of a small knoll which marks the end of a ridge. On the highest point there was a semi-intact *lovo*. Just below the *lovo* was a very dense concentration of pottery and below that again pottery and rock were spilling down the slope (see Fig. 4.2a). Directly above and west of this large scatter were two concentrations of pottery unassociated with a palaeosol. It appears that just here the Level 3 soil has been completely eroded off the top of the knoll, leaving deflated cultural remains on soft wind blown sand.

At 180M the Level 3 palaeosol reappeared and could be followed west along the 10 metre contour line for a distance of about 80 metres. At intervals along this exposure pottery was found eroding out of the palaeosol. Approximately 20 metres west of where the palaeosol disappeared a further concentration of Level 3 pottery was identified. The most extensively exposed example of these pottery concentrations, F7, was excavated (see Appendix B). Although F7 consisted of pottery scattered over an area 3.5 metres wide and extending downslope 10 metres, when excavated it was found that the pottery probably came from only 1 or 2 pots. This finding is probably also true for other pottery concentrations associated with the exposed Level 3 palaeosol.

Just past 400M, the Level 3 palaeosol reappeared as a short exposure 20 metres long. Trench excavations conducted a year later (Hudson 1994:10) established that this exposure continued and joined with a huge Level 3 exposure associated with a small amount of undiagnostic pottery between 480M and 550M. In 1992 this exposure had conflated onto an exposed section of the Level 2 paleosol, with Level 2 pottery spilling down the slope to the south. Testpit Transects 5–7 confirmed the identities of the two paleosols and indicated that in this area Level 2 formed a horizontal surface but Level 3 sloped up to the north at a gradient of c.1:6, thus conflating onto and possibly truncating Level 2 at the point of exposure, while overlying and preserving the Level 2 surface further into the dune face. Test trenching by Hudson in 1993 slightly higher on the dune slope confirmed the presence of both soil layers separated by sterile sand (Hudson 1994:11).

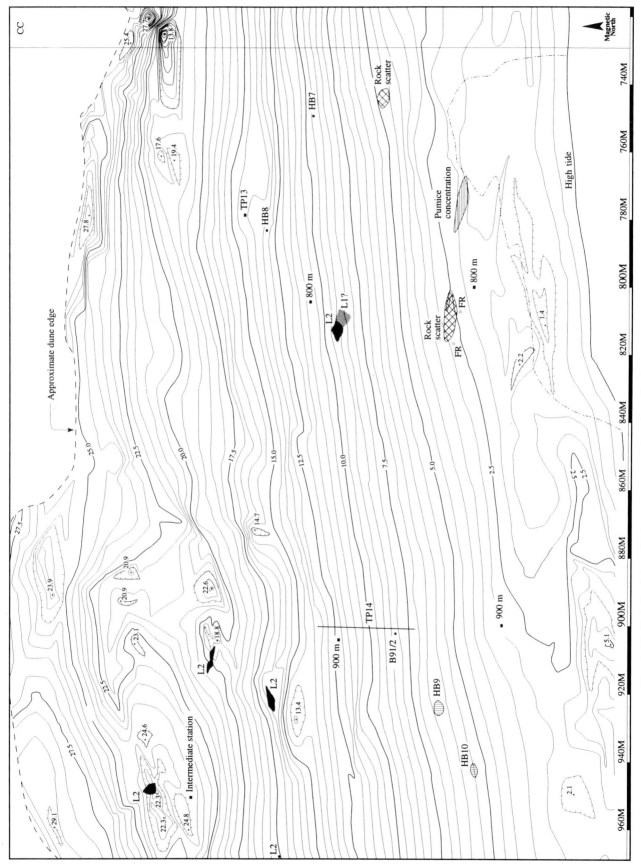

Fig. 4.2d Detail of the 1992 survey map, showing the far western section, M720 – M970

Beyond 550M there were no further definite exposures of Level 3. However, two small exposures high on the dune are thought to be Level 3. These are located at 590M and 15 metres elevation, and 610M and 20 metres elevation. No cultural remains were found in association with either soil exposure. As discussed above, two further exposures that contained Level 2 pottery may also have a Level 3 component. These are located at 640M and 20–21 metres elevation, and 680M–700M at 10–15 metres elevation. Finally, an area of dense grey compacted sand traversed by Testpit Transect 10 at c.690M, directly overlying Level 2 and associated with several scatters of human bone may represent the leached remains of Level 3 at its most westerly extent on the dunes.

Summary

In 1992 all three paleosols were exposed over a much larger area than had previously been recorded. In addition, a much greater variety of cultural remains were found than had been expected.

Level 1 was exposed intermittently over a distance of 650M. It appeared as a horizontal surface around 200M at an elevation of 2 metres. It was found rising steadily to the west to an elevation of 9 metres at 800M and forming a surface that slopes up increasingly steeply into the dune face. During the 1992 survey pottery was the only cultural material found in association with Level 1.

Level 2 was exposed intermittently across the entire mapped area. It appeared first below the 1992 high tide level at 80M. The exposed palaeosol could then be followed west for at least 1200 metres, along the course of which it rose steadily to above 20 metres in elevation. At the eastern end it formed a largely horizontal surface but was associated with a number of mounds and rises, two of which were associated with burial grounds. To the west it

formed a sloping surface, rising increasingly steeply into the dune face. Cultural debris was present across almost this entire length. However, most cultural remains occurred as concentrated pockets and the composition of these pockets was extremely variable. All concentrations contained pottery. Some also contained broken rock, coral, worked rock, faunal remains, charcoal, burnt posts and burnt clay in varying amounts.

The densest concentrations occurred between 600M and 700M and between 420M and 500M. Two further concentrations of pottery were associated with the two burial grounds, although these contained little in the way of rock or faunal materials. In particular several very large and well defined mounds of pottery with sherds from especially fine walled vessels were found in the vicinity of Burial Ground 1. Although scattered cultural debris was found between each of these four concentrations and further to the west, the concentrations represent distinct clusters of materials positioned at 150m intervals along the dune face.

Level 3 was exposed over a distance of at least 500 metres and possibly as much as 700 metres. Except where it first appeared at 80M, Level 3 was always exposed above 8 metres elevation. Unlike Levels 1 and 2 which rose steadily from east to west Level 3 exposures tended to occur at a consistent elevation close to the 10 metre contour. At the eastern end the palaeosol sloped down sharply to the north and east, indicating the back and end-slopes of the dune. To the west it formed a sloping surface, rising to the north into the dune face. Like Level 2, cultural remains occurred at low frequencies across the exposed distance but the vast majority were found in a single large cluster between 120M and 240M. Again, this cluster contained concentrations of pottery, broken stone, coral, worked stone, charcoal, burnt posts and burnt clay. The distribution of these materials elsewhere along the paleosol exposure was highly variable.

Chapter 5
Pulling together four decades of archaeology

Introduction

The 1992 survey provides a snapshot of the dune surface at a particular moment in time – namely August 1992. The value of this snapshot is that it can serve as a fixed reference point for understanding a surface that is never the same two days running. Earlier and subsequent investigations can be referenced to the 1992 map and plotted onto it. Once these archaeological investigations are located relative to one another it is possible for them to also inform one another – something which has until now been possible in only a very limited way. Although there has been strong archaeological interest in the human occupation of the Sigatoka Sand Dunes since pottery and human bone were first recorded eroding out of the dunes in the 1940s, this research has been conducted in a piecemeal fashion and much has been salvage in nature.

Listed below in Table 2 is a condensed synopsis of the more formal events that comprise the history of archaeological investigation on the dunes. These investigations are described in more detail in the following discussion. The main objective of this chapter is to collate as much of what we know about the dunes as possible and to locate it on the 1992 map so that it can be used to much greater effect in our efforts to understand both the formation of the dunes and the nature of the occupation which has taken place there. The chapter begins with an account of the investigations conducted prior the survey, then moves on to describe the investigations which followed the 1992 survey and Cyclone Kina. The following chapter brings together and locates all human remains recovered from the dunes up to 1998.

Re-locating pre-1992 investigations

Cultural remains were first identified on the dunes in 1944. Over the next two decades a number of archaeologists visited the dunes and reported on the expanding amounts of cultural material eroding from the sand. These reports in combination with analyses of a few collected sherds led to the development of Green's (1963a) four-phase chronological framework for Fijian prehistory. As described in Chapter 1, results from the Birks' extensive excavations at the dunes in 1965–6 neatly fitted this framework and established the Sigatoka Sand Dunes as the iconic type-site for Fijian prehistory.

Lawrence and Helen Birks 1965–6

During their excavations of Site VL 16/1 in 1965 and 1966, the Birks laid out a grid 1600 ft long, 200 ft wide in the western half and 100 ft wide in the eastern half (approximately 490 metres long by 61 metres narrowing to 30.5 metres). The location of this grid has been extrapolated onto the 1992 map (Fig. 5.1) using a combination of aerial photographs, topographic maps, the Birks' site plans, and copies of published and unpublished photographs taken during the Birks' excavations, some of which were kindly provided by Richard Shutler.

The precision of this extrapolation is confounded slightly by changes in the dune topography and magnetic variations occurring since 1966. However, we are confident that the error in any direction does not exceed 10 metres.

LEVELS 1–3

The Birks divided their grid into 5ft by 5ft quadrants and excavated 240 of these quadrants, representing 5% of the gridded area (see Birks 1973: Fig. 3). They defined three palaeosols which they called Levels 1–3. The excavations consisted of narrow bands that followed the eroding edge of each palaeosol, stopping c. 500ft from the western end of the grid (Fig. 5.1; Plate 8). Vast amounts of pottery, including an extraordinary number of

1944   Bruce Biggs first reports cultural remains on the sand dunes. Reference: Green 1963b:262.

1947   The presence of cultural materials and human bone is noted by American archaeologist E. W. Gifford. He describes two sites called Site 20 and 21 (Gifford 1951:251-2, 273, 278–9). Four sites, designated VL 16/1–4 are subsequently recorded on the Fiji Museum files: VL 16/1, areas of potsherds and human bone located on the seaward face of the dunes approximately 1km west of the mouth of the Sigatoka River; VL 16/2, located at Naqarai and composed of six scatters of pottery and bone; VL 16/3, a scatter of pottery on the dunes between VL 16/1 and the river mouth; and VL 16/4, an area of pottery located on flat land behind the dunes near their eastern end. References: Gifford 1951; Golson 1961.

1960-3 Further pottery collections are made at the dunes in 1960 by R. G. Ward and in 1961 by Bruce Biggs. These collections are analysed by Roger Green (1963b) who identifies the similarity of certain sherds to Lapita pottery in New Caledonia and Tonga.

1965-6 Extensive excavations are conducted at VL 16/1 by Lawrence and Helen Birks. They define three separate palaeosols on the dunes and recover different cultural materials from each. Level 1 contained Lapita pottery and was radiocarbon dated at 2460 ± 90 BP. Level 2 contained paddle impressed pottery and was radiocarbon dated at 1720 ± 80 BP. Level 3 contained plain pottery but was not dated by the Birks. Reference: Birks 1973.

1976   Simon Best visits VL 16/1 and notes the continuing presence of pottery and human bone.

1984   Geoff Irwin and Andrew Crosby visit the dunes and note the presence of large areas of pottery in the area of VL 16/1 and scatters of pottery and human bone on a disturbed and eroded dune surface between VL 16/1 and the river mouth – probably VL 16/3. They collect a large grinding stone from VL 16/1, which is deposited at the Fiji Museum.

1986   The presence of coral mounds on the dunes is reported to the Fiji Museum. Director Fergus Clunie investigates and finds fully articulated skeletons beneath coral mounds at the eastern end of VL 16/1.

1987-8 At Clunie's request, Simon Best directs excavations of an eroding burial ground at the eastern end of VL 16/1. He recovers 55 human skeletons that are radiocarbon dated to 1870 ± 70 BP. The bone is sent to the University of Otago for analysis by Edward Visser. References: Best 1987a, b; 1989; Visser 1994.

1988   Visser conducts an impact assessment survey of the land immediately north (inland) of the eastern end of VL 16/1 prior to the construction of a small surfing lodge, Club Masa. He finds cultural materials eroding from underneath the northern face of the dunes and an area of cultural soil on a low mound beside the river, which he interprets as a 19th century fishing camp. Reference: Visser 1988.

1991   Crosby and Fiji Museum Field Research Officer Sepeti Matararaba visit VL 16/1 and report 2 groups of skeletons eroding from the dunes. At the request of Fiji Museum they excavate 6 human skeletons from VL 16/1 which are sent to the University of Otago for analysis. They also map pottery and further human bone eroding from VL 16/1 over a distance of 900 metres along the dunes, noting that the processes of erosion on the dune are accelerating. References: Crosby 1991b, c.

1992   Crosby and Matararaba visit VL 16/1 on 3 further occasions. They note the presence of severely eroded human bone and extensive areas of pottery along the full length of the site. In July, Matararaba visits and notes the presence of a fully articulated skeleton beginning to erode from the eastern end of the site.

In August the survey reported here is carried out. The authors map VL 16/1 and excavate eroding pottery and burials. They also record two new archaeological sites, one with late Lapita pottery, on flat land immediately behind the dunes in the general location of VL 16/4. References: Crosby 1991a; 1992; Wood, Marshall and Crosby 1998.

1993   In April, Marshall inspects VL 16/1 for damage caused by cyclone Kina and maps the area of new sites on flat land lying between the dunes and Kulukulu village and conducts test excavations. Reference: Wood, Marshall and Crosby 1998.

In August, Crosby and Matararaba visit VL 16/1 and discover serious wave erosion has destroyed a major portion of VL 16/1 including Burial Ground 1 and threatens further burials to the west. They collect eroding dentate stamped Lapita pottery of a type apparently earlier then previously found on the site. With the Fiji Museum and University of Auckland, they seek funding from the European Community to mount an urgent salvage excavation.

In December, Elizabeth Hudson directs a joint Fiji Museum/University of Auckland salvage project funded by the EEC. Her excavations and additional mapping confirm massive loss of archaeological deposits at the eastern end of the dunes. They recover pottery and other cultural material from all three palaeosols including two new types of pottery from Level 1. References: Hudson 1994; Petchey 1994.

1994   Between April and June, Crosby, Marshall and Stefan Cabaniuk, of the Fiji Native Land Trust Board, conduct several brief surveys of sites along the seaward edge of the western dunes between VL 16/1 and the sandy point east of Naqarai (VL 16/2). They discover pottery-bearing archaeological deposits, often associated with exposed palaeosols, in almost all of the swales located between dune crests. Some of the palaeosols climb to considerable elevations northwards, into the dunes. They also note the presence of surface scatters of human bone. The pottery collected during their survey represents all three of the major periods of occupation on the dunes. It is deposited at the Fiji Museum.

1995   The Fiji Museum carry out four excavations at VL 16/1; two in Level 3 and two in Level 2. References: Burke 1995a, b; Waterman 1995.

1996   Atholl Anderson from the Australian National University visits VL 16/1 in July. He conducts a

Table 2: Chronology of archaeological investigations.

testpit and probe survey to search the eastern end of the dunes and the beach ridges behind the dunes for remnants of the Level 1 Lapita occupation layer. He also conducts test excavations at the Volivoli rock shelter, located behind the dunes at the western end, and the Malaqereqere rock shelter, located approximately 3km west of the dunes. Reference: Anderson et al. 1996; Dickinson et al. 1998.

Antoine de Biran and Geoff Clarke recover a date of c.600 BP from an inferred 'Level 3' paleosol in the western part of the dunes. Reference Dickinson et al. 1998:7.

David Burley conducts a field school with students of Simon Fraser University on and behind the dunes. They survey and record 14 sites at the western end of dunes; excavate two burials and record other scattered human remains, and conduct test excavations on the low beach ridges behind the dunes. Dickinson also begins a re-analysis of the sequence of dune formation. References: Dickinson et al. 1998; Burley 1997.

1997   Marshall and Crosby conduct a brief walkover survey of the dunes in December and discover

that wave erosion along the seaward edge of VL 16/1 has ceased and that a new beach flat and low fore-dune are beginning to form. They note that large areas of a steeply sloping Level 2 palaeosol surface are now exposed along the western part of the site which continues to yield Level 2 pottery and other cultural materials. In addition, larger areas of the Level 3 palaeosol are now exposed along the eastern part of the site. At the back of the dunes the small site bearing late Lapita pottery has been substantially destroyed by vehicles using the track alongside the site.

1998   In conjunction with the Fiji Museum and the National Trust of Fiji, David Burley conducts a second fieldschool with students from Simon Fraser University. They survey the full length of the dunes including Naqarai Bay; conduct test excavations at VL 16/22, and excavate a large area of Level 1 at VL 16/1. Reference: Burley and Shortland 1999.

Antoine de Biran and Geoff Hope recover a carbonised post from Level 3. Antione de Biran commences dissertation research on the geomorphology of the Sigatoka delta.

Table 2: Continued.

complete or near-complete vessels, and a small amount of stone, bone, shell and charcoal were recovered. The Birks' three palaeosols and the types of pottery identified from each palaeosol have provided the basis for all subsequent interpretations of archaeological finds on the dunes (Fig. 1.2; Plate 9).

As can be seen from Fig. 5.1 the Birks' excavations extend from approximately 400M to 700M on the 1992 map, an area which continues to yield the densest concentrations of pottery. Interestingly, the huge blow-out of very dense Level 1 and 2 pottery mapped around 650M in 1992 corresponds with an area in which the Birks were surprised to find no cultural material (Birks 1973:10). This demonstrates that, although the deposits of cultural remains appeared idiosyncratic on the basis of the Birks' narrow excavations, when the palaeosols are exposed in a wider north–south band the distribution of cultural remains becomes much more continuous.

EROSION

In general, at the time of the Birks excavations the three eroding edges of the palaeosols were located c. 25m further to the south than in 1992. At the point of their generalised profile (Fig. 1.3) Level 1 was approximately 1.65 metres in elevation (now c.5 metres). Level 2 was at 5.2 metres elevation (now approximately the same) and rose steadily toward the west reaching 10 metres at the point it disappeared. Level 3 was at 8.5 metres elevation (now 10–15 metres elevation) and dropped steadily to the east where it approached to within 24 metres

of the then high tide line. In the following 26 years up to the 1992 survey a huge volume of sand was stripped from the dune surface, deflating even the highest areas excavated by the Birks to less than 5m elevation. At the eastern end of the dunes the effect was particularly dramatic. At 400M the exposed Level 3 edge was pushed c.50m north into the dune face revealing extensive Level 1 and Level 2 exposures that had not been visible to the Birks.

The changes from 1966 to 1992 provide valuable information on the scale and nature of the erosion, and on the form of the palaeosol surfaces. At the eastern end of their grid the Birks supposed that Level 3 rose into the dune face. Subsequent erosion has demonstrated this to be true. They also supposed that Level 1 rose into the dune face and that Level 2 formed a horizontal or downward sloping surface into the dunes. This has also been demonstrated to be true, but only as far west as their generalised profile.

Further west the situation is very different. In 1966 the Birks found that "the dune system follows a rising course to the west from its origin near the river month, a trend following [sic] by each of the three earlier soil horizons" (Birks 1973:10). They encountered Level 2 rising to the west for a further 480 metres beyond the area they excavated, eventually attaining an elevation of 37 metres (rising to 120ft over a total distance of 2220ft, Birks 1973:10). This would take it to approximately 1250M on the 1992 map, placing it at the base of the large ridge. This is entirely consistent with the situation in 1992. On the 1992 map Level 2 rises constantly to the

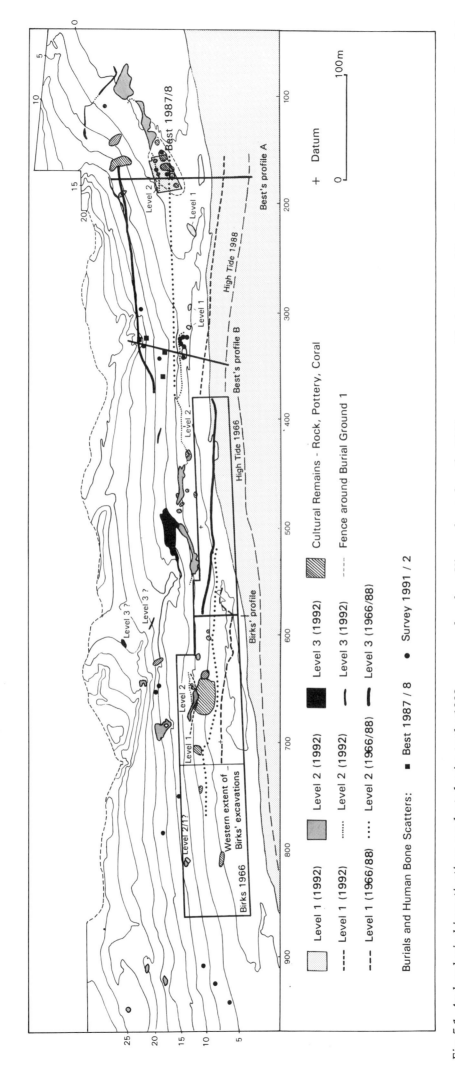

Fig. 5.1 Archaeological investigations conducted prior to the 1992 survey and cyclone Kina, relocated on the 1992 survey map. The locations of the eroding edges of the three palaeosols in 1965/6, 1987/8 and in 1992 are also shown.

west and by 960M is exposed at elevations up to 25 metres. The presumed exposure of Level 2 directly above the bone exposure at c.1150M and 31 metres elevation (Fig. 3.1) is virtually identical to the situation described by the Birks.

Far from being a horizontal deposit, at the western end of the surveyed area Level 2 has been demonstrated to rise to the west along the dunes to considerable elevations, presumably over an underlying dune formation. Level 1 also rises to the west but to date it has not been identified above 9 metres in elevation. Moreover, at the western end of the surveyed area Level 2 also rises to the north, into the dunes. The Birks failed to find the seaward slope of the Level 2 dune surface, excavating only along the eroding edge of a flat apron. The 1992 survey has now demonstrated that immediately inland of the Birks excavations the Level 2 surface slopes up steeply to the north, accounting for the presence of the palaeosol at such high elevations on the dunes surface west of 600M.

In 1966 the known extent of the three Levels in a westerly direction was therefore similar to our current understanding. However, no palaeosols were known east of about 400M and Levels 1 and 2 were unknown east of about 500M. The Birks had noted that Level 2 climbed to the west but found no evidence of it climbing north into the dunes. Between 1966 and the survey in 1992 the exposed edges of Levels 1 and 2 in the area of the Birks excavations had eroded back into the dune surprisingly little, about 25 metres. Level 3 in contrast, located higher on the dunes, changed much more dramatically, eroding back into the dune by as much as 50 metres.

Simon Best 1987–8

Over the two decades following the Birks' excavations cultural material was gradually exposed over an ever increasing area to the east of where they had worked. In addition, human bone began appearing in ever-larger concentrations (Best 1989: 6). It was the appearance of this bone that prompted the next major investigation (Plates 10–12).

BURIALS

In 1987 and 1988 Simon Best directed the excavation of what is now known as Burial Ground 1 (Best 1987a,b; 1989). The extent of these excavations is shown in Fig. 5.1 and Plate 11. Best removed a total of 55 individuals from a confined area measuring about 23 by 15 metres. These burials were associated with the Level 2 palaeosol. Those buried included women, men and children. Some were interred singly while others were in groups. Most group burials were capped with a mound of coral (Plate 10). The majority were buried with their legs flexed and orientated to the east and with their heads to the west. Four individuals were buried with grave goods. These included one adze and various shell artefacts. Seven large sherds of Level 2 type pottery were also found in direct association with the burials. In addition Best investigated four burials located further west around 300M. These four burials, W1–4, are shown in Fig. 5.1 as black squares. The skeletons from Burial Ground 1 have been fully analysed and written up by Visser (1994).

LEVEL 2

Best was also concerned with reconstructing the nature of the Level 2 landscape. He established that the burials had been placed on a small knoll (Best 1989:20–22). This may have been associated with the southeastern tip of a ridge that has since eroded. Identification of burnt wood recovered during excavations has established that the dunes were at least partially covered in Casuarina forest at the time of the Level 2 occupation.

EROSION

Best's investigations took place to the east of where the Birks' had worked. As illustrated in Fig. 5.1, the area of exposed palaeosols mapped by Best (1989: Fig 2) begins almost exactly where the Birks' grid ended. This near perfect juxtaposition was entirely fortuitous. Best's excavations can be accurately located on the 1992 map because he left in place a metal plate datum which was located and surveyed in on the 1992 map. However, his wider map of the area between 150M and 400M is not precisely surveyed, so the locations of the three palaeosol exposures in 1988, as shown in Fig. 5.1, must be considered approximate. Even so, they are extremely informative when placed alongside the Birks' grid.

Between 1966 and 1988 the high tide line moved very little. By 1988 Level 1 was visible directly behind and just above the high tide line in the area surveyed by Best, as was the case in the Birks' grid area. Therefore, although Level 1 was newly exposed in the east over a distance of 300 metres, it had been only minimally eroded north into the face of the dune. By 1992, only four years later, this had changed. The line of the Level 1 exposure was eroding rapidly and had moved north by up to 20 metres.

This erosion pattern was reversed higher up the dune. Between 1966 and 1988 the line of the Level 2 palaeosol exposure had already eroded north by perhaps 20 metres to approximately where it was located in 1992. Although Burial Ground 2 was not yet visible, Best recorded Level 2 in more or less the same location and at the same elevation as in 1992 (2 metres elevation along Best's Profile A and at 4 metres elevation along Profile B). This indicates that relatively little of the dune surface had eroded in the intervening four years. Indeed, by 1992 the section of Level 2 exposed between Burial Grounds 1 and 2 had become buried beneath a metre of drift sand.

A similar, though more extreme situation had occurred for Level 3. Between 1966 and 1988 the distance between the eroding edges of Level 1 and Level 3 at the eastern end of the dunes increased from 25 metres to 100 metres. Thus, between 1966 and 1988, most of the erosion occurred at relatively high elevations. Between 1988 and 1992, however, as for Level 2, little further change occurred in the recorded position of Level 3. On Best's Profile A, Level 3 was around 10 metres in elevation and it was still at this elevation in 1992. Along Best's Profile B Level 3 was exposed at around 13 metres elevation. In 1992 this location was around 16 metres elevation, probably because the side of the ridge had eroded and steepened. In 1988 Best recorded Level 3 as a continuous exposure from 150M to nearly 400M. By 1992 much of this exposure had been buried beneath recent drift sand and was no longer visible between 250M and 400M. By 1993 it became exposed again over some of this distance (Hudson 1994:3; see below).

Best's 1987–8 investigations, thus, increased by 300–400 metres the distance to the east over which all three palaeosols were known to extend. The excavations expanded the range of cultural materials recovered from the site to include structured burials. They also established that the most extreme erosion taking place between 1966 and 1988 was high on the dunes rather than low and close to the sea. Thus Level 3 was most seriously effected, Level 2 to a lesser extent and Level 1 only minimally. During the same period the high tide line hardly moved. In contrast, between 1988 and 1992 the greatest erosion occurred low on the dunes severely affecting Level 1 and moving the high tide line north by 10–30 metres (see Plates 6 and 7).

Andrew Crosby and Sepeti Matararaba 1991

In the three years following Best's excavations further scatters of mainly heavily degraded human bone appeared along the dune face west of his excavations, although no further coral mounds were uncovered. The fortuitous discovery of two groups of burials before they had become fully exposed prompted salvage excavations conducted for the Fiji Museum by Andrew Crosby and Sepeti Matararaba in July/August 1991.

BURIALS

Crosby and Matararaba excavated a group of four skeletons at 340M and a group of two skeletons at 900M (Crosby 1991b). These burials are described in detail in Appendix C. Although Best had previously excavated burials in the area of 300M, they were found relatively high on the dune and were not associated with a palaeosol. The burial of four skeletons at 340M in contrast was found lying within the Level 2 palaeosol and was identical in burial layout and orientation to those found by Best in Burial Ground 1. It signalled that Burial Ground 1 was not an isolated feature and that further burial grounds could be expected elsewhere on the dunes. The group of two skeletons at 900M, however, was not associated with a palaeosol, although the eroding edge of the Level 2 palaeosol was located nearby. Crosby and Matararaba also noted further scatters of human bone fragments between these two burials and further to the west, many at high elevations.

LEVEL 2

In the course of their excavations Crosby and Matararaba prepared a sketch map of the palaeosols and cultural materials exposed on the surface between approximately 100M and 950M (Crosby 1991c). This indicated the presence of Level 2 as a more or less continuous soil layer west of 340M and demonstrated the extension of Level 2 to 920M, almost 200m further to the west than encountered by the Birks. It also indicated, as suggested by the Birks, that it climbs up the dune face to the west, but is also associated with lower concentrations of cultural materials.

EROSION

The sketch map prepared by Crosby and Matararaba indicated the potential for recording the location of eroding materials on the dune face and for tying these into a permanent datum. Moreover, it indicated the potential for linking successive excavation and survey results to record the progress of erosion on the dunes. The new appearance of burials, human bone scatters, and new areas of palaeosol in the area west of 300M was to foreshadow a new period of erosion lower down on the dunes.

Summary

The general patterns of erosion occurring in the area of the Birks' grid and further east in the area surveyed by Best are similar. Up to 1988, in both areas, wind erosion had the greatest impact, hitting hardest high on the dunes. Thus Level 3 suffered more erosion than Levels 1 or 2. By 1991 Crosby and Matararaba found this pattern was changing so that by 1992 sea erosion had intensified along the shoreline while wind erosion had abated to some degree at higher elevations. As a result Level 3 stabilised while Levels 1 and 2 now came under increasing threat and began to erode quickly.

The erosional changes provided additional evidence on the palaeosol surfaces. At the eastern end they further confirmed the Birks' supposition that Level 3 rose to the north. The new exposure of Level 2 in the area of Burial Ground 1 at an elevation of only 2 metres, however, represented a considerable drop in elevation from further to the west where the Birks consistently found it to be a more or less horizontal surface at 4–5 metres elevation. Most of this drop apparently occurs between 200M and 300M. The indication was that, to the east of 300M, Level 2 dropped to form a lower lying terrace with Level 1 presumably exhibiting a similar form beneath. When the old river bank identified to the north behind the dunes is projected through the dunes it passes approximately along the line of this drop in elevation, indicating that the land surface during the formation of Levels 1 and 2 may have been similar to that now located behind the dunes (see Chapter 7). At the other end of the mapped area, the changes also added intriguing evidence to support the Birks' observation that Level 2 rises high up the dune face to the west, beyond their excavations.

After Cyclone Kina: post-1992 investigations

On New Years day 1993, only three months after the 1992 survey was completed, Cyclone Kina hit Fiji. Damage was particularly bad in the Sigatoka region. The bridge at Sigatoka Township was destroyed and the huge volume of water that flowed down the Sigatoka River washed away the long spit of beach sand which had built up on the western side of the river mouth. Immediate damage to the sand dunes was unexpectedly light but six months later the situation changed and huge sections of the eastern dunes were washed away. Much of the work carried out at the dunes since 1992 has been a response to this catastrophic destruction. The locations of these investigations and the information recorded on the locations of palaeosol exposures, cultural remains and tide lines are summarised in Fig. 5.2.

Yvonne Marshall 1993

On 10th April 1993 Marshall conducted a walkover survey of the mapped area in order to assess immediate damage caused by Cyclone Kina. She found the following changes:

DATUMS
The 1992, 0 datum was gone. The 500M and 700M datums were visible but the 1000M datum had disappeared. It later transpired that it was buried under wind blown sand and it was relocated in November 1993.

BURIALS
No new exposures of bone were found in the area of Burial Ground 1. Tarpaulins that had been laid in 1992 to protect Burial Ground 2 were still in place and completely covered with sand. However, new exposures of bone were appearing to the west of the tarpaulins at around 350M. In this area scatters of bone and teeth extended over a distance of 15–20 metres. At one point 5 metres above the storm toss the top of a newly exposed cranium was visible.

LEVEL 1
No new exposures of the Level 1 palaeosol or of Level 1 cultural remains were identified.

LEVEL 2
The greatest changes were to Level 2. Exposure of the Level 2 palaeosol had increased considerably and could now be followed in a semi-continuous line across the mapped area. Between 400M and 500M there was a continuous scatter of potsherds from the tide line up to approximately 10m elevation. Paddle-impressed pots and trays were both present. A hard yellow-brown sand, possibly the weathered basal sand, was exposed across much of this area. Two new blowouts had appeared at around 750M. The first consisted of potsherds and rock scattered over an area approximately 15 metres in diameter. It extended from about 5m down to 2m elevation. An adze fragment was collected from this exposure. The second was a high exposure located at 700–750M near the base of the ridge at approximately 20 metres elevation. It consisted of very large plain sherds and tray fragments. A further high elevation exposure was recorded around 800M. It was located approximately 15m upslope from the human remains designated HB8. This would place it at an elevation of at least 15 metres. The Level 2 palaeosol was exposed for a distance of 20 metres and paddle-impressed pottery was eroding from it. One intact, lightly paddle-impressed pot was photographed. At approximately 1200M, near the base of the high ridge a lovo oven was exposed. It was 15–20 metres from the high tide line and consisted primarily of burnt white stone and dense charcoal. Some red stone, coral and small bones,

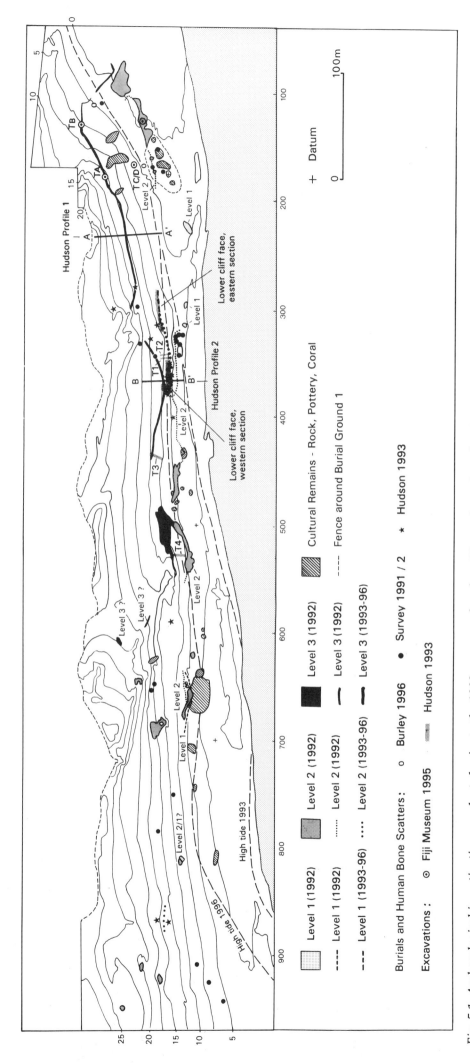

Fig. 5.1 *Archaeological investigations conducted prior to the 1992 survey and cyclone Kina, relocated on the 1992 survey map. The locations of the eroding edges of the three palaeosols in 1965/6, 1987/8 and in 1992 are also shown.*

possibly bird, were also noted. A few weathered sherds of Level 2 style pottery were collected.

LEVEL 3

No new areas of exposed Level 3 soil were identified. However, the extent of the Level 3 exposure between 100M and 200M had increased considerably, and between 400M and 500M pottery and rock which included material from Level 3 was scattered in a continuous drift from the high tide level up to approximately 10m elevation. This damage was surprisingly light given the strength of Cyclone Kina.

Elizabeth Hudson, University of Auckland 1993

During 1993, erosion at the eastern end of the dunes gathered pace. In July, Sepeti Matararaba visited the dunes and found the eastern section heavily eroded by both wind and high seas. The urgency of the situation was now apparent. In August, Crosby again conducted a walkover survey. By this time it was clear that a very large part of this eastern section of the dunes was about to disappear. A major section of the dune between Burial Grounds 1 and 2 had already collapsed, revealing a cliff-face exposure of Levels 1 and 2 (Plates 13 and 14). Elaborately decorated dentate stamped pottery of an early Lapita type from Level 1 (Fig. 5.3) and human bone from Level 2 was spilling out into the sea. Erosion further to the west did

not appear to be so severe. The Fiji Museum and University of Auckland secured funding from the European Community to carry out emergency salvage work. This salvage project took place in November 1993 and was directed by Elizabeth Hudson.

Hudson's mandate was to salvage the skeletons in Burial Ground 2. Unfortunately, November 1993 proved too late and few burials remained. Instead, therefore, Hudson carried out a general survey of the mapped area (Hudson 1994:2). This involved four kinds of investigation: burials; Level 1 excavations; trenches to establish stratigraphy; and mapping of the most heavily eroded areas.

BURIALS

Hudson located and removed all exposed human remains from 100M up to approximately 1200M. Ten burials (CF1–9) were removed from the western section of the newly eroded cliff face located between 300M and 400M. A further 19 scatters of human bone (SB1–19) were removed from isolated locations. The locations of the burials within the mapped area are shown on Figs. 5.2 and 6.1 and details of the burials are provided in the next chapter.

LEVEL 1

Along the eastern section of the lower cliff face (encompassing Areas B–E) Hudson excavated an

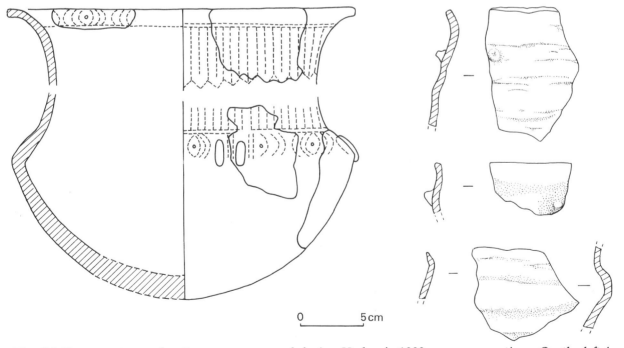

0   5 cm

Fig. 5.3 Two new types of pottery were recovered during Hudson's 1993 rescue excavations. On the left is a reconstructed Early Eastern Lapita pot with characteristic elaborate dentate stamp decoration. On the right are three wavy sherds, which are argued to represent a regional variant of very late Lapita wares.

area one metre wide and 35 metres long which yielded scattered sherds in what appeared to be a conflated deposit of Levels 1 and 2. Most sherds came from two concentrations. The first was located at the western end of Area B and yielded wavy-sherds, probably of a Late Lapita type dating to around 200 BC (Fig. 5.3). This type of pottery had not previously been found on the dunes but similar pottery dating to the same period was found by Crosby on the nearby islands of Beqa and Ugaga (Hudson 1994:24, 36–8; Crosby 1988:124, 214–6; Clark 1997). In Areas D and E a dense concentration of dentate-stamped, early Lapita sherds was recovered. These sherds were similar to those collected by Crosby in August. This pottery is older than any of the pottery recovered by the Birks in 1965–6 and extends the time depth of the Level 1 occupation. It is of an Early Eastern Lapita type and pre-dates 500 BC (Hudson 1994:24, 34).

LEVELS 2 AND 3

Hudson excavated four trenches to investigate the stratigraphic relationships between palaeosols exposed on the surface. Trenches 1 and 2, at the eastern end of the western section of the lower cliff face (Fig. 5.2; Plate 13), indicated that the palaeosol exposed low down in the cliff face was Level 2. It sloped down slightly to the north into the dune face. A second palaeosol, higher up the eroding dune face was established as Level 3. Trenches 3 and 4 (T3 and T4) were located further west around 440M and 520M respectively. They contained both the Level 2 and Level 3 palaeosols. The former sloped down very slightly into the dune face and was separated vertically from Level 3 by approximately 2 metres of sterile wind deposited sand (Plates 13 and 14).

EROSION

As part of Hudson's investigations Shannon Wood remapped the section of the dunes between 150M and 520M. The high tide line from this map (Hudson 1994:Fig. iii) is reproduced in Fig. 5.2. It shows extreme levels of sea erosion had taken place at the eastern end of the 1992 mapped area. Just west of 200M, Hudson's Profile 1 shows that the high tide line had moved inland by at least 50 metres. This had the effect of dramatically steepening the dune face as shown by Hudson (1994:4). This change is shown in Plates 13 and 14. At 370M, Hudson's Profile 2 shows the high tide had advanced 25 metres into the dunes, again dramatically steepening the dune face. By 600M, however, the effects of sea erosion were minimal and there was little change in the position of the high tide line west of 600M.

Hudson's excavations and survey thus confirmed that although the erosion occurring after the 1992 survey was catastrophic, wiping out both Burial Ground 1 and Burial Ground 2 and causing a new exposure of Level 1 pottery, it was a continuation of a trend that was already well underway by 1988. Major sea erosion was affecting the eastern half of the dunes at low elevations which encompassed both Levels 1 and 2, but the upper levels of the dunes and the western half of VL 16/1 remained largely unaffected. Although the rapid new erosion of Levels 1 and 2 in the area 200–400M was alarming, it did confirm that Level 2 extended horizontally or sloped down into the face of the dunes in this area and that it had become conflated with the slightly upward sloping Level 1 palaeosol in some places. They also established that significant Level 1 deposits remained preserved in the conflated deposit, although they were now severely threatened by further sea erosion. Moreover, Hudson's excavations confirmed what had been long suspected, that the individual palaeosols could not be considered as representing single occupation surfaces. As the now highly variable Level 1 pottery demonstrates, they represent surfaces that were occupied over prolonged periods, sometimes sequentially on different parts of the dunes.

Fiji Museum 1995

In 1995 the Fiji Museum undertook a new project at the dunes. Between 10 January and 2 February they carried out excavations at the far eastern end of the dunes under the direction of Christine Burke. The approximate locations of their four excavations and one testpit are shown in Fig. 5.2. The precise locations of these excavations on the 1992 survey map have not yet been established. This will be done following the completion of a report currently in preparation (Burke 1995a).

Two of the excavations, Trenches A and B, were specifically aimed at recovering Level 3 materials. This was the first archaeological work at the dunes to focus specifically on the much-neglected Level 3. The two excavations were located along the eroding line of the Level 3 palaeosol between 100M and 200M. Trench A consisted of a 3 by 3 metre square and Trench B was 2 by 2 metres (Burke 1995b). The stratigraphy in these trenches independently confirmed that Level 3 sloped down steeply to the east at around 100M indicating the location of the backslope of the dunes at the time the Level 3 palaeosol formed.

The other two excavations, Trenches C and D were put down to investigate the large Level 2 soil exposure between 100M and 200M. Trench C measured 1 by 17 metres. It began at the exposed Level 2 palaeosol and ran up the dune face. Trench

D measured 1 by 20 metres and ran along the exposed Level 2 soil line. Not all the squares in these two trenches were excavated (Burke 1995b). An eroded burial was excavated from the Level 2 soil exposure at the southern end of Trench C. On the basis of these excavations Burke (1995b) concluded that the Level 1 palaeosol probably remained intact beneath Level 2.

A considerable amount of pottery was recovered. Other important items recovered from Level 3, including a glass bottle, a clay pipe fragment and a possible gun flint (Burke 1995a), established that occupation on the dunes continued after European contact, considerably later than was previously assumed. Like Level 1, Level 3 may have been sequentially occupied at different times. The materials excavated in 1995, combined with the pottery recovered from the 1992 excavations of Features 6 and 7 will help to broaden our knowledge of the poorly understood Level 3 occupation.

Simon Fraser University 1996

In June 1996 David Burley of Simon Fraser University, in association with the Fiji Museum, brought a group of students to the dunes for an archaeological fieldschool. Three investigations were carried out.

Firstly, they surveyed the western part of the dunes recording 15 new sites including a burial (see Burley 1997:13 for locations). All but two of these sites were west of the area mapped in 1992. Site 2, a feature consisting of "a small number of undecorated sherds and burned rock eroding from Level 3 exposure" (Burley 1997:14) was located at the base of the high ridge and is almost certainly the same *lovo* feature recorded by Marshall in 1993 (see above). Since Marshall collected diagnostic Level 2 pottery from this feature it is probable that the palaeosol observed by Burley was Level 2 rather than Level 3.

On the western dunes they found that a "single exposed palaeosol was present in many of the erosional scarps" (Burley 1997:15). It commonly occurred around midway in the dune section and their impression was that it was probably Level 3. No superimposed palaeosols were identified. In association with the palaeosol exposures they identified 8 pottery scatters and features, 3 hearth features and 1 burial. No diagnostic pottery was found but the forms appeared to be late. One hearth, Feature 8, located at an elevation of 6.1m was excavated and a radiocarbon date of 230 ± 40 BP was obtained from charcoal recovered from this hearth.

Secondly the fieldschool excavated two exposed burials from the far eastern end of the 1992 mapped area (see Figs. 5.2 and 6.1 for locations). These are described in greater detail in the following section.

Thirdly, they carried out investigations in the area of undulating beach ridges between the dunes and Kulukulu village. This work was informed by and built on the investigations carried out by Marshall in 1993 (described below in Appendix D). Initially Burley's crew conducted a testpit survey of the area. Pottery recovered from these testpits included sherds diagnostic of periods ranging from Late Eastern Lapita (c.500 BC) to within the last few hundred years (Burley 1997:25), confirming Marshall's results. Burley then opened two excavations. Excavation Series One (ES1, see Fig. D.1) was located in the unpromising location of a swale between two beaches ridges. Sherds recovered included various paddle impressed, spot relief and incised wares. Burley argues these indicate post 900 BP occupation. Excavation Series Two (ES2) was larger and included a hearth feature. Charcoal from this hearth was radiocarbon dated to 510 ± 60 BP. However, the range of pottery recovered from ES2 was very broad and included, for example, 12 wiped sherds typical of the much earlier Late Eastern Lapita plainware style (Burley 1997:31). Again, a very extended period of occupation is indicated. This material is discussed in greater detail in Appendix D.

EROSION

Burley also recorded the approximate 1996 shoreline along the eastern end of the dunes on a simplified version of the 1992 map (Burley 1996: 17, Fig. 5 – note that the Birks' grid is miss-located on this map). This high tide line is shown here in Fig. 5.2 alongside the high tide lines for 1992 and 1993. Although only approximate, it indicates a dramatic shift had occurred in the erosion pattern. In the eastern section of the mapped area, up to around 300M there was little further change in the high tide line between 1993 and 1996 indicating that the sea erosion at the eastern end of VL 16/1 had stabilised. West of 300M, however, the opposite is true. By 400M the high tide line had moved inland by about 20 metres and by 800M this had increased to 50 metres. By 1996, therefore, the area of intense erosion had shifted to the western end of the area mapped in 1992.

Thus, when Cyclone Kina hit Fiji in January 1993 it set in motion an erosion cycle. This cycle began at the river mouth and gradually worked its way west. The initial impact of the storm was felt most keenly at the mouth of the river where the large sand bar was washed away. From the river mouth west to about 100M storm waves encroached up to 100 metres inland. Over the next year these invasive storm waves moved progressively further west.

By November 1993 when Hudson arrived they had scoured the dune edge back at least 20 metres up to 400M. By July 1996 the storm waves had progressed along the dune to 900M. As a result, between 40 and 60 metres was wiped off the seaward edge of the dune along the full length of the dunes mapped in 1992. In contrast, between 1993 and 1996 wind erosion higher on the dunes appears to have been fairly limited.

Atholl Anderson and William Dickinson 1996

In conjunction with Burley's work, William Dickinson of the University of Arizona, Atholl Anderson of the Australian National University and personnel from the Fiji Museum began an investigation into the geological history of the formation of the Sigatoka Dunes. The results are reported in Dickinson et al. (1998) and are discussed extensively in Chapters 2 and 7. One part of their investigation was a probe and testpit search for Level 1 at the eastern end of the dunes in the area between 100M and 500M and on the beach ridges behind the dunes. No evidence of Level 1 was identified. These results led them to the mistaken conclusion that "Level 1 cultural remains have been largely if not entirely removed by shoreline erosion since the Birks excavation" (Dickinson et al. 1998:6).

University of Southampton 1997

In November 1997 Crosby and Marshall conducted a brief walkover survey in order to assess the extent and nature of changes to the eastern dunes since their last visit in 1994.

Erosion

They found that the inland extent of the sea erosion had advanced approximately a further 15 metres north into the dune face in the vicinity of the large pottery and palaeosol exposure at 660M, almost completely removing that feature. In other areas, the sea erosion had not advanced beyond the high tide line recorded by Burley in 1996. The erosion process had now stopped and a wide beach shelf and partial beach ridge had started to build up again along the seaward edge (Plate 15). As a result the high tide line had returned to a position very close to that mapped in 1992. This new beach shelf was widest at the eastern end where a large flat had again formed in the area of Burial Ground 1 and further east. The area between 0M and 100M which had been completely underwater for part of the 1992 survey (see Plate 6) was now at least 2 metres above the high tide line. Further west, deep deposits of drift sand had accumulated against the "cliff-face" erosion profile experienced by Hudson and

Burley and the seaward dune slope had been restored to a relatively shallow gradient (see Plate 15).

Level 1

No Level 1 exposures were seen, although these would be expected to be buried beneath the new accumulation of drift sand low on the dunes. Level 1 is expected to survive beneath Level 2, particularly in the area 600–800M but also further east.

Level 2

Level 2 had been completely removed up to the high tide line indicated by Burley. Above this level, however, the palaeosol was visible as a semi-continuous surface exposure extending between c.450M and 850M and as large discontinuous deposits further west. West of c. 550M it formed an upward sloping surface extending to the north up the dune slope to elevations of c.15m, emulating the dune surface. No surface exposure of any palaeosol was seen above this elevation. Scatters of characteristic Level 2 pottery and other cultural debris continued to erode from the palaeosol although no pottery concentrations of the density mapped during the 1992 survey were seen.

Level 3

Level 3 had also been destroyed up to the high tide line indicated by Burley. In 1997 it was visible as a semi-continuous surface exposure extending from c.130M to c.550M. Over the western 100 metres it extended along the dune slope directly above the Level 2 exposure. Level 3 therefore remained more or less as mapped during the 1992 survey and Hudson's excavations, although it had advanced slightly north, up the dune slope, towards its western extent.

These findings suggest a 10 year cycle of sea erosion at the eastern end of the dunes has run its course and a period of sand accumulation has begun. Given the volume of sand washed out to sea following Cyclone Kina, the offshore sand reservoir is probably substantial and the amount of sand available for redeposition on the dunes quite considerable. The next few years may see rapid burial of the exposed palaeosols. The evidence suggests that all three of these palaeosols continue to exist and continue to yield cultural material. Indeed, a greater area of Level 3 appears to be now exposed than ever before and Level 2, while no longer evident to the east, now forms a major new exposure of sloping palaeosol surface to the west.

Simon Fraser University 1998

In June 1998 David Burley and members of the Fiji Museum returned with another team of students for a second fieldschool at the Sigatoka Dunes. Following up on the contradictory conclusions reached by Dickinson et al. (1998) and Wood, Marshall and Crosby (1998), they decided to focus on the "problem of the chronological origins for dune formation" (Burley and Shortland 1999:5). To this end they concentrated primarily on surveying the western section of the dunes. They found that "exposed features and eroded sherd scatters throughout the area were not abundant" (Burley and Shortland 1999:12). Only two new pottery features not previously recorded in 1996 were identified. Of these, Feature 8 was an extensive area of 33 scatters of 2–10 potsherds all located below 5m in elevation. Most of the pottery was undiagnostic, but one sherd had parallel ribbed paddle impressed decoration establishing that some early occupation probably did occur on the western dunes.

At Naqarai Bay, which marks the western extent of the dunes, the Birks had recorded a site which they designated VL 16/22. In test excavations at this site they had identified a stratigraphic sequence of four palaeosols from which pottery ranging from early Lapita to the last few hundred years was recovered. On his return to Naqarai Bay in 1998 Burley surface-collected pottery ranging in age from the late Lapita period to within the last few hundred years. He also relocated what he believes is the Birks' site. Test excavations revealed an intact palaeosol at 1.5m elevation from which Late Eastern Lapita pottery was recovered. More recent pottery was recovered from slump material overlying this palaeosol (Burley and Shortland 1999).

In the course of resurveying the eastern end of the dunes, a new exposure of Late Eastern Lapita pottery was identified and a salvage excavation measuring 8 by 13 metres was opened. Burley and Shortland (1999:30–1) locate this excavation on the 1992 map at around 740M which, as they point out, is almost exactly where the Birks' Level 1 excavations stopped (see Fig. 5.1 above). This is also precisely where in 1993 Marshall identified a new exposure of the Level 2 palaeosol and associated pottery, and where, based on the 1992 survey, Wood, Marshall and Crosby (1998:61, 67) predicted that Level 1 was likely to remain intact. The pottery recovered from these excavations was virtually identical to that recovered by the Birks. In addition a hearth feature was excavated. Two charcoal samples from contexts associated with Level 1 materials were radiocarbon dated to 2490 ± 50 BP and 2470 ± 50 BP. These dates are nearly identical to that obtained by the Birks.

Chapter 6
Human remains recovered from the dunes, 1965–1998

Introduction

Until the mid 1980's evidence of buried human remains on the site was sparse. The presence of "human bone fragments" was first noted by Gifford in 1947 (Gifford 1951:251). The Birks also found fragments of human bone during their 1965–6 excavations but they considered them unrelated to the cultural occupations associated with the site's three palaeosols (Birks 1973:62). It was not until Best's 1987/8 excavations of 55 human skeletons associated directly with the Level 2 palaeosol that burials were demonstrated to be an integral part of occupation on the dunes (Best 1987; 1989). The burials excavated by Best had been carefully and deliberately interred beneath coral mounds in an apparently bounded area on a low mound (Plates 10–12)

Since Best's excavations further human remains, mostly of an extremely fragmentary and degraded nature, have been found on the site. Some were clearly associated with the Level 2 palaeosol, but others came from loose sand and are unprovenanced to a cultural occupation. While officers of the Fiji Museum and other visiting archaeologists have maintained a vigilant watch for the appearance of human remains on the site, human bone is commonly exposed and destroyed in a matter of weeks, leaving only a powdery trace. Consequently, dozens of burials have been destroyed on the dunes over recent years and no record exists of their locations.

The 1992 survey has provided a base map on which the accumulating evidence for human burial on this eastern section of the dunes can be collated. Fig. 6.1 summarises this evidence. It shows the locations of all human bone recorded, mapped and excavated in the survey area during the period 1965–1998. For all burials the numbering used in the original reports has been retained. These include:

- All human bone identified and excavated during the 1992 survey. They are numbered in Fig. 6.1 as B92/A–C, B1–6 and HB1–10. One complete burial (B92/A), one partial burial (B92/B) and a scatter of teeth (B92/C) were excavated and the bone removed to the Fiji Museum. Details of these excavations are reported below in Appendix C.
- Burial Ground 1, excavated by Best in 1987–8.
- Four burials excavated further west on the dunes by Best in 1987. They are numbered in Fig. 6.1 as W1–4.
- Two groups of burials excavated by Crosby and Matararaba in 1991. They are numbered on Fig. 6.1 as B91/1 and B91/2. The locations of these burials were recorded during the 1992 survey. Details of the excavations are reported below in Appendix C.
- Exposures of human bone investigated by Hudson in 1993. These are in two series. The 10 burials associated with her cliff face trench excavations are numbered on the map as CF1–CF9. Their locations are established from Hudson (1994:16, Fig. x).
- Hudson also investigated 19 scatters of exposed bone. Of these, 5 were not human bone (SB1, 3,12,14,15) and the locations of 6 which contained human bone now in the Fiji Museum are not given (SB2,13,16–19). The remaining 8 are located on Hudson's Fig. ii (Hudson 1994:3). Of these, three are located to the west of the 1992 mapped area (SB4,5,9) and 5 are shown here in Fig. 6.1. They are numbered as SB6–8 and SB10–11.
- Two exposures of human bone excavated by Burley in 1996. They are numbered in Fig. 6.1 as BS and B2. Burley also excavated a double burial on the western section of the dunes, approximately 1 km beyond the mapped area. This burial is not shown in Fig. 6.1.
- An additional eroded burial was removed by the Fiji Museum during their 1995 excavations

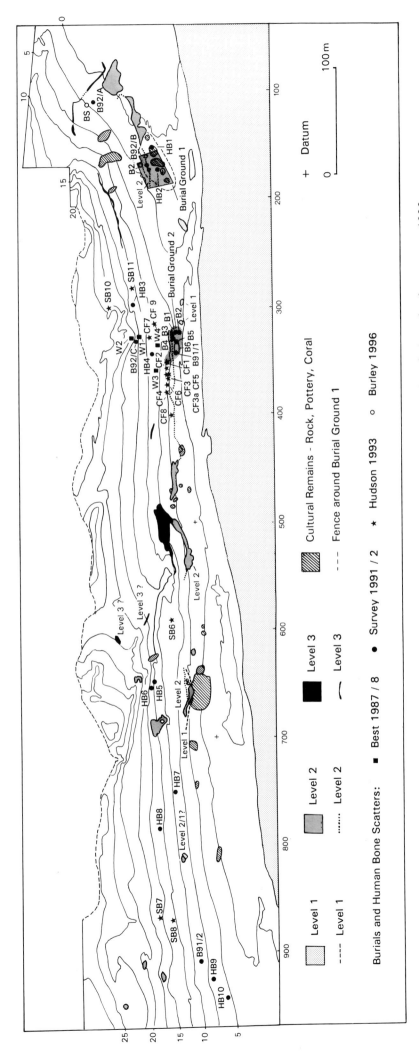

Fig. 6.1 Locations of all excavated burials and surface scatters of human bone identified on the dunes up to 1998.

(FM1). A report is in preparation (Burke 1995a). Its exact location on the 1992 survey map has not yet been established but it came from the general vicinity of B92/B and B2 on the northern side of Burial Ground 1.

- In 1998 a further burial was recovered by the Lautoka police from the vicinity of Burley's 1996 burial exacation on the western dunes (Burley and Shortland 1999:11).

In total, a minimum of 119 individuals are represented by these burials. They are described below beginning in the east and working west.

Eastern burials around 100M

B92/A

An isolated exposure of human bone was identified at around 2 metres elevation and 110M. This is below and approximately 12 metres seaward of the exposed Level 3 palaeosol. Investigation of the loose sand around the bone revealed a largely intact skeleton which was then fully excavated (see Appendix C for details). The skeleton had been placed in a semi-flexed position orientated east–west. The stratigraphic position of this burial, above Level 2 and below Level 3, but not directly associated with either, indicates only that it was probably interred after the Level 2 occupation. The excavation of Burial B92/A was recorded in the BBC television documentary, *Nomads of the Wind*.

In 1996 the Simon Fraser University Fieldschool excavated a scatter of human remains, BS, from around the same area. BS was located between 2.5 and 4 metres elevation and downslope of the Level 3 soil exposure. This places it somewhere between B92/A and the Level 3 soil exposure. Like B92/A the remains were not directly associated with a soil layer, but it is likely they were interred during the Level 3 occupation. BS consisted of scattered human teeth distributed over an area several metres in diameter. A total of 47 teeth were recovered. They represent at least 2, possibly 3 children (Burley 1997). In 1998 scattered bone and teeth fragments were again observed eroding from below the Level 3 palaeosol exposure at the eastern end of the dunes (Burley and Shortland 1999:11).

The remains of at least 3 and possibly 4 individuals have now been recovered from this general location. They suggest a small burial ground postdating Level 2 and possibly associated with the Level 3 occupation.

Burial Ground 1

Burial Ground 1 is a Level 2 cemetery. In 1987/8

Best removed a total of 55 individuals from a confined area measuring about 23 by 15 metres (see Best 1989:18, Fig. 4). These burials were associated with the Level 2 palaeosol (Plates 10–12). Women, men and children were all represented. Some individuals were interred singly while others were in groups. Most group burials were capped with a mound of coral. The majority were buried with their legs flexed and were oriented east–west with their heads to the west. Four individuals were buried with grave goods. These included one stone adze and various shell artefacts. Many small sherds of pottery were found in the course of the excavations, however, only seven large sherds, all with the cross-hatched paddle-impressed designs typical of Level 2 type pottery, were found in direct association with the burials. The skeletons from Burial Ground 1 have been fully analysed and written up by Visser (1994). His results suggest status and gender differences in the arrangement of burials within the cemetery. In addition Best investigated four burials located further west, around 300M. These four burials, W1–4, are shown in Fig. 6.1 as black squares (Best 1989).

B92/B, HB1 and HB2

In 1992 three areas of exposed human bone were found in the general vicinity of Burial Ground 1. B92/B, located just inside the northern limit of Best's excavation, close to Best's burial B24, was clearly the remains of an eroded but still in situ burial. It was fully excavated and removed to the Fiji Museum (see Appendix C for details). The burial was laid out in a semi-flexed position orientated east–west in a similar manner to the skeletons excavated by Best.

HB1 was a small concentration of exposed human bone associated with a concentration of coral. The bone appeared to be in situ beneath the coral suggesting an intact coral mound burial similar to those excavated by Best. Since HB1 is located just outside the eastern boundary of Best's excavation area it is assumed to be a previously unidentified burial with an associated coral mound. HB2 consisted of scattered human bone that had eroded from a point a few metres to the north-east of Best's datum. This places it in the vicinity of Best's burial SA1/ES, in the area between the 1987 and 1988 erosion edge of Level 2. Again, it is likely that HB2 represents the eroded remains of a previously undetected burial within Burial Ground 1.

B2

In 1996 the Simon Fraser University Fieldschool excavated another burial, B2, located close to where B92/B was removed (Burley 1997:42–44). It consisted of two individuals and the scattered remains of a possible third individual. The two largely intact individuals were interred in a tightly flexed position in a burial pit. This burial pit was not directly associated with any palaeosol but a large fragment of Level 2 type paddle impressed pottery was recovered from the pit fill. The north–south orientation of this burial did not conform to the generally east–west orientation of most burials in Burial Ground 1. However, the orientation of burials along the northern margins of Burial Ground 1 near where B2 was located was found by Best to be relatively irregular. Further scattered fragmentary bone was identified in this vicinity in 1998 but no further burials were found (Burley and Shortland 1999:11).

FM1

In 1995 the Fiji Museum excavated the remains of an eroded burial located on the northern side of Burial Ground 1. It came from the southern end of Trench C and had eroded out of the Level 2 soil horizon. The exact location of this trench on the 1992 survey is not yet established so the burial is not included on Fig. 6.1. However, it is clear that FM1 was found in the same general area as B92/B and B2.

In summary, it can be confidently assumed that the six, possibly seven, individuals represented by burials B92/B, HB1, HB2, B2 and FM1 were all part of Burial Ground 1. This rises the total number of individuals known to have been interred there from 55 to at least 61.

Burial Ground 2

In March 1991 Crosby and Matararaba examined an area of eroding bone located approximately 200 metres west of Burial Ground 1 and close to the high tide line (Crosby 1991b). They found an "area of fully intact and articulated skeletal material" which when excavated several months later revealed a group of four skeletons, B91/1. The four individuals were all adult and were interred parallel to each other in flexed positions. They were orientated east–west with their heads to the west in the same manner as the skeletons in Burial Ground 1 suggesting they were buried around the same time. This interpretation is supported by their stratigraphic position. The burials rested on or in the Level 2 palaeosol which formed a level surface extending into the dune face. Details of these burials can be found in Crosby 1991b and below in Appendix C.

The location of burial B91/1 was marked with a bamboo pole and in 1992 it was surveyed in at 340M and 4 metres elevation. In March 1991 Crosby and Matararaba had also noted the presence of a concentration of eroded and severely degraded human bone between 15 and 25 metres east of B91/1. This bone was located at or slightly below the eroding line of the Level 2 palaeosol. "Test excavations indicated that no in-tact skeletal material remained of these surface bone scatters. However, their configuration suggested the eroded remains of three individuals buried within 5 metres of each other" (Crosby 1991b:8). In 1992 a particularly large concentration of bone was identified in the same location between 300M and 340M, to the east of the pole marking the location of B91/1, at elevations between 1 and 4 metres (Plate 7). As virtually nothing remained in 1991 of the burials from which that surface bone had eroded, the 1992 bone must have come from different burials. Given the concentration of burials appearing in this area it has been designated Burial Ground 2.

In 1992 five in situ but eroding burials were recorded, B1–B5. B1 consisted of an exposed cranium; B2 was a 50cm diameter scatter of unidentified bone; B3 was a 50cm diameter scatter of eroded bone which included teeth; B4 was a confined scatter of bone which included long bone fragments eroding from the base of the Level 2 palaeosol; B5 was a one metre diameter scatter of bone which included teeth and jaw bone. Although only one of these 5 burials was directly associated with Level 2, their position directly below the eroding Level 2 palaeosol suggests they almost certainly derive from that soil layer. This interpretation is supported by the presence of two concentrations of eroded Level 2 pottery close to B4 and B5.

In addition, the 1992 survey recorded a large scatter of bone measuring 10 by 5 metres for which no in situ bone source was identified (B6). B6 covers the area between B91/1 and B1–5. Despite intensive testpitting and trowel probing in this area no intact skeletal material was found. The area may therefore have been previously partially exposed causing the degradation of skeletal material, then covered again with loose sand, and finally re-exposed yielding already degraded bone material. Nevertheless, given the excavation of the four substantially complete skeletons of B91/1 right on the edge of the B6 bone scatter, it was considered highly likely that the area would yield further intact burials.

At the time of the 1992 survey Burial Ground 2 was the most rapidly eroding part of the site and new scatters of bone were seen almost on a daily basis. Unfortunately, it was beyond the resources of the 1992 survey to excavate Burial Ground 2 so the area was covered with a tarpaulin held down by logs then completely buried with loose sand. It was no surprise when, less than a year later this area of the site collapsed under storm wave erosion to reveal further articulated bone material (Crosby personal observation). Unfortunately, archaeological excavations could not be mounted in time to recover this material in tact. In her 1993 excavations Hudson recovered only one in situ burial from this area, CF1. It was in direct association with the Level 2 palaeosol and consisted of the head, body and long bones of an adult individual buried with their head to the north (Hudson 1994:18–20).

CF1 brought to 13 the number of individual burials recorded in Burial Ground 2. In addition to these there are the unknown number of burials represented by the bone scatter B6, and the individuals lost to erosion during the year that lapsed between the survey in 1992 and Hudson's salvage excavations in 1993. It is therefore likely that Burial Ground 2 once contained at least 20 individuals and probably considerably more. These burials are confined within an area measuring no more than 25 by 15 metres. This would make it the same size as Burial Ground 1 and containing possibly half the number of individuals.

Possible Burial Ground 3

B92/C and HB3

Two exposures of human bone, B92/C and HB3, were identified in loose sand at around 12 metres elevation and between 300–350M. B92/C consisted of a scatter of human teeth. These remains were collected and removed to the Fiji Museum. More than one individual was probably represented. Further investigation in the general vicinity did not reveal evidence of any further remains. B92/C is therefore assumed to be the last remnants of one or more burials which were otherwise completely eroded away. HB3 consisted of a small amount of eroded bone suggesting the presence of an intact burial which would soon be exposed. These two sets of human remains occurred at the base of, and on either side of an eroding ridge.

Best (1989) had previously recovered two burials in loose sand, W1 and W2, from the western side of this ridge in locations very close to B92/C. W1 consisted of two sections of long bone and no information is available on W2 (Best 1989:43). Hudson subsequently investigated two further exposures on the eastern side of the same ridge, SB10 and SB11. SB10 consisted of a few eroded cranial or innominate fragments which may have been redeposited (Hudson 1994:18,47). SB11 consisted of unidentified bone fragments found in association with coral and "plain sherds identified as belonging to Level 3" (Hudson 1994:17, 47). Given the difficulties of locating any

position precisely on the shifting dunes, it is possible that SB11 is the same burial as that previously recorded in 1992 as HB3.

When the information on Level 3 from Birks, Best, Hudson and the 1992 survey are considered together, they show that Level 3 once extended much further south (seaward) than is now evident. The seaward end of the high ridge with which Level 3 is here associated has now been eroded away. It is therefore very likely that these burials were part of a Level 3 occupation associated with this high ridge.

HB4

A small scatter of eroded bone was initially identified on the surface of the sand at around 9 metres elevation and 340M. Careful investigation of the loose sand around the bone revealed in situ bone just beneath the surface. It was concluded that HB4 was an intact burial just about to be exposed. In 1987 Best identified two burials, W3 and W4, in the same area. W3 was located a few metres west of HB4 and W4 just to the east. Best (1989:43) comments that these burials appeared to be rather causally interred and to be much more recent than those from Burial Ground 1. The location and elevation of these burials, just in front of and below the current Level 3 exposure also suggests they may be associated with a Level 3 occupation.

In 1993 Hudson excavated 9 remnant burials, CF1–9, along an 80 metre exposure, between 300M and 380M. Of these, one burial, CF1, was associated with the Level 2 palaeosol as discussed above. However, one burial, CF7, was in direct association with the Level 3 palaeosol at an elevation of 10 metres. The remaining burials were all found in loose sand between the Level 2 and Level 3 soil exposures at elevations between approximately 4 and 6.5 metres. Plain pottery sherds of a type associated with Level 2 were found in the sand around CF2, but these sherds may well have been redeposited (Hudson 1994:18–9). Burials CF3–9, and probably also CF2, therefore appear to post-date the Level 2 occupation but only CF7 can be directly connected with Level 3.

In summary, there are at least 18 individuals identified in the area between 280M and 380M which are not part of Burial Ground 2 or otherwise associated with Level 2. Some are associated with Level 3, others are not. They cluster around three elevations:

• There is a group of 7 or 8 burials (CF2–6, CF8, 9) at 4–6.5 metres elevation none of which has a definite stratigraphic association, but all of which appear to post-date Level 2.

- A group of 4 burials (HB4, W3, W4 and CF7) is clustered around and just below 10 metres elevation. All post-date Level 2 and one, CF7, is directly associated with Level 3.
- A group of 6 burials at or above 12 metres elevation is located along the base and sides of the high ridge (W1, W2, B92/C, HB3, SB10 and SB11). Again all post-date Level 2 and one, SB11, was found in direct association with the Level 3 palaeosol.

It is possible that all three clusters will eventually turn out to be parts of a single burial ground, tentatively called Burial Ground 3, located on the sides and at the base of a now heavily eroded high ridge. This burial ground was probably associated with a Level 3 occupation.

Burials between 600M and 1000M

HB5, HB6 and SB6

Two burials, HB5 and 6, were identified at around 650M and 12 metres elevation. They were located 10 metres apart at the base of the western slope of a large steep-sided ridge in an area where scatters of severely degraded bone fragments had been noted a year earlier by Crosby and Matararaba (Crosby 1991c). HB5 consisted of a one metre diameter scatter of unidentified bone fragments. HB6 consisted of a 3 metre diameter scatter of bone which included cranium, long bones and vertebrae. It is likely that at least some of this bone was redeposited. These burials were not associated with a palaeosol. However, exposures of Level 2 pottery, frequently in direct association with the palaeosol, occurred on the dune surface directly to the west, east and north. One further scatter of human bone, SB6, was found in this area by Hudson in 1993. It was located at the base of the same ridge as HB5 and HB6, but approximately 60 metres to the east at an elevation of about 8 metres. SB6 consisted of bone from all parts of the body including head, arm, rib, leg and foot bones. It was found in association with plain pottery sherds identified as belonging to Level 3 (Hudson 1994:17, 47). This is around the western limit of Level 3 type pottery identified within the 1992 survey area.

HB7 and HB8

Two burials were identified between 700M and 800M. HB7 was located at 740M and 9 metres elevation. It consisted of scattered, unidentified human bone for which no in situ source was found. HB8 was located at 790M and 13 metres elevation.

It was an eroding but still in situ burial. After mapping it was covered with driftwood to help protect it.

SB7 and SB8

In 1993 Hudson investigated two human bone scatters located at approximately 870M and between 12 and 15 metres in elevation. Both were found in association with a palaeosol from which Level 2 pottery was eroding. SB7 consisted of assorted innominate fragments and was found with plain sherds thought to come from Level 2. SB8 consisted of long bone shaft fragments (Hudson 1994:17, 47).

Although the 7 burials described above (HB5–8 and SB6–8) are strung out over a distance of nearly 400 metres their elevations are fairly consistent at between 10 and 15 metres. Exposures of what is probably the Level 2 palaeosol also occur sporadically along this elevation. It is therefore likely that this string of burials is emerging as the face of the Level 2 palaeosol is progressively eroded.

B91/2, HB9 and HB10

In March 1991 Crosby and Matararaba investigated a group comprising two fairly complete skeletons and one partial skeleton consisting only of leg bones (Crosby 1991b). This group, referred to as B91/2, was subsequently excavated in August 1991. Its location was mapped in 1992 at 900M and 8 metres elevation. The two near-complete individuals were lying side by side on their backs orientated east–west, but facing west, the opposite direction to the majority of the burials excavated by Best in Burial Ground 1. They were buried in loose drift sand and the bone was of a relatively fresh appearance (see Crosby 1991b and Appendix C below for details). Nevertheless, their close association with Level 2 exposed approximately 20m to the north and identified in Testpit Transect 14 just to the east suggests they may derive from Level 2.

In 1992 two scatters of human bone were found just below B91/2 and slightly further west. HB9 was located at 920M and 7 metres elevation. It included long bone and jaw fragments which were also noticeably fresh in appearance. HB10 was located at 940M and 5 metres elevation. It consisted of scattered bone fragments most of which were from long bones. It was too eroded to evaluate its relative antiquity.

Western burials beyond 1000M

Additional exposures of human bone were identified between 1000M and 1200M during the 1992 survey. A scatter of human bone, HB11, covering an area about 1.5 metres in diameter was mapped at approximately 1150M and 31 metres in elevation (see Bone Exposure, Fig. 3.1). All the bone was heavily weathered and no in situ bone source was found. The bone occurred 10–20 metres down slope of a large soil exposure identified as Level 2.

In 1993 Hudson investigated three westerly exposures beyond the 1992 mapped area. SB4 was located at approximately 1110M and 10m elevation. It was a single interment in loose sand and was not associated with any palaeosol. Most of the upper body had been eroded away leaving scatters of cranial fragments, teeth and part of the left mandible. The lower body, however, including long bone shafts and innominate fragments were still in situ at the time of excavation. Hudson (1994:20) suggests it may be a "comparatively recent burial". SB5 was located at 1130M and 15 metres elevation. It consisted of two groups of bone, each of which included long bone, cranial and other unidentified bone fragments. SB9 was located at 1040M and 12 metres elevation. It consisted of long bone and other unidentified fragments including some possible cranial remains (Hudson 1994:17). Both SB5 and SB9 were found in recent dune sand and may also be comparatively recent.

The occurrence of human bone in the western section of the dunes, beyond the high ridge which marks the western extent of the 1992 investigations, is limited. In their 1994 walkover survey of this area Crosby, Marshall and Stefan Cabaniuk noted the presence of occasional human bone scatters. In 1996 Burley excavated two eroding burials in this western section. These are the first skeletons to be recovered from the western section of the dunes. They were located close to the sea, on steeply sloping sand, approximately 1 km beyond the 1992 survey area. They consisted of two directly superimposed burials. Both individuals were adult males and they had been interred in a fully extended position (Burley 1997). Occupation features were excavated in close proximity to the skeletons. A radiocarbon date of 230 ± 40 BP was obtained from a nearby hearth feature which indicates the burial may have been part of a Level 3 occupation (Burley 1997), although the nature and date of occupation of this Level remains ill defined. An additional burial was recovered from this area by the Lautoka police in 1998 (Burley and Shortland 1999:11).

Summary

From 1965 to 1998 human burials have appeared sporadically across the eastern section of the sand dunes. A minimum of 119 individuals have been mapped and excavated. Many more have eroded out and disappeared without trace. There is no doubt that further human skeletons are contained within the dune sands and will be revealed and destroyed from time to time as the sands erode. Subsequent to Hudson's 1993 investigations, further skeletal material has already been eroded from the area of Burial Grounds 2 and 3.

In the absence of any method for keeping track of the locations of exposed burials they have appeared to be unrelated to each other and to represent idiosyncratic events. However, when the locations of the burials are collated on the 1992 map, previously unrecognised patterns and clusters become visible. It begins to appear likely that most burials are associated with one of the human occupations and the majority are part of distinct clusters or burial grounds.

Level 1

No burials associated with Level 1 have yet been identified on the dunes.

Level 2

Burials associated with the Level 2 palaeosol occur intermittently across the full length of the mapped area. At the eastern end there are two Burial Grounds. Burial Ground 1 contained a minimum of 61 individuals and Burial Ground 2 contained at least 13 individuals although probably many more. In addition, between 600M and 1200M, at least 8 burials have appeared which are either directly associated with the Level 2 palaeosol or were found in the general vicinity of the eroding soil line.

Level 3

Burials associated with Level 3 have appeared in at least two areas in the eastern section of the mapped area. A small group of at least 4 individuals has been recovered from the far eastern end of the mapped area. A much larger concentration of burials has been progressively appearing above Burial Ground 2, probably in association with the base and sides of an eroded ridge. This area has been tentatively called Burial Ground 3 and at present contains at least 18 burials. Unlike the Level 2 burials, which were all relatively shallow inhumations within the palaeosol, the burials associated with Level 3 appear to have been placed in deeper pits excavated into loose sand beneath the palaeosol. In addition Burley's excavation of two burials in close proximity to dated Level 3 occupation features suggested burials were also taking place in the western section of the dunes during late prehistory.

Unprovenanced burials

Burials not associated with any of the three palaeosols also occur. However, it is becoming evident that such burials are exceptional and even these burials occur in clusters. One group of 5 apparently very recent burials has been identified low on the dunes around 900M. A possible explanation for these burials was provided by a local Fiji Indian man, who is a third generation resident in the area directly behind the dunes. He informed us that his grandfather remembered people burying bodies on the dunes, both singly and in groups, during the measles epidemics in the late 19th and early 20th centuries. Best (1989:6) also reports that Fergus Clunie told him he once found a skull on the dunes containing "a 30 calibre slug from an M1 carbine".

Chapter 7
Reconstructing the changing dune surface

Introduction

As described in Chapters 5 and 6 the 1992 survey map has provided a reference point for collating the large body of archaeological evidence which has accumulated since the Birks' excavations of 1965/66. Previously invisible patterns in the nature of occupation on the dunes and the form of the palaeosols on which those occupations took place have now come into view. Because of the diagonal erosion profile through the dunes, and the difficulties of excavating and probing through great depths of sand, reconstructions of the palaeosol surfaces have commonly been based on narrow strips of information collected from limited areas. Even the most recent attempt by Dickinson et al. (1998) suffers from being based primarily on a single season's work concentrated at the far eastern and western margins of the dunes. Because the interpretations presented here are based on all the information collected since 1965 they do not suffer from these limitations.

As outlined in Chapter 2, there is considerable debate over exactly when and how the Sigatoka dunes formed. It is widely accepted that dune formation could not have begun until after the stabilisation of sea levels at around 4–5000 years ago (Dickinson et al. 1998; Nunn 1990; Sheppard 1990). What is hotly contested is exactly how soon after this date dune formation began. Following Birks (1973) and Parry (1987), Dickinson et al. (1998) argue that significant dune formation did not begin until after human occupation took place and that human occupation of the Sigatoka River valley significantly accelerated dune formation. In their opinion, development of a prominent dune field, comparable to the present one, "is not indicated by available evidence" until after the formation of the Level 1 and 2 palaeosols (Dickinson et al. 1998:12).

When considering data collected exclusively from the area east of 400M this does appear to be the case. In this area, it is indeed true that "dune growth was substantially enhanced" after the formation of the Level 1 and 2 palaeosols (Dickinson et al. 1998:20) and that large volumes of sand were deposited on the dunes between Levels 2 and 3, and overlying Level 3. However, this is not the case for the area immediately to the west, between 400M and 1300M. When all the evidence compiled over the last 35 years for the area 0M–1300M is combined, a very different picture emerges.

Previous interpretations have been misled by the assumption that the entire dune field grew in a westerly direction from a single origin point near to the easterly extent of the identified palaeosols; in other words from around 0M on the 1992 map. Contrary to this assumption we argue that the dunes grew in several phases from at least two origin points: one at around 0M and an earlier one at around 5–600M. A schematic representation of this process is illustrated in Fig. 7.1. The evidence supporting this very different interpretation of the dune jigsaw is described below beginning with the period immediately prior to the formation of Level 1 and working through to the present day.

Pre-Level 1

Central to the debate over how and when the dunes formed is the question of where the Sigatoka River has exited over the past 5,000 years. Parry (1987) argued that prior to the development of the sand dunes the river exited several kilometres west of its present location, and ran along the base of the rock face which marks the western extent of the deltaic plain behind the present dunes. An abandoned palaeochannel marks this route (Fig. 2.1). Parry's contention was that the dunes began to form when the river mouth moved east to its present position. He went on to argue that on several subsequent

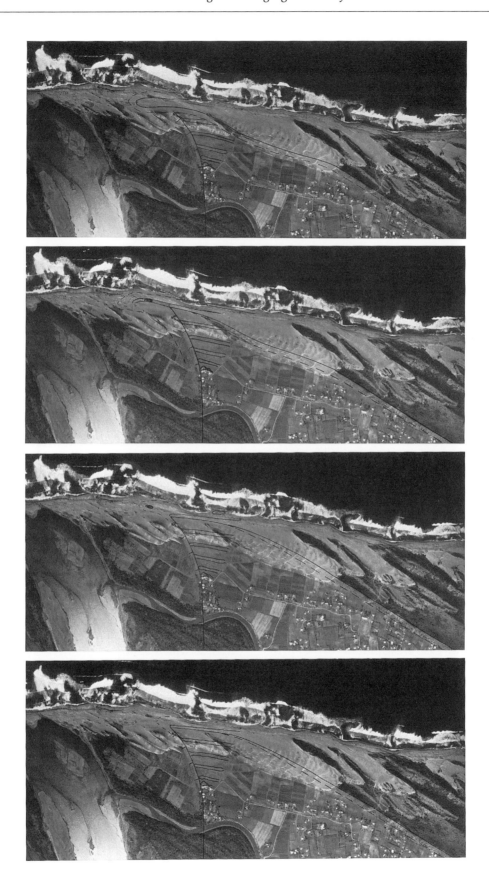

Fig. 7.1 Reconstructions of the sequence of dune formation at the eastern end of the Sigatoka dunes. The reconstructions are superimposed onto a 1983 aerial photograph. Top: Pre-Level 1. Second from top: at the time Level 1 was forming. Second from bottom: at the time Level 2 was forming. Bottom: at the time Level 3 was forming.

occasions the river mouth reverted to the west, allowing the dunes to stabilise beneath vegetation and creating the opportunities for paleosols to form. Recent work has now established that Parry's proposed palaeochannel has been blocked from the sea for at least 5,000 years. In addition, the shallow stratigraphy of the Volivoli Lagoon, located directly behind the western end of the dunes, "further implies that any such channel was blocked by beach ridges well before growth of the dune field" (Dickinson et al. 1998:14). The western channel could not therefore have played a role in the development of the dunes. However, given that the river has exited to the east for at least 5,000 years, dune formation could have begun at least this long ago.

Attention has now shifted to an old river channel located approximately 600 metres west of the present river. It is clearly marked by a steep 2–3m high palaeo-cutbank which runs north behind the dunes alongside Kulukulu village (Fig. D.1; Plate 18). This feature has been central to reconstructions of the dunes since its initial identification by Simon Best (1989:9). However, because most reconstructions assume an entirely westerly build up of sand they assume this old river course must have exited at the far eastern end of the present dunes. This would place it east of Best's burial ground, at around 50M on the 1992 map. This is the location suggested by Dickinson et al. (1998) and shown in their Figs. 3 and 5. We argue that the actual location of the channel mouth was around 250M, well to the west of Best's burial ground, at a point where the Level 1 palaeosol has been shown by Testpit Transect 15 to dip suddenly and disappear for a distance of about 50m along the dunes (Fig. A.6). This revised location is used in Fig. 7.1.

Extending to the west of the old riverbank, and behind the present dunes, is a series of at least four low ridges that run east–west, parallel to the current shoreline but at an angle to the dunes. They reach a maximum height of 5m a.s.l. (Fig. D.1; Plate 17). The presence of a fifth ridge, to seaward, is indicated on old aerial photographs but now lies buried under the advancing backslope of the dunes. Cultural remains found eroding from the back of the dunes by Visser (1988) are probably associated with this ridge. Even further to seaward, a sixth ridge is reconstructed as partly underlying the Level 1 and Level 2 occupations along the front of the dunes, as is discussed below. Following Dickinson et al. (1998) these ridges are interpreted as old beach ridges which formed progressively in a southerly (seaward) direction. The oldest ridges are therefore inland and the most recent ridge runs along the current shoreline. The formation of all these beach ridges pre-dates both human occupation and initial dune formation.

After the beach ridges had formed and while the river still exited at around 250M, the dunes began to form in a westerly direction from around 5–600M. This initial dune build-up must pre-date the formation of the Level 1 palaeosol because over much of the area west of 5–600M the Level 1 palaeosol formed on a surface well above the maximum 5m elevation of the beach ridges. Exactly how big and how high the dunes were at this time is not known, although the investigations carried out by Dickinson et al. at the far western end of the dunes indicate they did not extend west as far as the Volivoli rock face (Dickinson et al. 1998:19). One possibility, however, is that the old consolidated and vegetated dunes, which can be seen in aerial photographs emerging from beneath the higher and more recent wind blown dune sands, represent the pre-Level 1 surface. If the back face of these older dunes is extrapolated east, the origin point would be between 500M and 600M. This suggested reconstruction is shown in Fig. 7.1.

Level 1: the form of the dune surface

Our current knowledge of the dune surfaces at the time the Level 1 palaeosol was forming is collated in Fig. 7.2. It shows all 1992 exposures of the Level 1 palaeosol; all 1992 testpits in which Level 1 was identified (TP1,3,4,5,7,8,15,P2); Level 1 features excavated in 1992; the lines along which Level 1 was exposed in 1966, 1987 and 1993; and the probable location of Burley's 1998 excavations of Level 1.

Additional information comes from the beach ridges behind the dunes. Pottery recovered from Marshall's test excavations, supported by the results of Burley's 1996 excavations, indicate that this area was occupied at approximately the same time as the Level 1 palaeosol on the dunes. However, the 70 cm thick deposit of black soil, which covers the beach ridges behind the dunes, is of a different nature than the Level 1 palaeosol. On the front of the dunes the three palaeosols were often separated by the build up of loose sands, whereas behind the dunes a single soil layer formed as an uninterrupted deposit. It contains cultural materials relating to all periods of occupation. We know then that the beach ridges formed prior to the earliest human occupation and have remained largely unchanged through to the present day.

A reconstruction of the Level 1 palaeosol surface which uses the 1992 survey map as a base is illustrated in Fig. 7.3. This reconstruction is described from east to west. By the time the Level 1 palaeosol formed the river mouth had shifted east to around 100M. The area between this and the old

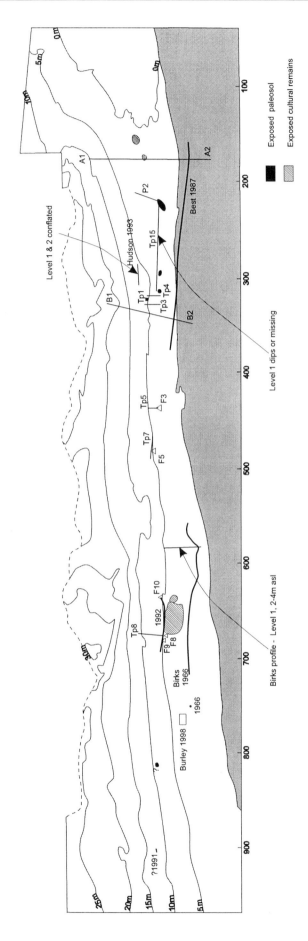

Fig. 7.2 Collated evidence from all investigations carried out on the dunes up to 1998 for the location and elevation of Level 1 palaeosol exposures.

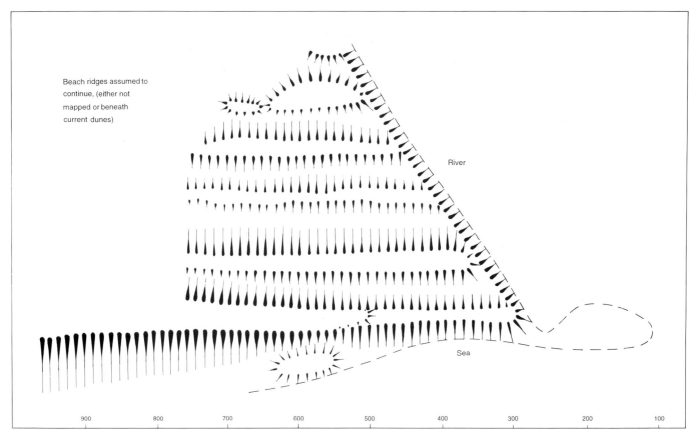

Beach ridges assumed to
continue, (either not
mapped or beneath
current dunes)

River

Sea

900   800   700   600   500   400   300   200   100

Fig. 7.3 Reconstruction of the eastern dunes at the time the Level 1 palaeosol was forming.

river mouth at 250M now comprised a flat sandy pan or sand spit elevated only 1–2m above sea level. The 1992 probe transect, P2, indicated the Level 1 surface sloped down slightly to the north, suggesting it formed the back slope of a low ridge or knoll-like feature. At this time the low-lying area further to the north, in the vicinity of Club Masa, may have formed a river meander or lagoon.

At the point where the old river channel originally exited at 250–300M, the surface of Level 1 dips and disappears over a distance of 50m along the dunes, indicating a dip in elevation across the base of the partly infilled river channel (see TP15, Fig. A.6). To the west, between 300M and 500M, Level 1 formed on the pre-existing beach ridges. The most seaward ridge rose gently but consistently up from the sea at a gradient varying between 1:5 and 1:10 (1992 TP1, 4, 7, Features 3 and 5) reaching a maximum elevation of about 5 metres above sea level. Its back slope was identified in Hudson's excavations (Hudson 1994:24). It can be followed west from the old riverbank for a distance of 200 metres.

However, between 500M and 600M the form of the Level 1 surface begins to change. In 1992, TP8 located at 680M identified Level 1 raising into the

dune at a slope of 1:10 from an elevation of 5 metres (Fig. A.4). Level 1 was also picked up briefly at around 8 metres elevation at 800M. The previous year, Crosby (1991) had found it at 900M, at an elevation of around 10 metres. We argue that west of 5–600M the Level 1 palaeosol formed on an early *dune* surface, not on a continuation of the undulating beach ridges, on the basis of three features. Firstly, in the area west of 5–600M Level 1 consistently rises northward into the present dunes and has never been recorded as a level surface or a downward slope. Secondly, in this area it rises to an elevation of at least 10m, far exceeding the maximum heights of any of the beach ridges. Thirdly, west of 5–600M, Level 1 changes orientation. It no longer forms a ridge parallel to the shore but begins to turn inland thus emulating the southeast orientation and wedge-like shape of the current dune configuration. This shift in orientation fits perfectly with the extrapolated back edge of the old vegetated dunes, as shown in Fig. 7.1.

This interpretation of the Level 1 dune surface is supported by the Birks descriptions of Level 1 in 1966. At the eastern end of their excavations Level 1 dipped into the dune. In the main excavation area, which is around 600M on the 1992 map, Level

1 was quite flat allowing the excavations to extend up to 50 feet into the dune face (Birks 1973: Fig.3, Fig.5a). West of this large excavation area Level 1 began to rise northward into the dune face, a tendency which became ever more pronounced as they moved west. This rise forced the Birks to narrow their excavations to only a few feet (Birks 1973:10). Our interpretation of this evidence is that the Birks' main excavation area was located on the top of a low foredune similar to the one mapped in this area in 1992. The Birks offered a similar interpretation suggesting the existence of an eroded south-facing promontory (Birks 1973:10). Further west, however, the Birks excavations were further inland and probably extended back onto the base of the relatively steeply rising seaward face of the main dune. The transition from one landform to another was obscured by the strip-like nature of their excavations.

Burley's 1998 excavations, located at 760M and probably abutting the western extent of the Birks excavations, were not located far enough north, to encounter this rising dune surface. He uncovered Level 1 at 5m above mean sea level, which is around 3m elevation on the 1992 map, and found that it "followed a roughly level course north into the dune face" (Burley and Shortland 1999:35). This suggests that Burley, like the Birks, also excavated on what was once a low foredune, or perhaps in a swale between it and the main dune to the north.

Our contention, then, is that the dunes had already begun to develop prior to the formation of the Level 1 palaeosol. We agree with previous interpretations, which suggest that the dunes built up largely in an east to west direction. However, we identify an initial phase of dune build-up, during which they formed only to the west of 5–600M, approximately 250–350m west of the old river channel. By the time of the formation of the Level 1 palaeosol the river channel had shifted some 300m to the east, perhaps creating the right conditions for the dunes to stabilise and consolidate. East of 5–600M, at the time the Level 1 palaeosol was forming, there were undulating beach ridges, and the newly formed sandspit, but no dunes.

No definitive evidence of the Level 1 palaeosol has yet been identified on the dunes west of the area mapped in 1992. We would expect Level 1 to be present as a separate and distinct palaeosol for some distance west of 900M but buried deeply under the current dunes. Both the Birks and Burley have found a palaeosol containing Lapita pottery at Naqarai Bay at the far western end of the dunes (Birks and Birks 1966; Burley and Shortland 1999). There is no good reason, however, for assuming that this represents an extension of Level 1. It is more likely to represent a localised soil deposit comparable with the beach ridges behind the eastern dunes.

Level 2: the form of the dune surface

All available information on the Level 2 palaeosol is collated in Fig. 7.4. This includes all the 1992 exposures of the Level 2 palaeosol, all the 1992 transects in which Level 2 was identified (TP1–5, 7–12, 14, 16, P2), the Level 2 features excavated in 1992, the lines along which Level 2 was exposed in 1966, 1987, 1993 and 1998, and all profiles and trenches in which Level 2 occurred. Based on this information a reconstruction of the dune at the time Level 2 was forming is illustrated in Fig. 7.5. This reconstruction is explained from east to west.

During the 1992 survey the eastern extent of the Level 2 palaeosol was defined in TP16 at around 80M where it formed a steep, downward sloping surface indicative of a bank, possibly marking the location of the river channel at this time (Fig. A.7). As for Level 1, from this point west to 300M the palaeosol formed on a low sandy rise, which never reached elevations much above 2 metres. The highest identified point is the area of Burial Ground 1 which Best (1989) has reconstructed as a small knoll about 2 metres high. The Level 2 palaeosol exposures surveyed around Burial Ground 1 in 1987 and 1992 indicate that it now formed a continuous surface across the low area of the old river channel at 250–300M where Level 1 had previously dipped or disappeared. In the intervening period between the formation of Level 1 and Level 2 the depression created by the old river channel had become at least partially infilled.

Around 300M Level 2 rises suddenly from 2m to 4–5m in elevation indicating the line of the old riverbank where the beach ridges start. This change is identified in Best's (1989) two profiles (A1–A2 and B1–B2), in Hudson's (1994) excavations, and in the 1992 P2 and TP1–4 (Fig. A.2). From this point west to 500M Level 2 formed on an undulating beach ridge surface but always remains below 5m elevation. In some locations in this area it has been encountered as an upward sloping surface, but has predominantly been found to form either a level or downward sloping surface. This is indicated by TP2–7 (Figs. A.2, A.3) and by Hudson's Trench 3 and 4 in which Level 2 is identified sloping down to the north into the dune from an elevation of around 4 metres a.s.l. (Hudson 1994:11). It can be reconstructed as having formed on a low ridge that runs east–west on the same orientation as the beach ridges and overlies the earlier Level 1 ridge. The intervening build up of sand between Level 1 and 2 along this ridge is fairly minimal. It never

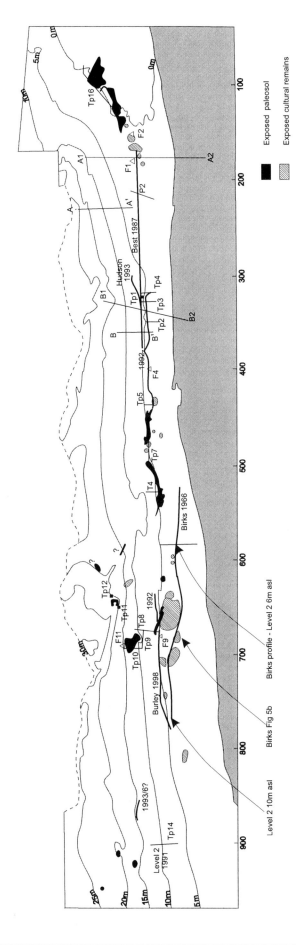

Fig. 7.4 Collated evidence from all investigations carried out on the dunes up to 1998 for the location and elevation of Level 2 palaeosol exposures.

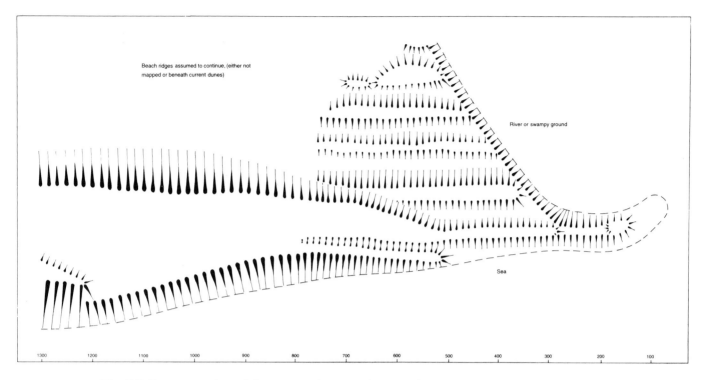

Fig. 7.5 Reconstruction of the eastern dunes at the time the Level 2 palaeosol was forming.

exceeds 3 metres and in many places the two palaeosols are directly superimposed or merged (see TP3, 4,7; Hudson 1994).

West of 500M no exposures of the Level 2 palaeosol have yet been identified at elevations below 5 metres a.s.l. The situation indicated by the Birks' excavations and later projects is of a foredune which probably formed over the older beach ridge, and was backed to the north by a much higher dune. Between 520M and 680M the Birks followed Level 2 as a surface that consistently sloped down into the dune face, but increased in elevation from east to west to 8m elevation by 680M. They followed the surface for a further 100m to the west, but are not specific about whether it sloped up or down into the dunes. By 780M it would have exceeded 10m elevation and was continuing to rise, suggesting that by that point the foredune and main dune had merged. Ten metres is at least double the height of any of the beach ridges east of 500M. Moreover, the orientation of the foredune identified by the Birks, is not directly east–west, but angles slightly into the dunes to the WNW.

From 500M west, behind the foredune on which the Birks excavated, the Level 2 surface changes character completely. From this point it rises steadily and dramatically. In 1992 an exposure of the Level 2 palaeosol at 700M was traced north into the dune face from the 5m contour. TP8–10 (Fig. A.4) established that this palaeosol rose steeply up into the

dune, and was continuous with a large area of exposed palaeosol directly above it which reached an elevation of 15 metres. A further exposure of the Level 2 palaeosol was identified at 20–23 metres elevation just 50 metres to the east. TP11 and TP12, put in to investigate this exposure established that the base of the palaeosol was at 19.26m and 21.025m elevation respectively. Since the two testpits were only 12 metres apart this equates to a very dramatic rise of 1:1.7, suggesting a steep dune crest. Two additional high elevation palaeosol exposures at 600M are tentatively identified as Level 3, but it is possible they are also Level 2.

These exposures unequivocally establish that west of 500M the Level 2 palaeosol developed on a substantial dune very similar to the present one. Between 500M and 800M the crest of this dune rose from 5m to more than 20 metres and its configuration closely resembled that of the dune in 1992. This dune developed over and behind the Level 1 dune. At its crest as much as 15 metres of sand could separate the two palaeosols. However, along the 5 metre contour line the two palaeosols are often directly superimposed if not actually merged suggesting the seaward edge of the dunes had not changed a great deal in the intervening period.

West of 800M intermittent exposures of the Level 2 palaeosol have been recorded. These are all at or above 10 metres elevation. There are six exposures between 800M and 1000M which vary in elevation from 9 to 24 metres. In TP14, at 900M (Fig. A.5) Level 2 was identified at 10m elevation and was rising steeply into the dune at a gradient of 1:4.5. Directly above it the Level 2 exposure at 20m elevation appeared to dive down to the north. This may mark the crest at the 900M point but it could also be simply an undulation in the dune surface. Two Level 2 palaeosol exposures have been recorded further west. During the 1992 survey it was visible at 1150M and 31m elevation (Plate 1). In 1966 the Birks followed the Level 2 palaeosol "on a diagonal course up the dune slope" for a distance of 2,220ft, by which time it had reached an elevation of approximately 120ft (Birks 1973:10). This would place the termination of the palaeosol at approximately 1250M and 37m elevation on the 1992 survey map, about halfway up the present dune face and close to the base of a large transverse dune ridge which runs the full width of the dune cutting off the eastern section from the western dunes.

Summary: For Level 2, as for Level 1, the 5–600M point on the 1992 survey map is the dividing line between two kinds of topography. East of 5–600M there is no evidence for Level 2 above 5m elevation; west of this point the Level 2 palaeosol has never been found below 5m elevation. From 80M–300M the Level 2 palaeosol formed on a low sandy rise up to 2m high. At 300M this surface rises 2–4 metres over the old riverbank and continues along the crest and flanks of an east–west beach ridge up to 5m high. Beyond 5–600M the surface widens and rises into a typical dune configuration. Over a distance of little more than 100m it rises to an elevation of at least 20m then maintains or increases this elevation west to at least 1250M. In front of this main dune a low foredune was present between 500m and 700M. This is the area in which the Birks excavated. The foredune rose to at least 10m elevation and beyond 700M would have merged with the main dune behind. In short, between 500M and 1250M the Level 2 palaeosol formed over a dune surface very similar to that mapped in 1992.

Level 3: the form of the dune surface

All available information on the Level 3 palaeosol is collated in Fig. 7.6. It includes all exposures of the Level 3 palaeosol mapped in 1992, all the 1992 transects in which Level 3 was identified (TP6, 16), all Level 3 features excavated in 1992, the lines along which Level 3 was exposed in 1966, 1987 and 1993, and all profiles and trenches in which Level 3 occurs. Based on this information a reconstruction of the dune at the time the Level 3 palaeosol was forming

is illustrated in Fig. 7.7. All recorded exposures of the Level 3 palaeosol occur within a 500m long section of the dunes between 100M and 600M. Unlike Levels 1 and 2 the vast majority of Level 3 exposures have appeared since the mid 1980s.

The eastern extent of the Level 3 palaeosol was established at 80M by TP16, which found the Level 3 palaeosol sloping very steeply down to the east just beyond the east face of Level 2 (Fig. A.7). Investigations by the Fiji Museum in 1995 found exactly the same configuration. The much steeper angle of the Level 3 palaeosol indicates its rapid descent from a far higher elevation than Level 2. From this origin point Level 3 palaeosol exposures have been recorded along a semi-continuous line to 560M. For much of this distance, up to 300M, they hover between 10m and 13m elevation and are always reported as sloping steeply down into the dune indicating that it is the backslope which is exposed, probably close to the crest. In the area east of 300M Level 3 therefore formed over a substantial dune, at least 10 metres high. The seaward half of this dune has been eroded away.

This dune overlies the older Level 2 surface. Between 80M and 300M, up to 10 metres of sand may intervene between the Level 2 and Level 3 palaeosols. However, to the west, the Level 3 surface drops between 350M and 500M to form a relatively low saddle. In this area the new dune formed very close to and in places right against the southern face of the older Level 2 dune surface. The intervening sand deposits between Level 2 and Level 3 would not have exceeded 5m in depth, and around 400M where the Level 3 palaeosol dips particularly low there may be as little as 2m of sand between the two palaeosols. At 500M, where remnants of the south facing slope of Level 3 were mapped in 1992, Levels 2 and 3 were conflated at an elevation of 6–7m. This conflation was confirmed in Hudson's 1993 trench, T4.

The Birks 1966 excavations of Level 3 were located in the area between 380M and 580M, well seaward of the 1992 shoreline. The eastern half of this exposure sloped up into the dune face indicating they encountered the south facing seaward slope of the dune before it was eroded away. The western half of the exposure, however, sloped down to the north into the dune indicating a northern backslope. The simplest explanation for this evidence is that this downward sloping western surface formed over the backslope of the same foredune the Birks encountered west of 500M for Level 2.

Two high elevation palaeosol exposures located during the 1992 survey around 600M are also tentatively attributed to Level 3. If this is correct then the Level 3 palaeosol must have formed over the crest and down the backslope of the Level 2

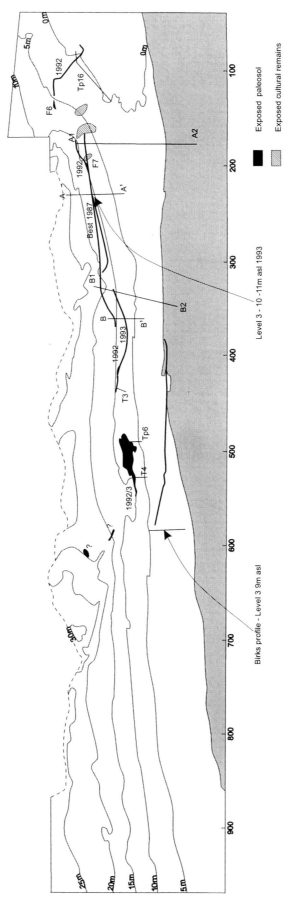

Fig. 7.6 Collated evidence from all investigations carried out on the dunes up to 1998 for the location and elevation of Level 3 palaeosol exposures.

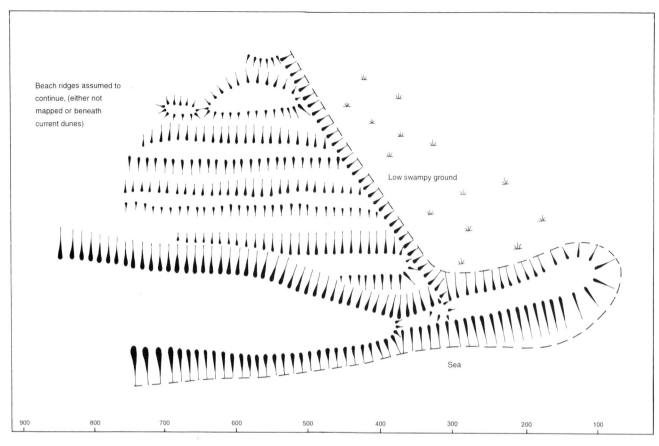

Beach ridges assumed to
continue, (either not
mapped or beneath
current dunes)

Low swampy ground

Sea

900   800   700   600   500   400   300   200   100

Fig. 7.7 Reconstruction of the eastern dunes at the time the Level 3 palaeosol was forming.

dune. This would have widened and heightened the dunes a little in this area but would not have significantly altered their overall shape and appearance. Thus, although in the intervening period between the formation of Levels 2 and 3 a 10m high dune formed to the east of the Level 2 dune, burying the Level 2 surface east of 500M, the Level 2 dune surface changed very little west of 500M and little further dune build-up occurred.

Summary: The formation of the Level 3 palaeosol is a localised event which had the effect of stabilising a large new parabolic dune which formed against and slightly behind the pre-existing Level 2 dune at 500M, and covered the low Level 2 beach ridge which ran from 80M to 500M. By extending the dune system 400m to the east, over an area of low beach ridges, this consolidation event gave the eastern dunes their present configuration but did not alter in any major way the form of the dunes immediately west of 500M.

Post-Level 3: the form of the dune surface

Following the formation of the Level 3 palaeosol, sand continued to build up in a northerly and easterly direction. As can be seen in the 1983 aerial photograph used as a base for Fig. 7.1 the dunes east of 500M widened considerably and a sand spit more than 500m long built up between the eastern extent of Level 3 and the river mouth. This recent build up significantly altered the shape and appearance of the dunes east of 500M. In contrast, post-Level 3 changes to the area between 500M and 1500M were minimal.

Summary

Previous reconstructions have made two fundamental assumptions: 1) a simple east to west progressive build up of dune sands from a single origin around 0M, and 2) the rate of dune formation accelerated after the Level 2 occupation. Detailed examination of the archaeological evidence has, however, revealed that the dunes grew in several phases, initiating from an origin point located around 5–600M on the 1992 map. Most of the dune build-up took place during this initial phase, which means it occurred prior to the formation of the Level 2 palaeosol, and probably even prior to Level 1. It is indeed the case that east of 500M there was a second phase of significant dune formation that did not take place until after the Level 2 occupation. But this was a local process which had very little impact on the substantial dunes already present west of 500M.

By chance, the Birks put their 1965–6 excavations right around the 5–600M origin point (see Fig. 5.1). The 3 layer sequence they recovered in this area was a chance effect specific to the area in which their excavations took place – namely a foredune located seaward of the main dune and at the intersection point of two formation processes: beach ridges to the east and dunes to the west. The Birks' excavations happened to straddle the only area on the dunes where the three palaeosols approach each other. The layercake stratigraphy they identified was a unique feature of the successive foredunes on which they excavated. It was a localised phenomenon and not at all typical of the stratigraphic structure of the dunes generally.

The reconstruction presented here refers only to the eastern dunes – to that section of the dunes, which stretches from the river mouth west to the large transverse ridge, which divides the eastern section from the western dunes. This is a distance of 2km. West of this ridge there are another 3 km of dunes. The sequence of palaeosol and dune formation identified for the eastern dunes cannot be assumed to be present on the western dunes. This is a matter for investigation. Given how context specific the nature of the formation processes identified for the eastern dunes are, it is extremely unlikely they will be reproduced in exactly the same sequence elsewhere. Burley's 1996 and 1998 surveys of the western dunes have identified intermittent palaeosol exposures, some of which contain cultural remains. They occur most commonly midway up the dunes (Burley 1997:15). No superimposed palaeosols have yet been identified. While these exposed sections may all be part of a single continuous palaeosol, the evidence from the eastern dunes suggests caution. They may not have all formed at the same time and may not equate with any of the palaeosol events identified on the eastern dunes. It is possible that they may instead result from localised events of consolidation, which took place at a number of different times. These events may or may not have occurred at same time as events which led to the formation of palaeosols in the eastern dunes.

Recent destruction of the dunes

The longitudinal study of the dunes over the last 35 years also provides a basis for understanding recent processes of erosion. Over the past three decades, the rates and locations of both wind and sea erosion of the eastern dunes have varied enormously and it has been difficult to identify overall patterns. However, with the 1992 survey map available to anchor our understanding of recent erosion, longer-term patterns are beginning to emerge. The process of eastern dune destruction since 1965 is described chronologically and is summarised in Fig. 7.8.

1965/6

In 1965/6 when the Birks carried out their excavations Levels 1 and 3 were each exposed over short distances of 200 metres or less, at elevations below 9 metres. Level 2 was exposed much more extensively. From a point around 500M and 5 metres elevation, it could be followed over a distance of some 700 metres before it finally disappeared to the west at around 37 metres elevation.

1966–1987/8

From 1966 until the mid 1980's the high tide line remained fairly stable and sea erosion was minimal. On the other hand, intense wind erosion took place at higher elevations, severely eroding the Level 3 palaeosol. The distance over which Level 3 was exposed expanded 300 metres to the east while the edge of the exposed palaeosol retreated inland by up to 50 metres and rose to a minimum elevation of 8 metres. Levels 1 and 2 were also affected by wind erosion but less extensively than Level 3. They too became exposed to the east of the area in which the Birks worked. By 1988 all three Levels could be followed east from 400M to at least 180M. However, it was not until the mid 1980's that wind erosion low on the dunes became intense enough to cause serious damage to Level 2. At this point the Burial Ground 1 skeletons began to appear and Level 2 was widely exposed at low elevations (Plate 11). Level 1, however, remained fairly intact.

1988–1992

Between 1988 and 1992 wind erosion seems to have been steady and general, but not intense. The main effect was to expose further sections of Level 2 but to begin to cover over the recently eroded sections of Level 3. It was during this period that the skeletons in Burial Ground 2 began to appear. It was also during this period that sea erosion began to escalate and the high tide line started to move inland, advancing at least 25 metres in 4 years (Plate 6). This advance was more pronounced in the east where the eastern sections of Levels 1 and 2 started to wash away.

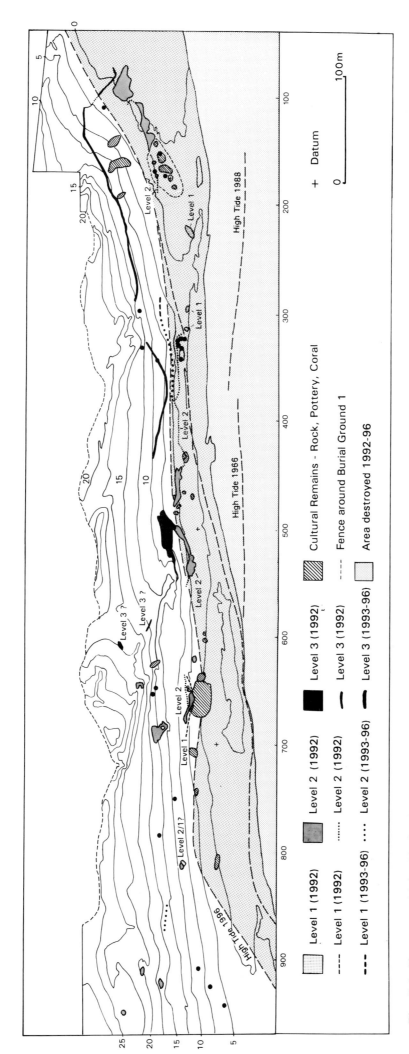

Fig. 7.8 Changes to high tide levels occurring between 1965 and 1996 and the approximate locations of the eroding palaeosol exposures between 1992 and 1996.

1992–1996

Following Cyclone Kina in January 1993 sea erosion accelerated further. Initially the erosion was concentrated in the east. During 1993 the high tide line advanced more than 100 metres at the eastern end of the mapped area but west of 600M the effects were minimal (Plate 14). By 1996, however, this dramatic advance had been repeated along the full length of the mapped area. By then the high tide line was at least 40 metres inland of its 1992 position, usually considerably more. This advance had a devastating effect on Levels 1 and 2. In contrast, between 1993 and 1996 wind erosion at higher elevations was fairly light and Level 3 suffered comparatively little damage in the aftermath of Cyclone Kina.

1997–1998

By November 1997 the cycle of sea erosion at the eastern end of the dunes had run its course. The high tide line had returned to a location close to that of 1992 and a wide beach flat was beginning to build up between the high tide line and the base of the dunes (Plate 15). Up to two metres of sand had already accumulated and the rate of build up was accelerating. In addition the foredune which had been present along the high tide line until 1992 was reforming. During 1998 some of this development was reversed and new erosion had occurred particularly around 700–900M. Despite this new erosion it is likely that the main changes taking place in the immediate future will involve the build up of sand along the seaward edge of the dunes.

Summary

Erosion processes along the seaward face of the dunes appear to be cyclical. Over a period of approximately 25 years the sea has alternately washed away and built up the seaward edge of the dunes. Wind erosion higher on the dunes has alternately stripped palaeosol surfaces bare and buried them beneath thick drift sands. These cyclical processes can be seen repeated in aerial photographs which provide a time lapse sequence extending back to the 1940s. The photographs emphasise, however, that the cumulative long-term effect is the steady redistribution of sand from the front of the dunes to the back. This process has seen the dunes migrate inland at the rate of approximately 20 metres per decade over the last 30 years.

Chapter 8
Understanding the nature of human occupation

"Available radiocarbon dates establish that there were three discrete periods during which the site was intensively used. …. The barren nature of the thick sand layers that intervene between the paleosol culture levels (Fig. 4) suggest sustained absences or periods of severely limited site use during two temporal intervals prior to the modern period. These intervals of abandonment correspond approximately to the periods from 400BC to AD 100, and from AD 400 to AD 1300" (Dickinson et al. 1998:8).

Introduction

The above interpretation of the history of human occupation on the Sigatoka Sand Dunes follows directly from the reductionist view of the dunes stratigraphy as a simple vertical layercake (see Figs. 1.3 and 1.5 above). By assuming in advance that the Birks sequence of palaeosols is typical of the entire dune system, and that the sequence of human occupation is identical to and co-incident with that of the palaeosols, Dickinson et al. eliminate from view all variety and diversity present in the archaeological data. Our detailed re-examination of the horizontal as well as vertical evidence for each palaeosol, presented in Chapter 7 brings this diversity back into view and shows that dune formation occurred as a series of localised events which built upon each other to create the overall dune system. Because the stratigraphic history of each part of the dunes characterises only the events taking place in that specific area there is no generalised stratigraphic sequence which typifies the dunes as a whole. There cannot then be a parallel sequence of human occupation on the dunes.

In this chapter we argue that a fuller consideration of the archaeological evidence from Sigatoka also indicates that human use of the dunes was not characterised by three brief periods of occupation interspersed by extended periods of abandonment. The three organic soil layers have certainly yielded the great bulk of the archaeological materials recovered from the dunes, but these palaeosols represent the dune surfaces during extended periods of stability, punctuated by relatively brief periods of instability and rapid sand accumulation, not the reverse. Furthermore, these periods of instability did not necessarily result in the abandonment of occupation: some parts of the dunes were disrupted more than others and archaeological evidence has now been recovered to suggest that occupation in the area of Burial Ground 2 – the eastern end of the most seaward beach ridge – included at least six periods of occupation indicating the continued use of the dunes from as early as 1000BC to the time of European contact.

Indeed human occupation of the dunes is far more complex than previously imagined. Some of this complexity can be summarised as follows:

- The palaeosols each have a complex micro-history and micro-stratigraphy. Although on the eastern dunes there are three broad soil formation periods corresponding to the Birks three Levels, these palaeosols are stratigraphically and geographically complex events. The formation history of each palaeosol is specific to its particular location and cannot be generalised to the dunes as a whole. Furthermore, the occupational history of any palaeosol is closely related to its context specific formational history.
- All forms of cultural remains found on the dunes occur in well defined spatial clusters or concentrations. These tend to be confined to narrow stratigraphic bands like micro-layers or lenses within the deeper palaeosols. They are not usually mixed through a depth of soil. This

clustered patterning needs to be understood within the context of the micro-geography of each palaeosol.

- Human occupation spans a much wider time period than previously recognised. Occupation associated with each palaeosol is more appropriately characterised as an extended series of events rather than a single short period. Considered in this way the archaeological evidence preserved in the dunes approaches a near-continuous record of occupation from the earliest human arrivals in Fiji through to European contact.
- Cultural remains are geographically more extensive than previously recognised and their known distribution is still growing.
- Cultural remains are more varied than previously recognised. The range of pottery types present in cultural deposits has expanded considerably since the Birks excavations and the presence of features such as burials, *lovo* and possible built structures indicative of a much wider range of activities, are now known. In view of these results the extremely small amount of faunal material recovered from the dunes can reasonably be attributed to taphonomic processes. Since even carefully buried human bone does not survive well unless it is protected with a covering of rock or coral, discarded and scattered faunal remains could only be expected to survive in exceptional circumstances.

A detailed re-examination of the archaeological evidence recovered from the dunes is presented below. Its purpose is to highlight the complexities summarised above with a view to rethinking the way we understand the nature of human occupation on the dunes over the past 3000 years.

Lapita occupations

The range of pottery recovered on the eastern dunes from stratigraphic positions below, in and above the Level 1 palaeosol, indicate an extended period of occupation which commenced by 1000 BC with Early Eastern Lapita pottery, continued through Late Eastern Lapita pottery, and ended at or after 200 BC with a possible late form of Lapita plainware or an early form of paddle impressed ware (called "late Level 1 ceramics" by Petchey 1994: 34, 38; 1995:154). The predominant Late Eastern Lapita pottery recovered by the Birks merely represents the middle of a complex sequence of occupation spanning 800 years or more.

The locations of the major deposits of Lapita cultural materials are shown in Fig. 8.1. Two features

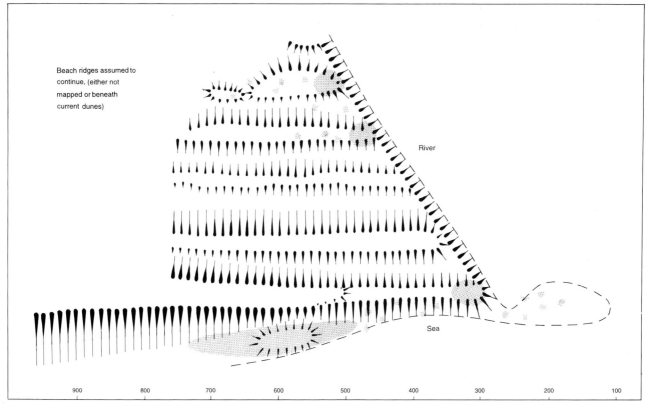

Fig. 8.1 Collated evidence for Lapita occupation of the eastern end of the Sigatoka dunes mapped onto the reconstructed Level 1 dune surface.

of this distribution stand out. Firstly, they hug the shoreline and secondly, they are concentrated in three discrete places along that shoreline. Scattered remains are, however, found right along the most seaward beach ridge and foredunes as far west as 800M. Additional pockets also occur on the eastern ends of the beach ridges behind the dunes in locations, which at the time of occupation would have overlooked the old riverbank. This pattern is very typical of Lapita settlements generally (Kirch 1997:165–6) and suggests that the Sigatoka River flowed close to or even right up to the old river bank at the time of first human settlement more than 2500 years ago. If this were the case, all Lapita cultural remains recovered from the dunes would have been deposited within 50 metres of the shoreline or riverbank.

Scattered Lapita artefacts have been recovered from a wide area but most materials have come from concentrations deposited in three locations: on the eastern ends of two beach ridges behind the present dunes; on the eastern end of the seaward beach ridge; and on the foredunes between 500M and 700M. The material recovered from each of these areas differs significantly and suggests they were used in different ways and at different times.

Early Lapita occupation of the seaward beach ridge

The oldest archaeological evidence for occupation on the dunes consists of a small concentration of cultural remains recovered from the eastern end of the seaward beach ridge (Fig. 8.1). At the time of occupation this location would have stood at, and overlooked, the junction between the beach and the river bank. Cultural remains were recovered from consolidated beach sand, below and therefore pre-dating the formation of the Level 1 palaeosol. They came from a very restricted area measuring only 1.5m by 10m (Hudson 1994:24; Petchey 1994:28). Material recovered included 333 potsherds of which 156 had dentate stamped decoration; five chalcedony flakes; several scatters of fire-cracked rock and very fine fragments of charcoal. Additional dentate-stamped pottery collected by Crosby in 1993 also came from this location. The complex dentate-stamped decoration on this pottery (Fig. 5.3) and the range of vessel forms represented are similar to Early Eastern Lapita assemblages recovered from other Fijian sites and suggest a date of between 1000BC and 500BC (Petchey 1994; 1995), but may be as early as 1200BC (Kirch and Hunt 1988),

Late Lapita occupation on the foredunes

The largest concentration of Lapita cultural remains is dominated by pottery of the Late Eastern Lapita

plainware style and comes from the foredune which once stood in the area between 500M and 700M. From 550M where the Birks began their excavations to the end of Burley's excavation at around 760M a semi-continuous deposit of pottery has been identified. Although in 1966 the Birks found a hiatus in the middle of their excavation this gap has since been filled by the large blowout mapped in 1992 between 640M and 690M. Small numbers of sherds of similar pottery have also been found along the most seaward beach ridge to the east and over the low-lying sandspit in the area of Burial Ground 1. But these are scatters not concentrations.

The Birks recovered 70 reconstructable pots of which many have rim-notching, 31 bowls, 11 restricted orifice vessels which are probably water jars, 2 covers, 14 pot rests, and 13 worked sherd discs (Birks 1973; see Fig. 1.2 this volume). To this total Burley's excavations added another 12 pots, 7 bowls, 1 water jar, 2 flat-bottomed vessels unlike any described by the Birks, 2 potstands and fragments of at least 35 more vessels (Burley and Shortland 1999:43). Further collections from this area await analysis at the Fiji Museum. Aside from pottery, artefacts were scarce. The Birks recovered 3 complete adzes and one roughout plus a few grinders and flakes. Burley's excavation added another adze. Unworked pieces of stone, pumice and coral were recovered in small numbers.

No faunal remains or human bone were recovered from either excavation. Structural evidence identified by the Birks was limited to a few shallow stakeholes and "three places where fires had burned" (Birks 1973:14). Two of these contained rocks, sherds and charcoal and the third was a simple scoop of discoloured sand and fine charcoal. All were located at the eastern end of the excavation and rested on or in the basal sands below Level 1. One further hearth containing rocks was found in Burley's more westerly excavations (Burley and Shortland 1999:40).

As described above the radiocarbon date obtained in 1966 and the two obtained in 1998 on charcoal from this area are virtually identical and indicate a short period of occupation around 550–500 BC (Burley and Shortland 1999:44). The Birks describe Level 1 as having an average effective depth of 28cm with cultural material right down to the compact sand below. All materials recovered by Burley were in Level 1 and were distributed through a depth of 20cm. As both the Birks (1973:9,12) and Burley and Shortland (1999:35) point out, Level 1 in this area was not a well consolidated soil but rather soft sand only slightly darker and finer than the overlying sands. An extensive but fairly brief occupation on the foredune at a time when it was not well stabilised by vegetation is therefore likely.

Rapid burial of the area in drift sand followed quickly after abandonment and resulted in the excellent preservation of semi-complete pots combined with the destruction of virtually all charcoal and bone.

Late Lapita Plainware occupation on the beach ridges

Concentrations of Late Lapita Plainware pottery, unlike that recovered from the foredunes, has been identified at the eastern ends of Beach Ridges 2 and 3, and on the most seaward beach ridge. A total of 384 sherds were excavated from the eastern end of Beach Ridge 2 and 706 sherds were recovered from excavations and surface collections at the eastern end of Beach Ridge 3. As described in Appendix D, these assemblages were dominated by Late Lapita Plainware vessel forms commonly finished by wiping and scraping of the exterior surfaces. The vessel forms are similar to the Late Eastern Lapita forms recovered from the foredune except that their rims are generally less expanded, more rounded and lack the rim-notching so typical of the Birks Level 1 assemblage. In addition the beach ridge assemblages have occasional heavy rib relief and some early paddle impressed finishes such as irregular hatching and wavy relief which Crosby (1988:215) has described as a possible indication of a transitional potting technology between the Lapita plainwares and paddle impressed styles. Late Lapita occupation on the eastern ends of Beach Ridges 2 and 3 may therefore have spanned the period from 2350 BP to 1850 BP (400 BC – AD 100). The presence of postholes and other features in the testpit put down in Beach Ridge 2 further suggests actual habitation in this area rather than passing expedient use.

The greatest concentration of this very late Lapita pottery comes from the eastern ends of Beach Ridges 2 and 3 but it also occurs in other places. Burley (1997) recovered small numbers of wiped sherds from further west along Beach Ridges 2 and 3, and Hudson (1994) recovered a small assemblage of distinctive wavy sherds from within but near the top of the Level 1 palaeosol, approximately 10–20m west of where she recovered the Early Eastern Lapita sherds (Fig. 5.3). Crosby has provisionally dated these unusual wavy sherds to around 200 BC (Petchey 1994). Again, these wavy sherds are suggestive of a brief transitional potting style between Lapita and paddle impressed wares.

Summary

Close examination of the full range of archaeological evidence for Lapita occupation at the dunes does not indicate a single brief occupation directly associated with the Level 1 palaeosol. The earliest cultural materials come from a concentrated lens on the eastern end of the seaward beach ridge at the junction between the river and the sea. They were deposited beneath the Level 1 palaeosol and therefore pre-date its formation. From there people moved briefly onto the foredune at the south-eastern corner of the dunes proper. This more extensive occupation was directly associated with the Level 1 palaeosol. It seems, however, that people quickly moved away from this unstable environment, back onto the crests of the beach ridges along the riverbank. In this area evidence for Lapita occupation continues for another 500 years. This move may have been prompted by increasing dune instability, which eventually rendered the foredune environment too inhospitable for occupation. Aside from a brief foray onto the dunes at 200 BC, reoccupation of the dunes proper did not occur until after they consolidated following the formation of the Level 2 palaeosol and the growth of extensive tree cover. So-called Level 1 occupation of the dunes therefore encompasses occupation in at least three discrete locations, only one of which is directly associated with the Level 1 palaeosol, and it spans a time period of up to 1000 years.

Level 2 occupation

By far the most extensive archaeological evidence for human occupation of the dunes comes from the Level 2 palaeosol (Fig. 8.2). Semi-continuous deposits of cultural debris have been found in association with the Level 2 palaeosol from 100M to 800M and isolated Level 2 features have been found as far west as 1200M. Between 100M and 500M Level 2 materials are not found above 5m in elevation but west of 500M Level 2 pottery has been identified at elevations up to 25m. All the large concentrations of debris, however, occur below 6m in elevation and are located close to the shoreline. Scattered sherds of Level 2 pottery indicate human activity may also have occurred on the beach ridges behind the dunes, but no specific locus of occupation has yet been identified in this area (Appendix D; Burley 1997). In contrast to Lapita times when occupation was closely associated with the old riverbank, habitation during the Level 2 period shifted to the shoreline along the seaward beach ridge and foredunes.

Unlike the Lapita occupations, the Level 2 cultural material appears to be relatively homogenous and the three available radiocarbon dates suggest a compressed occupation within the period AD200–400. Caution should be exercised, however, in light of the fact that pottery from this period is far less

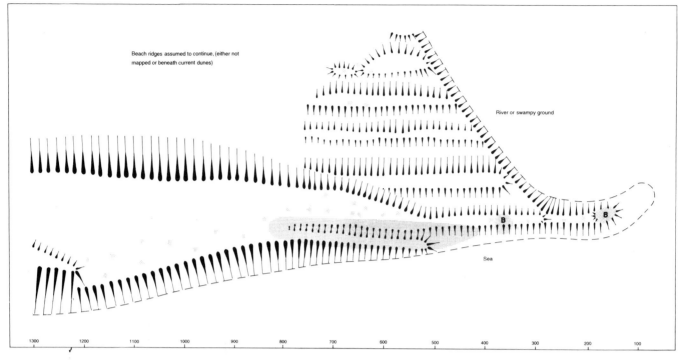

*Fig. 8.2 Collated evidence for Level 2 occupation of the eastern end of the Sigatoka dunes mapped onto the reconstructed Level 2 dune surface. **B** marks the locations of burial areas.*

well studied than the various Lapita wares and the Level 2 materials may therefore prove to be more chronologically diverse than realised. Moreover, as further Level 2 materials are recovered they are beginning to suggest patterns of movement along the dunes, or use of different parts of the dunes for quite different purposes.

400M – 800M

The densest deposits of Level 2 pottery have been found between 400M and 800M, and at 2–5m in elevation. Thick carpets of pottery were mapped in this area during the 1992 survey and it is here that the Birks carried out their excavations. Both excavations and survey found the pottery was concentrated in clusters. The Birks recovered pottery from 4 main clusters (Birks 1973:22) and the survey identified a great many more. Unlike the Birks' Level 1 pottery, which was often recovered as semi-complete vessels, their Level 2 potsherds were scattered and broken. This was also the case for the Level 2 surface pottery identified during the 1992 survey.

The Birks recovered parts of 58 cooking pots (Birks 1973:41–5). These were generally larger and heavier than their Level 1 equivalents (Fig. 1.2). All had some decoration. Most were decorated on the shoulder and/or body with a variety of paddle-impressed designs and some had additional finger-pinching or asymmetrically incised detail around

the shoulder and neck. Lip notching was also found on 29 of the 37 vessels with remaining rims. Gone were the bowls, jars and potstands of earlier Lapita times, although one completely new vessel form appeared. This is a large flat-bottomed dish or tray (Plate 9). The Birks recovered 17 trays of which 12 had leaf impressions on the underside and 5 had mat impressions. These impressions have been analysed by Lambert (1971). During the 1992 survey occasional tray sherds were found across much of the eastern dunes but the vast majority were confined to the area of concentrated deposits. The presence of these trays along with pots decorated with distinctive rim notching and asymmetric incision represents a highly distinctive and short lived aberration within an otherwise relatively undistinguished sequence of paddle impressed pottery. It can therefore be used to date it to a narrow envelope of one or two hundred years around AD 200 (Best 1989:59). The recovery of sherds with these features along the full length of the Level 2 deposits suggests they represent contemporary occupations.

Aside from pottery, the Birks recovered very little. A few pieces of worked stone were found on the surface, and broken pieces of rock, pumice and coral, and scatters of charcoal were found in those areas where pottery was most common. A few fragments of fish bone and shell were recovered. No evidence at all for structures was identified (Birks 1973:16). Enough charcoal was collected to obtain a single radiocarbon date of 1720±80 BP or AD 230 (Birks 1973:57).

The 1992 survey identified a greater range of materials within this area. The composition of Level 2 features varied a great deal. Some were composed entirely of pottery, some were almost exclusively broken rock and others were mixed deposits of rock, coral and pottery in varying proportions. Usually, each feature was a discrete entity and clearly separate from its neighbours. One unique feature, a scoop containing burnt clay, ash and small fire-cracked rocks may have been a small kiln (see Appendix B, Fig. B.3). When the 1992 survey results are considered in conjunction with results from the Birks excavations this large area of Level 2 occupation can be seen to be a highly structured deposit containing a wide range of materials and features with distinct spatial patterning. In particular, the exceptionally dense concentration of pottery and other materials between 600M and 700M suggests an area of concentrated settlement.

Less concentrated cultural debris associated with the Level 2 palaeosol can also be found all around the main settlement area and scattered pottery and occasional features continue north up onto the high dunes to an elevation of 25m and are found west to at least 1200M. This indicates a more generalised dispersal of other activities. However, as is discussed below, this generalised dispersal of debris does not extend to the east beyond 400M where the two Level 2 burial grounds are situated.

250M – 400M, Burial Ground 2

Hudson's 1993 excavations recovered very little Level 2 cultural debris confirming the pattern established during the 1992 survey that only small scatters of pottery were deposited in the area between 250M and 400M. However, at the eastern end of the seaward beach ridge, around 280M, Hudson (1994:25) found scattered Level 2 sherds, sometimes associated with rock and charcoal, in the top of a palaeosol she assumed to be Level 1. The Level 2 sherds were at the same depth but in different locations to the very late Lapita/early paddle impressed, wavy sherds. This depositional association was confusing because it did not fit the Birks' model. It makes sense, however, once this area is identified as the crest of a beach ridge where there was no depositional sequence of palaeosols separated by sterile sand. Levels 1 and 2 are here a single soil.

Within this area of relatively concentrated cultural debris is one of the two cemeteries that have been attributed to the Level 2 occupation. Burial Ground 2, located between 300M and 350M contained 13 identified skeletons. Many more are known to have been present but were eroded away before description or recovery could take place. Excavated skeletons rested on or in the Level 2 palaeosol and most were buried with their heads to the west and feet to the east. No associated artefacts, rock or coral were found but few of these burials were intact at the time they were identified or excavated (see Chapter 6 and Appendix C for details). It appears to represent the selection of the slight rise afforded by the crest of the beach ridge for a small cemetery situated approximately 100m east of the main area of settlement.

100M – 250M, Burial Ground 1

Further to the east is a larger cemetery: Burial Ground 1 (Plates 10–12). It is also located on what was at the time a small rise, which overlooked the junction of sea and river (Best 1989:20–22). Between 1988 and 1996 a total of at least 61 individuals have been removed from this cemetery. Of these 55 were excavated by Best in 1987–8 and 6 further skeletons have appeared over subsequent years. As described above these skeletons were buried in a highly structured manner. Almost all were orientated with their heads to the west and feet to the east and many were placed in groups then covered with cairns of large coral boulders (Best 1989). Ed Visser's (1994) detailed analyses of these skeletons indicate a centralised distribution of high status individuals – both men and women – surrounded by groups of lower status individuals including some burials of women and children. Two radiocarbon dates were obtained for Burial Ground 1. A date of 1680±57 BP (AD 266–494) was obtained on material from a burnt stump, and a date of 1870±80 BP (38 BC–AD 282) was obtained on human bone from Burial F.C.1 (Best 1989:48–9).

Relatively few sherds or other materials have been recovered from the area between Burial Ground 1 and Burial Ground 2 to the west. Furthermore, only 7 sherds representing 5 paddle-impressed cooking pots were recovered by Best (1989:33–5) from within Burial Ground 1, although Burley (1997:44) also recovered a single sherd from an unusual paddle-impressed bowl. However, during the 1992 survey three pottery concentrations which included characteristic Level 2 type sherds were mapped just outside the burial ground. The largest and densest concentration, Feature 2, which appeared to be composed almost exclusively of very fine walled, highly decorated paddle-impressed pots, was excavated (see Appendix B, Fig. B.2). The pottery recovered from this unique feature has yet to be analysed, although it was noted during excavation that it appeared to lack the distinctive trays and incised pots found associated with the Level 2 occupation on the dunes to the west.

Summary

Only the Level 2 occupation still appears to be relatively homogenous and short-lived. This is curious since it also forms the most highly structured and geographically extensive deposit. Despite much variation in the composition of concentrations of cultural debris, the Level 2 pottery is all broadly contemporary with early Paddle Impressed Ware vessel forms and decorative styles, and reported radiocarbon dates span a range of less than 200 years, from 1870 BP to 1680 BP. Significantly, along the full length of the exposed palaeosol, the key appearance of many sherds with new decorative techniques, including asymmetric incision and finger pinching, can be used to very precisely date the pottery at around AD 200. It has also been used to suggest renewed contact between Fiji and the west, probably New Caledonia and Vanuatu (Best 1989:59–61). It is likely Best is correct then when he states that "the three events – the village occupation, the use of the cemetery, and the appearance of new ceramic traits, all occur at the same time, about the middle of the third century AD" (Best 1989:49).

Best, however, is inaccurate in his description of the occupation as a single village and cemetery. The evidence now suggests the presence of two clustered settlements to the west, separated from two burial grounds to the east. The separation between the area of settlement and the burial grounds is of special interest. It reinforces the ritual significance of the Level 2 burial practices indicated by the highly structured arrangements of burials within the cemeteries. The location of these cemeteries to the east of the settlement may increase the significance of the large and, as yet, unanalysed mound of pottery situated slightly further to the east and excavated during the 1992 survey (see Appendix B, Fig. B.2).

Later occupations

Areas of later, post-Level 2, occupation on the dunes have been identified in four spatially discrete locations (Fig. 8.3). Two are on the beach ridges behind the dunes and two are on the eastern dunes proper. In addition late occupation has been identified on the western dunes (Burley 1997). None of these occupations are well understood. However, a wide range of cultural materials, including

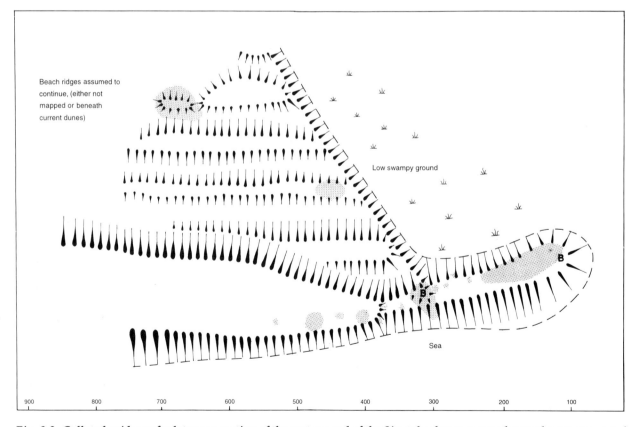

Fig. 8.3 Collated evidence for later occupation of the eastern end of the Sigatoka dunes mapped onto the reconstructed Level 3 dune surface. B marks the locations of burial areas.

pottery forms from as early as AD 1000 and materials from the early European contact period have been recovered. This suggests that occupation took place over an extended period of time and that people used the dunes in a number of different ways during this time.

Later occupation of the back beach ridges

Following the destabilisation of the Level 2 surface, sand began to accumulate quickly at the far eastern end of the dunes. High dunes developed up to and over the old riverbank. As a result the beach ridges behind were visually cut off from the sea and the Sigatoka River was pushed further east well away from the old riverbank. The area behind the dunes would therefore have been some distance away from both fresh and salt water, as is the case today.

Behind the dunes on Beach Ridge 3 Burley (1997:26) opened an excavation area measuring 3x3 metres. It was placed over a hearth that had been identified in earlier shovel tests. The hearth turned out to be a substantial feature measuring approximately 1m in diameter and densely filled with stones and charcoal. A radiocarbon date on charcoal from the hearth was 510 ± 60 BP, which calibrates to AD 1330–1430 (Burley 1997:31). Pottery recovered from the area was dominated by late *kuro* style cooking pots with paddle impressed or incised decoration. These styles are indicative of late period occupation. However, some Late Eastern Lapita and Level 2 pottery was also present, so multiple occupation remains a possibility. As Burley (1997:34) points out, the range and abundance of ceramics in this area combined with the large hearth "suggests a habitation as opposed to expedient use occupation". Unlike earlier occupation on the beach ridges, this habitation was not directly associated with the river or shoreline and was placed more than 100m to the west of the old riverbank.

Moving south toward the sea, a second area of late occupation was identified on the eastern end of Beach Ridge 1. During the 1992 survey an assemblage of 137 sherds was surface-collected from a deep depression which had been cut into the old riverbank and ridge by sand mining trucks. The high incidence of *kuro* style cooking pots, oil lamps and *dari* bowls, all of which are typical of late period pottery assemblages, combined with a low incidence of paddle impressed rib and spot relief decoration indicate an occupation between AD 1000 – AD 1500 (see Appendix D for details).

Later occupation on the dunes proper

By far the most extensive evidence for later human occupation occurs at the eastern end of the dunes where a large amount of cultural material has been found eroding from the exposed edge of the Level 3 palaeosol. It is distributed over a distance of 170m between 100M and 270M. The density of material declines, however, toward the western end of this area, with the bulk of the cultural materials spread over a distance of 100m. The cultural remains were concentrated in a narrow band only 20–30m wide and 5–10m in elevation. Although this area overlooks the sea it is well back from the shoreline compared to the locations favoured for earlier occupations.

During the 1992 survey four large, complex *lovo* features and numerous pottery concentrations were mapped in this area. One large pottery concentration was excavated. The collected material has not yet been analysed but the sherds appeared to come from only one or two large vessels and were directly associated with the Level 3 palaeosol (see Appendix B, Feature 7). The universally plain nature of the assemblage suggests a date of around AD 1000. The *lovo* features consisted of very dense concentrations of rock and pottery indicative of large earth ovens. One feature was excavated. In addition, small cores of chert, an area of baked clay and 6 concentrations of charcoal interpreted as burnt post bases were identified in this area suggesting a structured work area associated with a small building or settlement (see Appendix B, Feature 6). This is the first structural evidence yet recovered from the dunes surface. The largest of the unexcavated features, located at 160M, was situated at the summit of a high ridge or promontory which jutted out in a south-easterly direction overlooking and perhaps also commanding the meeting point between sea and river.

Additional excavations were carried out in this area in 1995 by the Fiji Museum. Large amounts of pottery were recovered along with several historic period items that included a glass bottle, a clay pipe fragment and a possible gun flint (Burke 1995a). Details of these excavations and the pottery analyses will be included in a report currently in preparation.

On the eastern and western margins of this Level 3 settlement are two areas of burials. At very low elevations around 100M, the remains of at least 3 individuals have been recovered (see Chapter 6 and Appendix C for details). This would have been at the eastern extent of the dunes at this time. The burials were placed above the Level 2 palaeosol and therefore post-date it, but were not directly associated with the Level 3 palaeosol. At the western edge of the Level 3 settlement, between 280M and 380M, is the proposed Burial Ground 3. At least 18 individuals have been recovered in this area which at the time formed the crest of another southeasterly facing ridge or promontory. Burials associated with this ridge are distributed in three clusters placed at different elevations. Around 5m there is a group of 7 or 8 individuals, all of which post-date Level 2. Around 10m is a group of 4 burials which post-date Level 2. One was directly associated with the Level 3 palaeosol. At and above 12m are another 6 burials of which one was directly associated with the Level 3 palaeosol. Given their high elevation, all must post-date Level 2 and some may also post-date Level 3.

Additional burials, which are assumed to be late, have been recovered from numerous parts of the dunes (see Chapter 6). Few of these burials were directly associated with a palaeosol and none were found in association with other cultural remains. They are therefore assumed to be isolated events, although some may be contemporary with late period occupation on the dunes and back beach ridges.

Late period remains have also been recovered from the area of foredune excavated by the Birks between 380M and 580M. They recovered the remains of only 22 pottery vessels, including 18 *kuro* cooking pots and one bowl, from an excavation extending for more than 200m in length (Birks 1973:17, 45). They also recovered one worked stone artefact and some fragments of weathered volcanic rock and, more recently, Antoine de Biran and Geoff Hope have recovered the remains of a carbonised post which they believe to be associated with Level 3 in this area (Antoine de Biran, personal communication). The pottery was deposited in a series of six discrete clusters, each of which contained the remains of semi-complete vessels (Birks 1973:22). The limited range of evidence found in the Birks excavations compared to the relatively full range of settlement evidence identified further east suggests this seaward foredune saw only brief, expedient use and lay on the margins of the main settlement area.

Finally, late occupation has been established for the western dunes (Burley 1997). In a dune valley located approximately 1km west of the area mapped in 1992 Burley excavated two superimposed burials. In close proximity to the burials were other exposed features, which included rock and pottery. One of these features, a semi-intact hearth, was excavated. It was located fairly high on the dunes, at 6.1m above the high tide level, and consisted of a shallow scoop 10–15cm deep and at least 75cm in diameter filled with broken rock, charcoal and pottery. Sherds from a large *kuro* style cooking pot and another sherd with shell impressed decoration were recovered. Both the style of this pottery and the location of the hearth high on the dunes suggested the occupation was late. Charcoal collected from the hearth was radiocarbon dated to 230 ± 40 BP (Burley 1997:39). A comparable radiocarbon date of AD 1300–1600 has been collected by Antoine de Biran from an eroding section of paleosol on the western dunes (Antoine de Brian, personal communication; Dickenson et al. 1998:7)

Summary

Later occupation of the dunes area was substantial, complex, and extended over a considerable time period. It began by around AD 1000 and final abandonment of the dunes for human settlement did not occur until the historic period. Human use of the dunes for subsistence activities continues today. Occupation occurred in at least four locations at the eastern end of the dunes area and at least two on the western dunes. They included habitation areas on both the back beach ridges and the dunes proper. The largest settlement is directly associated with the Level 3 palaeosol and centred on the now eroded promontory located at the southeastern point of the dunes. Here a number of large earth ovens and other features have been found, including a possible structure. They are surrounded by dense deposits of pottery and are flanked to the southeast and west by two areas of burials. The range of activities represented by these later cultural deposits is comparable to those identified for the Level 2 occupation. However, the locations chosen for occupation changed. They are much further away from the water and are now situated relatively high on the dunes.

Summary of human occupation

A vast amount of evidence for human occupation has been recovered from the Sigatoka Sand Dunes. The results of the 1992 survey, in combination with information accumulated over the last four decades of archaeological investigation at the dunes, demonstrate that this evidence is much more varied, covers a much greater time span and has greater integrity than had previously been thought. Our understanding of the variety and patterning of cultural materials on the dunes has increased considerably since the Birks' excavations, but still the nature of human occupation remains strangely enigmatic.

Detailed examination of the archaeological evidence does not support a model of three short occupation phases separated by long periods of abandonment. Only one possible gap in the temporal sequence of occupation at the eastern end of the dunes is identified: AD 400–1000. However, this coincides with a relatively poorly understood period of the Fijian ceramic sequence during which pots become increasingly plain. Ceramics from this period may easily be misidentified to later periods. Given how much material already removed from the dunes is sitting in the Fiji Museum awaiting analysis, and how little attention has been paid to Level 2 and the later occupations, it is unlikely this gap will last for long.

Close analysis of the horizontal as well as the vertical stratigraphy of human occupation reveals a striking picture of shifting settlement location. During Lapita times there was a long and continuous tradition of use of a wide area of the dunes. The most frequently occupied location was the eastern end of the most seaward beach ridge which, flanked by both sea and river, has yielded pottery covering the full range of Lapita occupation spanning a thousand years. This location was not used intensively, however. Intensive use of the dunes area did not occur until relatively late when, around 500 BC, a short-lived but extensive foray onto the seaward margins of the dunes proper took place before settlement moved inland to take advantage of the series of beach ridges along the riverbank.

Subsequent settlement on the Level 2 palaeosol appears to have been extensive but brief. It was concentrated along the foreshore at the southeastern corner of the expanding dunes. Less intensive occupation spread onto the higher dunes and the beach ridges to the north. The seaward beach ridge and an associated foredune formed the main locus of a settlement that included two cemeteries: one at the eastern end of the ridge and one on a sandy knoll situated below it to the east. At this time the major area of settlement was focused on the sea, and not the riverbank. During later post-Level 2 periods settlement moved higher up the dunes and back onto the beach ridges behind. All occupied locations were now some distance from both the sea and the Sigatoka River.

The nature of human use of the eastern dunes and beach ridges, therefore, varied through time and space. Archaeological attention has tended to focus on the Lapita occupations, yet they indicate a much more restricted range of activities than the later occupations. Archaeological evidence for Lapita occupation consists almost entirely of pottery. While this may be partly due to taphonomic factors, the fact that a broader array of evidence survives for the later occupations suggests that use of the dunes during the Lapita period was indeed relatively restricted. The subsequent occupations on the dunes and on the ridges behind have yielded evidence of burials, fires, ovens, structures and a greater variety of lithic and faunal remains, all of which suggest a broad spectrum of activities associated with settlement. Just why, at different times, this settlement was focused on the dunes or the back beach ridges is not yet understood. However, the mere process of mapping the many and varied deposits of archaeological materials at least provides a basis for such questions to be addressed.

Chapter 9
Working with complexity

Introduction

Our aim in this volume has been to present the Sigatoka Sand Dunes in all their complexity, to highlight their variety and diversity and to allow enigmas and gaps in our knowledge to inform the way we understand the dunes. For many readers we may have presented too much complexity. But details matter. The full body of available evidence must be thoroughly understood if our models of both the dunes and Fiji's prehistory are to move on. In the 1970's the Sigatoka Dunes played a foundational role in the creation of the Fijian culture history sequence. Three decades on, the volume and variety of evidence recovered from this site have overtaken the four-phase model it helped bring together. But Sigatoka remains vital to Fijian prehistory because the conceptual demands imposed on us by the expanding body of evidence challenge us to build new models, which are equal to its complexities.

The power of Sigatoka and the problem with its interpretation lie in the way a reductive geological structure has been imposed onto the archaeology. Once enshrined in the Birks' stratigraphy diagram the three geological palaeosols became in some sense iconic of the culture history approach in Fiji. In this book we do not dispute that the palaeosols exist; nor do we dispute that they were often the focus for human settlement. But we caution that the geological separation between these palaeosols is for archaeologists a red herring. It implies there is discontinuity in a sequence of human occupation that is actually close to continuous. No such separation exists behind the dunes where there is a single conflated soil representing all periods of occupation. Nor does it exist *on* the dunes where the three paleosols do not form 'horizons' or even 'levels' as the Birks originally thought. They are not brief moments of extensive occupation in a sequence dominated by long periods of abandonment. Nor do they run horizontally under the dunes. Instead they developed during and after the main build up of dune sands had occurred and therefore form broken, undulating and highly varied surfaces. Nevertheless these surfaces were sought out and exploited by the people who came and occupied them. Understanding the variation within them will help us to understand the purpose and nature of the many occupations on the site.

Accordingly, our models of Fijian prehistory must be rewritten to take much greater account of continuity – to theorise continuity – and to allow for, indeed to seek out, anthropological complexity and detail in the archaeological record. It is one thing to develop archaeological models of change; it is another to propose theories of society and culture that can incorporate events and moments of both change and stasis. Perhaps it is too much to claim that simply mapping the archaeology on the Sigatoka dunes and drawing together decades of research, including some of our own, can provide a basis for the construction of new models. But we do believe that such models must be written from the ground up – securely based in archaeological data – and we hope that our reanalysis at least widens the view so that in future the horizontal complexity of sites such as Sigatoka will not be sacrificed and squeezed into a vertical sequence.

With this in mind we now consider the implications for the prehistory of Fiji and the wider region. We commence with a few specific points and work towards a more generalised model of society and change which is presented in the concluding chapter. Our objective is not the construction of a new sequence, but an attempt to ask detailed questions about the changing constitution of Fijian society and culture.

On the origins of the dunes and first colonisation of Fiji

The commonly held assumption that the bulk of the dunes formed following human occupation has given rise to the further assumption that they formed as a result of human induced degradation of the surrounding environment which in turn led to increased sediment discharge from the Sigatoka River (Birks 1973; Burley 1997:4; Dickinson et al. 1998:20–2). Encapsulated in these assumptions is a theory of colonisation and progressive adaptation. In the face of demographic growth there was a move to the interior, increased deforestation and ultimately conflict. All this is attested to by a spread of fortifications, agricultural terraces and irrigated pond-fields up the full length of the Sigatoka Valley behind the dunes. It is a simple thing, but it belies a whole trajectory of thought exemplified in Pat Kirch's *The Evolution of the Polynesian Chiefdoms* (1984): an initial maritime focus to Fijian settlement, a logarithmic course of population growth, a gradual evolutionary shift towards an increasingly agricultural economy, and an accompanying escalation of socio-political complexity. This is not to say that such a scenario is incorrect. But the assumption underlying all of this at Sigatoka is based on the erroneous calculation by Birks (1973:61) and then Parry (1987:13–14) that the rate of deposition of sands increased exponentially with human occupation.

A rapid increase in the volume of sand deposited has only been demonstrated for a small area at the extreme eastern end of the dunes. Elsewhere, the great bulk of the dunes probably formed early, certainly before the AD 200 date of occupation for Level 2 and, we argue, prior also to the first human occupation of Level 1. This occurred by at least 700 BC although the Early Eastern Lapita pottery excavated by Hudson in 1993 indicates Level 1 may have been occupied as early as 1200 BC (Petchey 1995:104; Dickinson et al. 1998:6; Kirch and Hunt 1988). Such a date matches the earliest occupation of the nearby Yanuca rock shelter at 1150 BC (Hunt 1980) and places the first occupation of the dunes only a few centuries after the earliest known date of occupation for all of Fiji at circa 1450 BC (Davidson et al. 1990). Even if the early Lapita people moved into the interior of Viti Levu and started rapidly chopping down trees as soon as they arrived, there is simply not sufficient time available to account for the formation of a massive dune system at Sigatoka prior to 1200 BC, or even 700 BC. A much earlier movement of pre-Lapita people into the interior would be necessary. It is implausible that such a people could have caused environmental damage on such a scale without leaving some definitive archaeological trace, yet no material culture evidence of a pre-Lapita occupation has been found anywhere in Fiji, or even in Remote Oceania. While prehistorians will doubtless continue to speculate about the possibilities of much earlier human colonisation of Fiji, it seems that the chances of finding dates of the same Pleistocene order as those now known for the Bismarck Archipelago, the Solomon Islands and other parts of Near Oceania are remote (Allen et al. 1989; Gosden 1993; Gosden and Robertson 1991; Pavlides and Gosden 1994; Spriggs 1997).

We believe the answers lie in understanding the geological processes of dune formation in similar exposed coastal situations in Fiji and the effects of Holocene sea level changes prior to human occupation (Nunn 1990, 1994, 1997; Shepherd 1988, 1990). Antoine de Biran has already begun a dissertation project on this topic. His aim is to survey the underlying structure of the entire Sigatoka delta region. The results of this enterprise will help identify the true origins of sand deposition at the dunes. In the meantime, archaeologists will have to look elsewhere than Sigatoka for evidence of demographically induced adaptation and settlement pattern change.

On the nature of the first settlers

There is a longstanding debate over the nature of the economy of the Lapita colonisers. Were they maritime "strandloopers" colonising ahead of agriculturalists (Groube 1971:312), were they agriculturalists, utilising tropical root and tree crops (Green 1979:37), or were they one of many other possible variants in-between (Clark and Terrell 1978)? In this debate much attention has focused on the location of Lapita sites. Were settlement locations selected with regard to marine, terrestrial or a mixed mosaic of resources, and is the size and complexity of early settlements indicative of a permanent, horticultural resource base? Within Melanesia the debate has been rendered murky by the presence of earlier colonisers, and the complex interaction between them and the "Lapita peoples" is only beginning to be understood (Kirch 1997; Smith 1995; Spriggs 1997; Gosden 1992, 1993; Gosden and Specht 1991). Within Fiji and Polynesia, however, there has always been the promise of a clearer picture and indeed models from Polynesia have provided much of the basic information about the Lapita economy (Poulsen 1967; Groube 1971; Kirch 1988).

But no clear understanding of the nature of early settlement has as yet emerged. Best has reported that the first occupations on the island of Lakeba in the Lau Group (Fig. 1.1), which took place at around 1000 BC, were seasonal camps, with no evidence of domesticates in the earliest levels. He argues they represent the arrival of a highly mobile group of people who subsisted on wild birds and turtles and maintained long distance trade and exchange for 100–200 years prior to the establishment of permanent settlements (Best 1984:641). Conversely, Hughes et al. (1979) have employed evidence of early deforestation and significant human modification of the Lakeba landscape to argue for the early introduction of swidden agriculture. At Yanuca, Hunt has argued that the presence of domestic animals of Lapita association and the presence of anthropophilic land snails are strongly suggestive of early agriculture, particularly since they are found in combination with a wide range of inshore fishing strategies, unspecialised shell fishing, and turtle hunting (Hunt 1980:195). At Naigani, a small island in the Lomaiviti group, the dominance of fish and turtle bones suggests mainly lagoon exploitation (Kay 1984:143–144). In general, therefore, the Fijian evidence is contradictory and inconclusive, and one suspects the nature of early settlement varied considerably from one island to another.

Evidence from Lapita occupation at Sigatoka has not contributed greatly to this debate. The Birks decided that none of the occupations at the dunes were likely to have been villages or permanent settlements. In their view, the large trays from Level 2 (Plate 9) were most suitable for dismembering turtles or evaporating brine, suggesting the dunes were used simply for turtle fishing or the manufacture of salt (Birks 1973:61–64). Lapita occupation on the dunes has therefore been considered specialised and atypical and therefore of only limited value for understanding the general nature of first settlement in Fiji. Nevertheless, the presence of specialist sites would itself argue for a degree of complexity in the wider settlement pattern of the region, especially if they pointed to the existence of a centralised centre for the production and distribution of salt, an important exchange resource throughout the prehistory of many world regions. Moreover, the manufacture of salt on the kind of scale suggested by the quantity of pottery present at the dunes would raise questions about the scale of food production for which the salt was presumably intended.

The Birks specific objections to the possibility of more permanent settlement on the dunes relate to the absence of a fringing reef and a nearby freshwater supply, the absence of built structures, and the restricted range of vessel forms found at Sigatoka. Each of these arguments can now be rejected. We have argued that at the time of the Level 1 occupations the Sigatoka River flowed around or past the low dune and sandy flat on which occupation took place, possibly creating a fresh water lagoon

immediately to the north. Indeed the earliest occupation appears to have been right at the junction of the river and the sea, a location which is entirely typical of Lapita settlements generally (Kirch 1997). Subsequent occupations spread both up the river and along the foreshore. From these locations they had maximal access during all periods to fresh water, canoe entry, and open sea resources. The lack of built structures and ceramic variability, as we discuss below, is common to all late Lapita occupations in Fiji and is in no way unique to Sigatoka. We argue therefore that there is no strong basis for claiming that Lapita occupation on the dunes did not constitute permanent settlement. Unfortunately more detailed information about the precise nature of the economy on the dunes is hampered by the poor survival of faunal remains on the site. Nevertheless, the implication should be that the site was selected for the purpose of settlement, that its successfulness as a settlement grew over time, and that it can make a significant contribution to our understanding of first settlement in the region.

On the enigmatic nature of occupation at the dunes

If you stand on the Sigatoka dunes in a howling gale with sand driving into your eyes and ears, no vegetation or fresh water in sight, it is simply impossible to imagine why anyone would chose to live there. And yet we know that people did so, again and again. Even today they continue to use the dunes to collect special resources including driftwood, seafoods and certain plants. Given the inhospitable feel of the dunes today it is hardly surprising that archaeologists have assumed they were only used for specialist activities such as collecting turtles or making salt and not for general habitation. In 1973 this view seemed justified by the lack of general occupational evidence in the Birks excavations. As a result, the Sigatoka occupations were seen to be fantastically useful for constructing the Fijian ceramic sequence but, because of their atypical nature, of little value in reconstructing the nature of settlement pertaining to each phase.

Such a view is hard to maintain in the light of accumulating evidence for cemeteries, structures, ovens, hearths and utility areas, and much more extensive settlement than the Birks recovered. The astonishing recovery of an internally structured cemetery on the dunes caused Best to first reconsider the nature of the Level 2 occupation and to suggest a permanently occupied village (Best 1989:50). In addition, evidence that the eastern dunes once formed a remarkably stable living surface was found when Best recovered burnt stumps of *Casuarina littoralis* in Level 2 (Best 1989:47). These stumps indicate that the vegetation around the cemetery was probably very similar to that now existing over the western half of the dunes where habitation seems eminently more sane. Furthermore, if as our 1992 map suggests, the dunes had reached close to their present size and volume by the time of the earliest Lapita occupation, then very little of the dunes surface has changed since that initial occupation. Only the extreme eastern end has changed radically (Fig. 7.1). The dunes as a whole have therefore been much less volatile than previously thought and much more hospitable to settlement than previously imagined.

Occupations on the dunes were not, then, atypical camps. They were probably close to the norm for settlements of their respective periods. This is an important revelation given the paucity of our knowledge about even the basic dimensions, let alone the layout, of early sites in Fiji. Typically, archaeological records for sites older than a thousand years consist of a locational dot on a site distribution map coupled with an estimate of site area based on the spread of pottery brought to the surface by the actions of land crabs and Fijian gardeners. Excavations have typically been deep and narrow. There was little opportunity to investigate a wide areal expanse at Yanuca (Hunt 1980), Navatu (Gifford 1951; Shaw 1967; Clark n.d.), Natunuku (Davidson et al. 1990; Anderson et al. 1996) or any but a few of the early sites on Lakeba (Best 1984). Only a few excavations have therefore yielded information about the nature or layout of settlement at early sites. The exceptions are Best's 74 square metre excavations of Site 196, a large coastal Lapita settlement on Lakeba (Best 1984:89–105) and his excavation of an 83.5 square metre portion of a similar site located on Naigani Island in the Lomaiviti group (Best 1981; Kay 1984). More recently, Geoff Clark returned to a site originally identified by Crosby (1988) on tiny Ugaga Island within the Beqa lagoon, where he excavated 56 square metres in an area bearing Lapita and paddle impressed ceramics (Clark 1997).

So far Best's excavation at Site 196 is the only one to provide a representative sample across the width and breadth of a site. Moreover, this is the only early Fijian site for which any attempt has been made to reconstruct the internal settlement pattern. By mapping the distribution of surface collected pottery Best was able to conjecture about the orientation and relative centralisation or dispersal of settlement during three broad periods represented by early Lapita, late Lapita, and paddle impressed and early incised wares. For the early Lapita period he identified an early, clustered form of settlement with a formally demarcated perimeter and a well defined centre marked by a cluster of relatively high status pottery. This

gradually changed during the following two periods to a dispersed pattern of relatively short lived, scattered occupation along the coast. Houses were now "strung out through an area rather than pulled together within the confines of a settlement" (Best 1984:603). Interestingly, for this later, dispersed form of settlement Best found that the houses tended to be oriented parallel to the coast, as is the norm in Fiji today. Best (personal communication) counsels caution with regard to these findings. However, Crosby (1988:225) has noted from surface pottery collections that the first similarly oriented structural features on Beqa appear during the same broad period, almost certainly before AD 1000.

The data is not yet available from Fiji to make village reconstructions like those for Lapita communities on the Mussau Islands, the Reef Islands and Niuatoputapu (Kirch 1997:168–183). For these sites Kirch has been able to reconstruct settlement sizes, individual houses and other structures, activity areas, clusters of high status objects, and internal divisions within settlements based on geographical and material culture features. The potential exists to accomplish similar reconstructions in Fiji, particularly at sites such as Sigatoka where nature has exposed so much of the site to our view. Unfortunately, the bulk of the archaeological materials from the Sigatoka dunes have not been collected in a way which would allow us to make detailed reconstructions. However, at the level of conjectural trends, Sigatoka does provide evidence to support the changing pattern of settlement identified by Best at Site 196.

Level 1

The sketchy data we have at Sigatoka for the earliest Lapita occupations indicate only that they were small and located at the junction of the river and the sea. All of the early Lapita pottery – that excavated by Hudson and the few sherds collected by Crosby – have been found in this confined location (Fig. 8.1). At this time there is no sign of dispersal across the dunes or beach ridges. In size, these earliest settlements are most similar to the comparably dated small "hamlet" excavated by Green at Nenumbo in the Reef Islands. It covered little more than 1000 square metres and consisted of a central house surrounded by a "palimpset" of smaller structures (Sheppard and Green 1991; Kirch 1997:175–178).

There is much better data for later Lapita occupation at Sigatoka. It suggests the same pattern found by Best: fragmented settlement which left small clusters of ceramic debris, typically no more than 30m in diameter, distributed along the shoreline and riverbank. The Birks' excavations found these pottery clusters formed spatially discrete sites (Green 1979:56). Sufficient material has now been recovered to indicate a near continuous spread of these pottery clusters for at least 200m along the reconstructed foredune, although scattered sherds are found over a much wider area (Fig. 8.1). Radiocarbon dates obtained from two separate locations indicate that these concentrations represent contemporary occupations of short duration taking place around 550–500 BC (Burley and Shortland 1999:44). The recovery of a number of hearths and the general conclusion that most of the vessels represent primary deposition of pots broken in situ around these hearths (Burley and Shortland 1999:40) suggests a pattern of settlement strung out along the foredune without any evidence of centralisation or activity specialisation within. As yet, the east and west boundaries of Lapita settlement on the foredune are undefined, as is the internal boundary to the north. But given the presence of a steep dune slope to the north, this occupation probably consisted of a linear arrangement of semi-discrete settlements inhabited by a loosely linked alliance of households with little internal stratification. The further fragmentation of settlement is indicated by the abandonment of the foredune and subsequent spread of late Lapita settlement north to the beach ridges along the riverbank.

Level 2

With Level 2 a new style of pottery and a new form of settlement appear. The new paddle impressed pottery is remarkable for the extensiveness of its dispersal along the foreshore, covering a distance of at least 700m (Fig. 8.2). However, this is a highly structured deposit. Some areas comprised almost exclusively pieces of broken rock and coral, others contained only pottery, while yet others contained only human burials. Pottery was primarily concentrated in two clusters along a 400m length of dune. The larger of these clusters, identified in both the 1992 survey and the Birks 1966 excavations, occurred along a 100m length towards the western end (600M–700M). The second, smaller concentration was found between 520M–550M. A third concentration was found some distance to the east, around Burial Ground 1 (Figs. 4.2a–d). In addition, there was considerable variation in the kinds of sherds recovered from each of these three areas of very dense pottery. Unlike the Level 1 deposits, this pottery is less assuredly in primary deposition, and it is therefore possible that some of these deposits are refuse dumps. However, given the wider evidence for spatial demarcation of specific areas for different purposes, a well co-ordinated and highly structured

form of settlement is suggested. Both the ceramic and radiocarbon evidence indicate this settlement was very short-lived at around AD 200.

The most startling evidence for social stratification and complex social structuring within the Level 2 settlement is afforded by the two cemeteries, particularly Burial Ground 1. Best (1989:51–58) suggested that this cemetery, with its bound and internally structured arrangement of coral capped burial mounds (Plates 10 and 11), probably represented the burial ground either of a chiefly clan or of a village with internal social and political divisions. The subsequent discovery of a second burial ground points to the former option whereas osteological analysis of the skeletons from Burial Ground 1 points more to the latter. Edward Visser's (1994:170–186) analysis indicates that the cemetery contained the remains of a reasonably stable, well-fed community and probably included burial of mothers with their children as well as group and individual internment of both men and women. His analysis also identifies status and gender differences within the cemetery. Arguing largely from dietary evidence and burial position, Visser found that each sex might have been stratified into at least two social tiers with each group performing different specialist tasks. In short, high status men and women were buried at slightly higher elevations towards the centre of the cemetery while lower status individuals were buried towards the edges. Notably however, the degree of separation between these two groups does not seem sufficient to mark a clear dualistic structure within society. Lower status women appear to have worked harder than other females, but even high status women showed evidence of non-dietary tooth wear, a possible indication of the working of fibre between the teeth in tasks such as mat making.

Although no evidence of structures has yet been recovered from the Level 2 deposits at Sigatoka, it is clear from Best's burial ground excavations, that there was some degree of unity to this settlement and that models of centrality and status occupied the minds of those who buried their dead there. Moreover, it is notable that the paddle impressed wares are the only deposits not found behind the dunes. It seems that at this time there was a particularly fierce attraction to the coastal edge or the linear boundary between land and sea. Certainly this appears to have been the case on Lakeba, where Best was unable to find a site of this period at any distance away from the foreshore.

Level 3

Later occupations on and behind the dunes remain the least well understood, although our understanding of these deposits is accelerating with the recovery of new materials every year. On the basis of evidence recovered from the Level 3 settlement exposed at the eastern end of the dunes in 1992, the beach ridge site excavated by Burley behind the dunes, and the Level 3 material excavated by the Birks, these sites are strongly clustered, less extensive than the Level 2 occupation, but larger than the clusters of Lapita deposits (Figs. 4.2a, 8.3). They probably range from 60m to 100m in diameter. These are also the first major sites on the dunes to be located above 5m in elevation. Such sites fit well within Crosby's site types 3 and 4a on Beqa (Crosby 1988:31–35) and Best's categories 1–4 on Lakeba (Best 1984: 45–53). These are small hillside, hilltop or stream valley sites containing late paddle impressed and early incised pottery (pre-18th century) with, significantly, small numbers of raised house mounds and structural terraces. Most sites appear to have been occupied prior to or contemporary with the construction of larger ridge, hilltop and ring-ditch fortifications after AD 1500. They form a component of small hillside and streamside settlements within Elizabeth Shaw's similarly dated Class IV sites on Taveuni which typically contain around 5 house mounds within a confined area of settlement (Shaw n.d.:107–131).

The implication again is that the Sigatoka sites are not atypical but instead fit the general Fijian trends for settlement pattern change. This fit extends to the appearance in the Level 3 occupations of evidence for built structures in the form of carbonised house posts in two locations; one at the eastern end of the dunes (Fig. B.4) and one approximately 300m further to the west (Antoine de Biran, personal communication). Although the possibility of recovering house remains cannot be excluded for the earlier occupations, it seems more than coincidence that the appearance of raised house mounds elsewhere in Fiji is mirrored by the first appearance of substantial house posts on the dunes. This development bespeaks the investment of new cultural significance in defining and demarcating the dwelling, as well as a possible continuation of the trend toward status differentiation by elevation found earlier in Burial Ground 1. The trend, then, is one of increasing movement of settlement away from the extreme coastal fringe onto areas of slight elevation on low knolls, hillside flanks and saddles and to stream or riverside locations up alluvial valleys. Whether these shifts were due to changes in the agricultural economy, to an increased desire for defensive locations, or to other socio-cultural reasons is not yet clear, but the congruent development of a preference for alluvial soils, defensive locations and formally defined and arranged house structures in slightly elevated positions suggests that all three factors were involved.

The key areas where this trend does not seem to occur are the major river deltas on Viti Levu at Rewa, Navua and Ba and upstream of the dunes at Sigatoka. On the Rewa delta, Rosenthal (1991:157–159) records none of these types of settlement other than a small number of single house mound sites, no wider than 15 metres in diameter, usually located on upland regions or low ridges within the delta. All other settlements are encapsulated within defensive banks or ditches, or are massive nucleated village sites comprising many clusters of house mounds. John Parry's (1977, 1982) air photo surveys of the Rewa and Navua deltas similarly make no mention of small, undefended settlements, although he does record a few such settlements on the upper reaches of the Sigatoka Valley (Parry 1987). Such sites probably did once exist in these alluvial deltas; but low rises in areas of flat, boggy land are rare, and almost all were later reused as defended villages during the last 500 years of Fijian settlement. Evidence for this comes from recent excavations by Crosby and Marshall at Cautata on the Rewa Delta. This site contains paddle impressed pottery, provisionally dated at AD 950, sealed beneath a later ring ditch fortification dated at circa AD 1500 (Crosby and Marshall 1998). Further evidence comes from the recovery of paddle impressed pottery in the lower deposits of testpits excavated by Geoff Irwin in the early 1980s into several ring ditch fortifications on the Navua Delta (Geoff Irwin, personal communication). Even in these areas then, where fortifications appeared to have developed spontaneously out of no prior form of settlement, a precursive shift to settlement on relatively elevated and/or alluvial locations as indicated at Sigatoka may have occurred.

On the origin of fortifications

Excavations conducted by Burley behind the dunes and at the western end of the dunes have yielded radiocarbon dates of approximately AD 1400 and AD 1700 (Burley 1997; Burley and Shortland 1999). These dates complete what now amounts to a near continuous sequence of settlement of the dunes and their immediate environment. While this occupation on the dunes appears to have been relatively constant and harmonious, further inland the situation was entirely different. By the time of European contact the Sigatoka Valley had become dotted with ring-ditch and ridge fortifications attributed to the period after AD 1000 (Parry 1987:119). In a curious way then – as negative evidence – the Sigatoka dunes contributes to one of the continuing debates of Fijian prehistory; the origin of fortifications.

This debate is reviewed in detail by Rechtman (1992) and Best (1993). It stems originally from a polemical argument between Palmer (1969) and Frost (1974, 1979). Palmer argued that fortifications initially developed within Fiji as ring-ditch forms on the alluvial deltas. These places were ideally suited to the intensive cultivation of taro (*Colocasia esculenta*) and *via kana* (*Cyrtosperma edula*) and were therefore capable of satisfying the demands of a rapidly rising population. The early ring ditches doubled as drainage ditches and thus performed a dual agricultural and defensive function. When they later spread throughout Fiji their circular form was adapted to ridge and hilltop locations where they performed a purely defensive function. Frost on the other hand argued that on Taveuni both upland and flatland fortifications appeared simultaneously around AD 1200. This is shortly after the appearance of the new incised pottery styles. He invoked a migrational hypothesis suggesting conflict between the local population and new arrivals from Vanuatu or New Caledonia (Frost 1974:120). A reanalysis of Frost's pottery by Thomas Babcock (1976, 1977) has, however, indicated that the ceramic changes on Taveuni can be explained through purely local development.

Various alternative scenarios have since been proposed. These tend to reflect the nature and location of the specific region under study. Best pointed out that on Lakeba defence, if not fortification, was a feature of Lapita occupations as early as 500 BC. He proposed a model of elevated inland settlement and warfare precipitated by population stress, based on evidence for environmental degradation occuring by the end of the Lapita period (Best 1984:642–643). A similar situation is found on Taveuni, where Frost obtained a date of 100 BC from a site located on the flanks of a volcanic cone (Frost 1974:58). However, formal fortifications with defensive entrenchments, do not appear on Lakeba until AD 1000 when Ulunikoro, a massive coastal limestone fortification large enough to accommodate the entire population of the island was built and occupied (Best 1984:644). This fort, along with six smaller examples, represents a complete break with the preceding thousand-year period of undefended coastal settlement on the island. The recovery from within Ulunikoro of Samoan style adzes led Best to argue that it could have been built as a Tongan outpost within Eastern Fiji. From Ulunikoro, Tongans could manipulate long distance exchanges of wood products from neighbouring islands such as Kabara and basalt from Samoa (Best 1984:657–661).

The developmental relationship of these early limestone forts on Lakeba to fortifications elsewhere in Fiji, or even to later styles of fortification on Lakeba is enigmatic. On Lakeba no further significant developments in settlement pattern occurred until AD 1500. At this point the interior of Ulunikoro became spatially differentiated by elevation and status, and house mounds become a visible feature of settlements. Shortly after this date settlement shifted to smaller inland forts constructed on hilltops and narrow ridges, before finally shifting back to the coast where flatland ring-ditch fortifications were occupied towards the end of the 18th century. Best associates the eventual appearance of these ring-ditch fortifications with the arrival of further Tongans and the internal migration of a Fijian group originating from the island of Bau, located just off the Rewa Delta (Best 1984:661–662). Although this pattern of inland ridge forts followed by coastal ring-ditch fortifications may be corroborated throughout Lau (see Smart 1965; Palmer 1967; Lawlor 1981), the opposite appears to have happened in coastal areas of western and central Fiji, particularly those associated with Rewa. Crosby found that on Beqa, an island closely connected with Rewa in oral histories, ridge fortifications developed out of small, crude ring-ditches which appear by AD 1500 on small hillocks or on alluvium in marginal locations between the coast and the interior (Crosby 1988:228). Similarly, Crosby and Marshall's excavations of the small though complex ring-ditch fortification at Cautata on the Rewa delta indicate that it was constructed by AD 1500, some 350–400 years earlier than the first ring-ditch on Lakeba (Crosby and Marshall 1998).

During these events, settlement on the Sigatoka dunes continued unabated. There is not the faintest hint of the tumultuous changes occurring only a short distance away up the Sigatoka Valley, and indeed throughout Fiji. This disjunction highlights two points. Firstly, it emphasises that change was occurring in different ways and for apparently different reasons in different parts of Fiji. Something was happening throughout the Lau Islands and on Taveuni and something different was happening in regions closely connected with Rewa. Something different again was happening in the Sigatoka Valley. Secondly, it is important to remember that settlement pattern is a mosaic composed from a wide range of settlement activities, each occurring within a given context. Scrutiny of just one aspect of this context can never reveal the complexity of the wider picture.

On complexity and regional differences

Keeping the problem of Fijian fortifications in mind, we return to the four-phase model. It has completely failed to recognise, never mind account for, regional or even intra-site difference. Nor is it able to identify specific causes of cultural change with anything like the degree of complexity demanded, for example, by the interaction of specific events and developmental processes on Lakeba after AD 1000. The exclusion of horizontal variation from the simplified layercake model of the Sigatoka dunes can be seen as a metaphor for the more general failure of the culture history approach to accommodate regional complexity within Fiji. If Lau and Rewa followed such different trajectories in the acquisition of fortifications, we should expect similar differences for changes taking place earlier in prehistory. Best has already warned that this is the case for the early part of the Lapita sequence by pointing out that the pottery sequence on Lakeba more closely resembles those of Tonga and Samoa than western Fiji (1984:653–654). He raises the spectre of an east–west Fijian cultural divide running through the Koro Sea, an argument for which there is linguistic support (Hunt 1987), and goes on to suggest that the east may have been colonised later than the west, perhaps even by back-voyaging from Western Polynesia.

Our focus on regional difference also sheds new light on the transition from Lapita to paddle impressed ceramics in Fiji at around 200 BC. This has been the subject of long standing disagreement and debate among archaeologists (Frost 1974; Hunt 1980:126–136; Hunt 1986; Best 1984;), partly because it is so fundamental to the way Polynesian culture history has been understood. Because the new paddle impressed ceramics do not occur in Western Polynesia, the Sigatoka/Navatu transition marks the shift from Fiji as portal to Polynesia, to Fiji as cultural frontier. After this transition in Fiji, Polynesia is isolated and becomes a closed and separate cultural environment (see Chapter 1). This debate is about to be reviewed in detail in a forthcoming dissertation by Geoff Clark (personal communication), but it is still worth briefly considering here.

Debate centres on the question of whether paddle impressed pottery developed out of the Lapita potting traditions or whether there was radical replacement of Lapita by new traditions. Clarification has been hampered by the lack of well stratified separation between the two kinds of assemblages, with the result that many archaeologists report the presence of paddle impressed pottery among even quite early Lapita assemblages (Davidson et al. 1990; Hunt 1980). This has created an impression of gradual transition which Hunt (1986), notwithstanding the problem of stratigraphic mixing, has formalised as a model of continuity between the Sigatoka and Navatu phases by recognising transitional forms of vessels at Yanuca. On Lakeba, in contrast, Best (1984:654) demonstrates an almost complete break in almost all aspects of vessel decoration, form and fabric between the Lapita and paddle impressed potting traditions. These changes are rapid and comprehensive.

At Sigatoka, the unusual "wavy" or "Late Level 1" pottery recovered by Hudson from the Level 1–Level 2 transitional zone at the eastern end of the dunes may provide a further regional clue (Petchey 1995:118–120). This distinctive pottery, dated to around 300 BC, appears to be an early form of paddle impression on a Lapita plainware-like vessel (Fig. 5.3). Crosby (1988:215) has reported a similar and equally unusual type of "ribbed" pottery from sites on Beqa and nearby Ugaga Island, which also belong to the transitional Lapita/Navatu period. Given that similar pottery has not yet been reported from elsewhere in Fiji, the Sigatoka and Beqa sherds may represent a short-lived regional response to whatever influences ultimately caused the complete adoption of paddle impression throughout Fiji. This is not to say that these vessels provide the "missing link" between the two ceramic traditions. Merely that during a period in which there seems to have been widespread change, pre-existing local cultural circumstances would have affected the way change proceeded in different parts of Fiji. What has been phrased as a debate over the nature of a pan-Fijian Lapita/Navatu transition, may actually be better understood as a series of equally valid contributions each of which is situated by its unique regional perspective.

Chapter 10
Modelling change and continuity in Fijian prehistory

All this brings us to the wider question of the relationship between cultural change and continuity in Fijian prehistory. We have followed Best (1984) and Hunt (1986, 1987) in challenging the cultural historical, four-phase model. Because it focuses our attention so heavily on breaks in the material culture sequence it completely fails to address continuity and complexity. We have urged a more anthropological approach that seeks to model change rather than merely acknowledge its presence. Moreover we have urged that such models should be socially and culturally informed so that archaeologists can be clear about exactly what it is that is changing and what it is that is remaining the same.

A wide range of processes and circumstantial factors are involved in promoting both cultural change and continuity. It is an issue of great anthropological complexity yet Pacific prehistorians have tended to favour just one cause at a time. Mathew Spriggs (1992, 1997:152–186) reviewed some of the alternatives in his assessment of how and why Lapita cultures changed throughout Island Melanesia. These include (a) the contraction of the long distance Lapita trade system to more locally oriented exchange networks (see Allen 1984, 1985); (b) local adaptation to the colonised environment allowing increased self sufficiency and severing of homeland ties (see Pawley 1981; Kirch 1984); (c) sociopolitical transformation of a prestige economy (hierarchical control of prestige goods within a dualistic kinship and political structure) to a more generalised economy without hierarchical structures (see Friedman 1981, 1982; Kirch 1988); (d) absorption of the Lapita colonisers into a pre-existing local population involving a homogenisation of the two cultures (see Bellwood 1975:14); and (e) secondary migration again involving homogenisation of the two cultures (see Bellwood 1975, 1989:41; and for Fiji, Frost 1979).

At the Sigatoka dunes there is potential evidence for all of these alternatives, except (d). But how do we choose? Clearly we shouldn't, because as Spriggs (1997) himself shows for Island Melanesia each of these potential causes of change is interrelated. Each affects the others (see for example Gosden and Specht 1991; Terrell et al.1997). Migrations, contractions of trade networks, changes in society, and adaptations to the economy are all important elements but none outweighs the other. The effects of migration for example are unpredictable. When does the structured movement of people as part of a long-established exchange network become a migration? When is contact with other peoples merely part of the existing structure and when is it an event of social and cultural significance? There are no simple answers, but the archaeological evidence from the Sigatoka dunes does allow us to model some of these complex interactions.

At Sigatoka the bulk of the Level 1 pottery is fairly standardised compared to the wide variety found in earlier Lapita assemblages. This simplification or winnowing out of earlier complexity and the gross reduction in decoration prompted Green to identify within the Late Eastern Lapita pottery of the Sigatoka dunes a trend towards plainwares that was carried on to a greater extent in Tonga and Samoa (Green 1974:253 and Fig. 90). This trend is gradual and does not indicate the radical imposition of a new tradition of potting. The simple, undecorated forms of the Late Eastern Lapita assemblages are all present in earlier Lapita assemblages from Fiji and elsewhere (Hunt 1980; Best 1984: Fig.3.54; Davidson et al. 1990; Kirch 1997:Fig. 5.10). That is, plainwares are a feature of even early Lapita assemblages. Thus, although a few new forms appear through the Lapita sequence, it is more the case that a whole suite of elaborately decorated types of vessels drops out of production. These are flat based vessels, ring-foot vessels, small bowls and elaborately carinated and collar rimmed vessels.

They are vessels which might be interpreted as prestige goods – more useful for ritual presentation than for the tasks of cooking and storage. What is left are the standard utility wares that were always present in the assemblage but eventually came to constitute its bulk.

Kirch (1997:168–175) has used the remarkably well preserved evidence recovered from the early Lapita site of Talepakemalai in the Mussau Islands of the Bismarck Archipelago to develop a sociocultural model to explain this trend. At Talepakemalai Kirch found that the plainwares were generally thin, paddle-and-anvil finished, and well fired whereas the dentate-stamped, decorated vessels were commonly less skilfully made, thicker walled, often slab built and frequently low-fired. To account for this difference he builds on Marshall's (1985) hypothesis that Lapita pottery was made by women for a trading industry operated by men. Kirch (1997: 150–153) suggests that the plainwares were manufactured by women who exercised great technical control of the pottery-making process. In contrast, the decorated pottery was made by men for ritual purposes in which the decoration of the vessel surface was all important and functional considerations were of little interest. The two types of vessels moved in different long distance exchange networks. The plainwares moved as utilitarian exchange commodities while the decorated vessels circulated through ceremonial gift exchanges. Support for this argument can be found in the spatially differentiated distribution of the two pottery types at Talepakemalai. Decorated vessels along with shell ornaments and other exchange valuables, adzes and fishhooks were found along the littoral zone beneath stilt-supported houses built immediately offshore. Plainwares were found amid beach terrace deposits consisting of middens and cooking debris located immediately behind the shoreline. This evidence points to a dualistic separation within a prestige goods economy. The implication is that over time the impetus of this dualistic economy was lost, leaving only the plainer wares which continued to fulfil a useful role in later Lapita settlements.

What is the evidence that such a system ever operated at Sigatoka or elsewhere in Fiji? Unfortunately the exceptional conditions of preservation Kirch encountered at Talepakemalai have not yet been encountered in Fiji, but promising parallels can be found in the ceramic and settlement evidence. Within Fijian Lapita pottery assemblages paddle-and-anvil finishing techniques are found alongside both slab and coil building construction techniques (Best 1984:636). On Lakeba, Best found inconclusive evidence from a small sample of early Lapita wares (his Period 1) that dentate stamped vessels were relatively thick walled (8–14mm) and heavily cracked whereas two plain vessels appeared more evenly textured, were less heavily cracked and showed stronger evidence of anvil impressions on the interior – an indicator of paddle-and-anvil finishing (Best 1984:369–373). Among a sample of later Lapita plainwares (his Period 2) he found clearer and more general evidence of paddle and anvil finishing on simple cooking pots.

At Sigatoka the assemblage of Level 1 pots excavated by the Birks falls within a notably restricted range of simple cooking pots, pot stands, open bowls and narrow mouth jars, with only a few more complex inverted rim bowls (Fig. 1.2; see Birks 1973; Green 1974:Fig. 90). Of these, only the latter have complex dentate stamped decoration. The Birks failed to find any clear evidence for the use of paddle-and-anvil finishing within this principally plain assemblage but they note that the "overall impression of pots from Level 1 is that they exhibit considerable technical ability in construction, as exemplified by such features as thinness of body walls and reinforcement of the rim, and a final result that allies practical requirements with a definite aesthetic appeal" (Birks 1973:21). Of the few dentate stamped bowls, the Birks found they had been made with "more than usual care", although this seems to refer to the deliberate selection of an unusual temper rather than the quality of manufacture. In fact, while signalling these pots as special, they found this temper had been poorly sorted and produced heavier pots with large gravel inclusions (Birks 1973:26–27). Of the earlier Lapita pottery excavated at Sigatoka by Hudson, Petchey (1994, 1995:107) reports that 54% of the assemblage is decorated, mostly with dentate stamping. She notes that this earlier, more elaborately decorated pottery may have been predominantly slab built and is relatively thick-walled compared to the later, plainer Lapita wares excavated by the Birks.

A similar characteristic has been noted at the Natunuku Lapita site by Davidson et al. (1990: Fig. 11) who report that plain body sherds are, on average, significantly thinner than dentate stamped body sherds from the same deposits. In a similar vein, Rosalind Kay (1984:108) notes that at Naigani only the Lapita plainwares show paddle-and-anvil impressions, although she warns that this could be because the final finishing of decorated vessels may have obliterated such marks. Finally, from the Yanuca Lapita assemblages Hunt (1980: 137–140) has constructed a general model in which he argues that the complex flat based forms and heavily decorated vessels were slab built and only the simpler, plain globular pots, bowls and dishes were paddle-and-anvil finished. There is, then, a strong suggestion that technological differences in construction quality existed between the Lapita decorated and plainwares in Fiji, that the two types of vessel were contemporary within early assemblages, but that over time only the technologically superior plainwares continued to be produced.

Associated with this shift, there was a clear decline in the long distance exchange of pots or potting materials within the Lapita period in Fiji. Early Lapita sites such as Naigani contain pottery with mostly non-local tempers (Kay 1984:104). The two most elaborately decorated vessels excavated from early deposits at Yanuca were found to contain pyroxenic tempers, probably from the Natunuku region of Viti Levu's north coast, while at Natunuku, Fiji's oldest known site, a small number of sherds were found to contain tempers likely to have originated at the Sigatoka dunes (Dickinson 1980). At Lakeba, there is a great reduction in the proportion of sherds with exotic tempers between the Period 1 and 2 Lapita assemblages, indicating a diminishing amount of pottery was moving around (Best 1984:636). The trend at Sigatoka is also significant. Petchey (1995:129) found that a clear distinction could be made between the early and late Lapita assemblages on the basis of a higher proportion of biotite in the former suggesting early exchange of pots from the Vuda area of Viti Levu's east coast. The later assemblage excavated by the Birks was more predominantly of local origin. These trends indicate an increasing localisation of pot manufacture over time. However, the plainwares may always have been locally produced and what we see is the abandonment of the long distance exchange of prestige pots while the plainwares continued unchanged through the Lapita period. Unfortunately, in each of these studies only small numbers of sherds have been petrographically provenanced so the results must be treated with caution.

What settlement evidence is there for differential use of decorated versus plain vessels in Fijian Lapita settlements? There is only one site where such an analysis has been attempted – Site 196 on Lakeba. There Best found that within the centralised settlement pattern represented by the early Lapita wares there were two concentrated areas of ceramics: a larger central area and a smaller area to one side. In the later Lapita periods this pattern had fragmented into a series of smaller clusters with a more dispersed distribution. Best (1984:613) explained the earlier pattern as the result of status differentiation citing the lower concentration of dentate stamped sherds in the smaller area. A comparable situation has been encountered at the Nenumbo site in the Reef Islands (Green 1976: 254; Sheppard and Green 1991). Both sites indicate a dualistic patterning of decorated versus plain ceramics during the early

Lapita period, and at Site 196 this pattern fragments during the later Lapita period. Although no comparable analysis has been attempted elsewhere in Fiji, the shift from early concentrated forms to later fragmented forms of settlement may be a general pattern within the Lapita period. Certainly the large, early site of Naigani appears to be a concentrated settlement (Best 1981; Kay 1984:23) but other early sites such as Natunuku cannot be evaluated due to their disturbed condition (Davidson et al. 1990; Anderson et al. 1996).

If Site 196 on Lakeba does represent the norm, then, by the time late Lapita sites like those at Sigatoka were occupied an early dualistic form of society may have transformed into something less structured. However, this need not mean a radical transformation of society. Continuity in the basic industries, and perhaps underlying gender divisions and cultural perceptions are indicated by continuity in the plainwares. Perhaps just one aspect of the economy was lost: elevation of a status group to a position of economic prestige. At the end of the Lapita period there is also an escalation of inter-settlement conflict on Lakeba and Taveuni. But we do not know how generally this situation applied throughout Fiji, nor do we know the nature of the connection between this evidence of conflict and the hypothesised social change. Best suggests the conflict on Lakeba was related to environmental degradation and demographic pressure but it is difficult to imagine how a large volcanic island such as Taveuni could have been similarly affected. Moreover, by the time environmental degradation and conflict occurred on Lakeba the prestige elements had already been almost completely removed from the ceramic inventory. For the time being, we will return to the question of what continued throughout the course of this disruption.

In the previous chapter we considered the question of whether the introduction of paddle impressed ceramics represented a complete break with the Lapita ceramic traditions. This change might have been precipitated for instance by an episode of major contact with people from New Caledonia, perhaps taking advantage of the heightened state of volatility of Fijian society indicated on Lakeba. Certainly the view from Sigatoka is of radical change. The differences between the Lapita and paddle impressed assemblages are, as Best claimed for Lakeba, like chalk and cheese. It is difficult, coupled with the dramatic stratigraphy of the site, to see anything other than complete cultural discontinuity between them. But, alongside the obvious differences, continuity is also present.

What is similar about the late Lapita and paddle impressed pottery is that both assemblages are dominated by utilitarian and highly standardised wares manufactured with a high degree of techno-logical control. In fact, this represents an increasing trend through the paddle impressed assemblages. With the appearance of paddle impressed pottery at Sigatoka for instance the variation in pot forms becomes even more restricted. The Birks' Level 2 assemblage is dominated by globular/ovoid cooking pots and by large flat-bottomed trays or platters (see Fig. 1.2; Birks 1973:41–45). The pots have highly standardised rim forms and many have carbon deposits on the base. They are beautifully manufactured from local tempers, are extremely thin walled and generally display paddle-and-anvil finishing, if not carved paddle decoration. This carved paddle finishing or decoration is incorporated into the pot as part of the construction process. It is intergral to the pot rather than added to it; it creates the vessel's surface rather than decorating it. Conceptually, this is the opposite of what was happening with the dentate-stamped Lapita pots. These pots seem to have been built specifically in order to create a surface to which the defining decoration could be applied (Crosby and Marshall 1998).

In contrast to the pots, the trays are crude (Plate 9). They were made simply by pressing a mass of clay onto a bed of leaves or matting, resulting in extremely variable thicknesses within individual vessels (Birks 1973:45). Birks speculated that their most likely use was for dismembering turtles or evaporating brine into salt. Such a marked difference between the vessel types may seem odd but it has parallels in other parts of the world. An identical difference exists for example between pottery and briquetage (salt manufacturing troughs) within European assemblages from the Bronze Age to Roman periods. There, pots usually conform to rigid technological and stylistic criteria whereas the briquetage is usually crudely manufactured, often by the saltmakers themselves (de Brisay and Evans 1975).

Rather than representing something entirely new then, the Level 2 pottery at Sigatoka continues the established pattern of dominant and highly specialised production of utilitarian pots but also brings a new dualistic separation within the ceramic assemblages. We argue this represents the persistence of an underlying tradition in the gendered division of labour. We argue that the technologically specialised pots continued to be made by women and that they circulated within society quite independently of the crude trays which were a functionally specific set of wares, made quite differently and with much less expertise.

The trays may have been a purely local phenomenon as they have only been found in the vicinity of the Sigatoka dunes. But they are connected with a much wider phenomenon. Throughout Fiji at about AD 200 or possibly earlier we see the brief but generalised appearance of incised and finger-pinched elements, together with rim notching on some paddle impressed and plain pots. The brief appearance of the trays at Sigatoka with the equally brief appearance of new decorative elements throughout Fiji is unlikely to be coincidence, but the significance is not clear. As yet we are not aware of any studies of the distribution of the incised and finger-pinched vessels within paddle impressed assemblages of this period. We only know that such vessels are relatively rare and, at Sigatoka, they appear to be confined to small clusters within and to the west of the main area of settlement on Level 2. They do not represent a separate "breed" of pots because there is no distinction in vessel forms: the new elements have simply been applied to the same range of well made, utilitarian pots. Thus the new decorative elements do not seem to be part of the strongly dualistic separation indicated by the trays.

The situation is particularly curious given the speed with which these new decorative elements appear around Fiji. This rapid spread and the high degree of similarity achieved between paddle impressed assemblages after AD 200 suggest that inter-regional communication and interaction networks were in place across the Fijian archipelago (Geoff Clark, personal communication). This is especially curious, because Best's petrographic evidence from Lakeba indicates that the paddle impressed pots on Lakeba were almost all locally made even though obsidian from as far away as Vanuatu appears in Lakeba sites at around AD 200 (Best 1984:656). That is, the pots themselves were not moving around despite the fact that there was a long distance trading capacity for them to do so. Again, this emulates or continues the plainware tradition of the Lapita period.

If the pots themselves were not moving around then the idea of pots must have been. Terry Hunt (1987) has already suggested that people were on the move constantly within Fijian prehistory. He wished to explain the ultimate diversification of Fijian cultures and dialects through the variable degrees of isolation of different regions within the archipelago. Two sorts of movement of people are well known from recent Fijian history. Firstly the movement of whole villages or populations as a result of war, and secondly the movement of women through exogamous marriage. We have already discussed the difficulty of extending a generalised model of warfare across Fiji for this late Lapita/early paddle impressed period – evidence of warfare before AD 1000 is restricted to just two islands. It seems more likely that whatever communication networks were in place in Fiji at this time, they involved the movement of women and their knowledge of potting, but not pots.

Friedman (1982) has argued that the abandonment of a prestige economy, as appears to have been the case in Fiji, may signify a shift from an exogamous to an endogamous society. The assumption is that exogamous marriage was accompanied by the exchange of valuables and the monopoly-like control of such valuables by an elite group. Such a system, Kirch (1988:113) has argued, may have been useful to colonisers for maintaining links to homeland communities in order to augment demographically small and unstable groups with marriage partners. But within modern Fijian history large, ritualised presentations of prestige goods only accompanied important political marriages between high ranking chiefly groups. Generalised exogamous marriage between lower ranking groups occurred on a more local and less ritualised scale (Sahlins 1962). Thus the loss of exogamous marriages among a ranking elite early in prehistory may not have had any effect on an established practice of exogamous marriages between local groups on neighbouring lands. In fact the loss of a prestige economy could have *increased* interregional exogamy on a generalised scale by relaxing prohibitions on marriages across political and economic boundaries.

Thus, the loss of the capacity for monopolistic control of the exchange of prestige goods need not have affected the everyday production of utility items by women for use in their own villages. The capacity for women to move freely around Fiji may actually have increased during the late Lapita and paddle impressed periods. In this case women may well have been moving pots, but only over short, archaeologically undetectable distances implied by down-the-line marriages. Over time, the constant movement of women away from their birth place may have weakened the persistence of local potting idiosyncrasies and traditions and seen a collective pooling and standardisation of potting knowledge. Any perceived improvement in potting technology could have rapidly circulated as an idea, unhindered by political-economic barriers. Non functional decorative elements, such as the incised and finger-pinched decorations of AD 200 could have passed out of fashion as quickly as they passed into it. Indeed the very ephemerality of this decoration suggests it was mere whimsy, perhaps a new idea picked up from Vanuatu, but of no consequence in re-establishing a prestige economy or altering the fundamental basis of Fijian society. In contrast, the persistence of paddle impression, not just as a decoration but as a construction technique, combined with changes in fabrics and neck and rim forms, indicates that this offered a real advantage in producing lighter yet more durable utility wares. Paddle impression was thus embraced by women and became the standard to aspire to.

What then of the third major transition at Sigatoka, to the so-called Vuda phase? The pooled evidence from around Fiji suggests that the changes in potting tradition were at this time more gradual, much less of a clean break. Significantly, however, the settlement pattern evidence suggests that the cultural changes after AD 1000 were dramatic and far reaching. What are we to make of this?

At Sigatoka there are only relatively slight and subtle differences between the Birks' Level 2 paddle impressed assemblage and the later plainwares of Level 3 (Fig. 1.2). The main component of both assemblages, Type 1 cooking pots, are very similar in form, the distinguishing features being a lack of carved paddle impressions on the Level 3 wares, the presence of a more sharply angled neck and a more general incurving of the rim (Birks 1973:60). Both assemblages show predominance of paddle-and-anvil finishing and in Level 3 the pots continue to be extremely thin walled and well made. These changes do not constitute a complete replacement of the earlier paddle impressed technology, as demonstrated by the mixture of paddle impressed and incised decorative elements in the assemblages excavated behind the dunes by Marshall (Appendix D) and Burley (1997:29).

Elsewhere at Vuda and Navatu, the sites where the phase distinctions between Navatu, Vuda and Ra wares were originally made, Shaw determined that while a complete break can eventually be seen between Navatu and Ra ceramics, the intermediate Vuda phase – Gifford's "Middle Period" (Gifford 1951:225) – represents an extended transition from one to the other, with few diagnostic criteria of its own (Shaw 1967:117). This is partially borne out by Best's seriations from Lakeba which identify only one decorative element (spot paddle impression) and two vessel forms (oil lamps and high shouldered vessels) which are restricted more or less to the period AD 900 to AD 1600.

On Lakeba the two new vessel forms appear together with small numbers of sherds with incised and appliqué decoration at around AD 1000. At the same time the huge limestone fortification on Lakeba – Ulunikoro – is occupied and there is a commencement or re-commencement of Tongan influence in Fijian affairs (Best 1984:657–663). It appears to mark a significant pan-Western Polynesian event of some sort. At AD 1000 Samoa emerged as a centre for the export of basaltic adzes around Near Oceania, possibly as far as the Solomon and Cook Islands (Best et al. 1992; Leach 1993; Weisler et al. 1997). At the same date Fijian-made pottery suddenly appears in small numbers on Rotuma, Tuvalu and the

Tokelau Islands (Simon Best and Thegn Ladefoged, personal communications). According to Tongan oral histories, the powerful royal dynasties also emerged in Tonga around this time (Bott 1982; Campbell 1992). It appears that a new long distance exchange system – probably controlled by Tongans – emerged that had settlement repercussions in Samoa and on 'Uvea (Herdrich and Clark 1993:60; Sand 1993) and ultimately saw Fijian chiefs engaged in high ranking marriages with royal Tongan women (Kaeppler 1978). The impact and effects of this event were different everywhere, but the repercussions would eventually be felt throughout Fiji in one form or another.

On Lakeba this event saw the mooted establishment of a Tongan outpost which radically changed settlement patterns and catalysed a great increase in the flow of exotic pottery and other materials into Lakeba from elsewhere in Fiji and (in the case of Samoan adzes) from further afield. But it had only a minor initial effect on the pottery. A similar, though slightly later event may be indicated on Taveuni by the appearance of fortifications there at around AD 1200 (Frost 1974). Taveuni and the Lau group were certainly the centres of Tongan involvement in Fiji at the time of European contact. Yet corroboration from elsewhere in Fiji of a similarly dramatic impact on settlement immediately after AD 1000 has not been found. As already discussed, the process by which fortifications appeared on Beqa and Wakaya and in the delta regions of Viti Levu appears to be different, and to be both later and more gradual. Throughout Fiji there was a move away from uniformity to increasing regional diversity.

The area of greatest complexity during this final period was the Rewa river delta and the surrounding hills and small offshore islets. This area was home to four of the major chiefly centres encountered at European contact – Rewa, Bau, Verata and Viwa – and saw the development of Bau and Rewa into political confederations of near state-like proportions (Routledge 1985; Sahlins 1990). Parry (1977) and Palmer (1969) have argued that the emergence of this tributary socio-political system in Bau and Rewa was promoted by demographically driven intensification of agricultural production on the delta. However, Rosenthal (1991:278) has shown that far from showing signs of demographic stress, the population of the Rewa delta never approached capacity even in the 19th century. She argues instead, following Sahlins' (1985) and Hocart's (1970) models of ceremonial chiefly exchange, that the pre-existing role of the chief as a ritually important mediator of exchange between the different components or "sides" of a polity created a ceremonial demand for agricultural products (Rosenthal 1991:269–279). This accounts

for the final development by the 19th century of the typically nucleated form of settlement found on the Rewa delta and in the other great chiefly centres of Fiji including Taveuni and Lakeba. These are typically very large, highly structured and internally demarcated settlements which bring together a number of previously dispersed groups around centralised chiefs.

Rosenthal (1991) has constructed an archaeological model to explain the transformation of settlement on the Rewa delta from dispersed to nucleated, and the associated appearance of *yavu* (housemounds) and other features. According to Rosenthal the housemounds indicate a new ritual need for a group to locate themselves on a landscape. The *yavu* defines the group and their relationships with others. When previously dispersed groups amalgamated in nucleated settlements their *yavu* in a sense moved with them. *Yavu* allowed each group to maintain a separate identity within the nucleated clusters at the same time as trace their historical movements as a succession of *yavu* – or nodes – on the landscape. These highly specific pathways provide an idiosyncratic set of historical connections – or node-to-node relationships between the nucleated chiefly centre and adjacent lands. They are in a sense a 'constitution' for the historical power base of each chiefdom and a charter for ceremonial gatherings and exchanges that re-enact those connections (see Hocart 1929, 1952; Sahlins 1962, 1985; France 1969; Ravuvu 1987). The other key impetus for ceremonial exchanges was through strategic marital alliances between chiefly centres whereby new connections were forged between previously unrelated nodes.

Unfortunately Rosenthal's analysis lacks detailed information on chronology or ceramic change. Crosby and Marshall's (1998) test excavations at the Rewa delta site of Cautata, however, give some sense of the processes involved. They show a series of transformations occurring between the two occupation levels which they have provisionally dated at around AD 1000 and AD 1500. Over this time there was continuity in basic utilitarian cooking pot forms, although they become increasingly plain. These pots form the basis of the assemblage at both times. However, at AD 1000 they are almost exclusively locally made, while by AD 1500 at least 25% of sherds are exotic. Most exotic sherds contain pyroxenic tempers from the Ra region of northern Viti Levu. At AD 1000 two new vessel forms – oil lamps and high shouldered vessels – are both present, but only in very small numbers and there are none of the new decorative features of incision or tool impression. However, by AD 1500, carved impression continues only minimally as a decoration and is supplanted in frequency by incision and tool impression as well as new techniques including appliqué and finger-modelling. Several new vessels forms are also present, including *dari, vuluvulu* (finger bowls) and *saqa* (water jars). These latter forms are associated ethnographically with the ritual consumption of kava (*Piper methysticum*) in chiefly ceremonies, as well as being dishes for the personal use of high status individuals. It is on these vessels that the great bulk of the new decorative elements are found.

Attendant on the ceramic changes identified at Cautata is a settlement shift from what was probably a small open settlement on the fringe of the delta to a ring ditch fortification. By AD 1500 the site is defined by an outer circular ditch concentrically enclosing a second, inner ditch which itself encloses three small house or temple mounds. The bulk of the decorated bowls came from within this inner area, whereas the bulk of the cooking pots come from the surrounding area between the two ditches. Notably, the heavily decorated bowls and other vessels from the inner area appear from low power microscopy analysis to be manufactured almost exclusively of local tempers. It is primarily the plain cooking pots that have been imported from afar. The ditches at Cautata, particularly the inner ditch, can be seen as enclosing and defining a node on the landscape as well as providing defence for the occupants. Within the ditches ceremonial exchanges between groups from other nodes would have taken place. Defence was necessary, because such nodes were targets for warfare. Indeed they motivated warfare because their capture was a primary mechanism by which competing chiefdoms could erode the constitution of their enemies and garner the ceremonial exchange or tribute to themselves. It is the enclosing nature of these fortifications that defines them as a component of a very Fijian form of warfare, and differentiates them from the larger and less formally structured early limestone fortifications on Lakeba (but see Clunie 1977 and Best 1993 for an alternative view on Fijian warfare and defensive arrangements). This explains why even on naturally defended hilltops and ridges elsewhere in Fiji the fort-makers have gone to great trouble to extend the defences in order to maintain a specific spatial structure even though it was not necessary for strictly defensive purposes (see Crosby 1988: Figs. 2.9 and 2.13).

Thus, Cautata traces the chronological development of a nodal form of settlement on the Rewa delta marked by the imposition of symbolic boundaries around housemounds, the marking off of an internal zone dominated by new pottery vessels associated with ceremonial kava consumption and inscribed with new decorative elements, and the appearance of new long distance exchanges of pottery. But how did this new form of settlement and exchange emerge? Part of the answer may be that it was always there – at least the cultural tradition or idea of chiefly exchange may have survived from the Lapita period. But this would not explain why this high level of stratification disappeared for two millennia and then re-emerged in the specific form that it did.

The key appears to lie, again at Lakeba. In the early ceramic deposits on Ulunikoro there are a number of sherds from Rewa and other parts of Fiji but as yet no evidence of stratification in the pottery or the settlement pattern, and no evidence of a definitively Fijian form of warfare. We suggest that the creation of a Tongan outpost at Lakeba set up a current or eddy of circulation, probably commencing in eastern Fiji and rapidly taking in Taveuni and Rewa. There are strong oral historical and linguistic grounds for supposing that there were groups of people, probably located in the Lau region who were supplying valuable red feathers from Fiji to Tonga and Samoa and who were instrumental in founding new chiefly lineages in those places (Geraghty 1993). There are also strong grounds for supposing that many of the key material culture items vital to the operation of the Fijian chiefdoms were inspired or supplied from Tonga. These include new designs of canoe and possibly two essential elements in Fijian chiefly ceremonies: bowls for drinking kava and the most precious valuable of all, *tabua* or whales teeth (Clunie 1986).

Initially the trade may have been directly between Tongans and Fijians. But Fijians would have been quick to exploit the opportunities for monopoly control that would give them an edge over their allies and enemies. The chiefs of Rewa and its environs were early to exploit these opportunities, for Rewa tempers appear early, and in the largest numbers among exotic sherds on Ulunikoro after AD 1000, particularly among the new vessel forms found on Lakeba after AD 1000. The development of a new prestige economy appears to have happened relatively quickly and it is this that accounts for the new ceramic forms. They are vessels for the personal use of chiefs in ritual ceremonies. They may have been inspired by Tongan or Samoan vessels, such as wooden bowls for the consumption of kava, but they were quickly Fijianised in ceramic forms. Indeed, the entire exchange momentum would have been Fijianised. And so, although originally inspired by a desire for foreign valuables from Tonga and Samoa, this system was turned around and ultimately transformed into an internal Fijian trade system whereby agricultural products were exchanged for sea products. This exchange was characterised in terms of the reciprocal flow of indigenous and foreign goods (Sahlins 1985).

The Fijian potting industry appears to have been affected in a number of ways. There would have been a new demand for difference, for the exchange system was characterised by conceptual differences between indigenous and foreign or exotic goods and on status differences between chiefs and others. The venues and forums for exchange changed – no longer based on down the line exogamous marriage but on highly specific node-to-node connections between often widely spaced groups. These long distance exchanges were assisted by the presence of Tongan sailors. At the time of European contact such Tongans were regularly plying backwards and forwards between Lau and Rewa and were even engaged as mercenary fighters in wars between Fijian chiefs (Clunie 1977:28–29; Sahlins 1990; Routledge 1985:86). They resembled a fishermen class of Fijians whose role it was to sail widely, securing war victims for Fijian chiefs. In prehistory, certain potters would have had better access to such warrior/traders; others would have been restricted further by the new imposition of political frontiers between warring lands. The vagaries of these influences are difficult to determine. However, they could easily have transformed the Fiji-wide, highly standardised, paddle impressed ceramic industry into a series of specialised potting centres manufacturing and trading widely varying vessels distinguished by different elaborations of the competing designs and vessel forms known for the later historic period (Rossitto 1987, 1992; Geraghty 1981; Thompson 1938).

To conclude we return to Cautata and finally to Sigatoka. Crosby and Marshall (1998) argue that by AD 1500 a Fijian chiefly system of exchange had been instituted on the Rewa delta. Two types of pottery were now made. One was elaborately decorated and crudely made. This was the central preserve of chiefs and differentiated their ritual and personal status. This pottery was not imported into Rewa. Rather, Rewa appears to have been a production centre for these types of vessels, probably signifying its importance as an early Fijian centre of chiefly exchange. Rewa people were now receiving many of their plain utility wares from Ra in northern Fiji and probably also elsewhere. Kuhlken and Crosby (1999) have noted the presence of a massive but enigmatic agricultural terrace complex at Nakauvadra in Ra Province, which was capable of supplying production well in excess of local populational demand. It is conceivable that pots may have been moving directly from Ra to Rewa alongside agricultural products as part of a highly specific node-to-node historical connection. Certainly the chiefly groups of the Rewa region trace close oral historical connections to Nakauvadra today. These products were then redistribu-ted and dispersed through chiefly nodes throughout the Rewa settlements.

At Sigatoka, the initial impact of all this appears to have been slight, with only small and gradual changes in the pottery, and similarly subtle changes in settlement pattern between the paddle impressed and later periods. Perhaps there was a new preference for slightly elevated and agricultural locations evidenced in the movement of settlement up the dune face and onto the flats behind the dunes. There may also have been a new emphasis on the dwelling or its housemound foundation as a structure of greater social significance. In most other respects there is continuity, even to the use of very similar areas of the dunes for burials that had been used during the Level 2 occupation. By the 1800s, however, when Lakeba had to all intents become a Tongan colony, Tongans had also made their presence felt as far as the Sigatoka River. The Tongan chief Maile Latumai established settlements adjacent to the Sigatoka dunes at Korotoga and at several locations up the Sigatoka Valley (Parry 1987:41–42). His people no doubt sailed past the dunes, possibly even stopping off there. They would have found the dunes still occupied.

Even at the end of the prehistoric period pottery made in the lower reaches of the Sigatoka River region remained surprisingly little changed from that seen on the dunes. 20th century accounts of pottery traditions in the Lower Sigatoka Valley record the manufacture by women of the same basic forms of undecorated, paddle-and-anvil finished cooking pots as those recovered from Level 3 on the dunes (Palmer et al.1968; Rossitto 1987:34–36). Included within the 20th century assemblages are wide rimmed bowls (*dari*) and small finger bowls (*vuluvulu*) decorated with incised and impressed elements. But this is much less variety than found in the uppermost layers of sites such as Navatu and on Lakeba or, especially, at Rewa where the fullest range of ceramic elements represented by the so called Ra phase is found. This regional variation in the impact of the new ceramic styles holds the key to understanding what continued and what changed during the last 800 years of Fijian prehistory.

It is to be expected that the movement of ideas and goods through the exchange system created in Fiji during the last millennium would be highly idiosyncratic, and that the impact would be highly variable throughout Fiji. This was indeed the case both in the transition from paddle impressed to highly incised wares and in the emergence of fortifications and nucleated settlements. In both of these respects the Sigatoka dunes were now a backwater, no longer of consequence in the shifting sands of Fijian prehistory.

Appendix A
Testpit and Probe Transects 1992

The results of the 1992 testpit and probe survey are summarised below. The locations of all testpits and probes are shown in Fig. A.1. More precise locations can be found in Figs. 4.2a–d, and below in Figs. A.2–A.7.

Testpit Transects 1, 2, 3 and 4

Testpit Transects 1, 2, 3 and 4 were excavated in the area 320–350M on a steeply sloping section of the dune face crossed by two exposed palaeosols and covered by human bone scatters (Fig. A.2). They identified the palaeosols as Levels 1 and 2 and indicated that the human bone was almost certainly eroding from Level 2. They further indicated that immediately west of Testpit Transect 2 the Level 2 surface is relatively level or dips slightly to the north, but immediately to the east both palaeosols rise slightly into the dune face. Level 1 rises at a slightly higher gradient such that at approximately 4 metres above sea level it is truncated by Level 2 above. Similar indications were subsequently obtained by Hudson (1994:12–13, Figs. viii, ix). At the time of the Level 2 occupation, therefore, the dune surface to the west of Testpit Transect 2 was relatively flat. Just to the east it rose towards the dune crest which currently protrudes to the north separating Burial Grounds 1 and 2. On early photographs of the dunes this crest can be seen extending nearly to the foreshore (Birks 1973:151, Plate I). It is possible that Burial Ground 2 is located on a shallow rise or knoll at the base of this crest, thus resembling the locational situation of Burial Ground 1 to the east (Best 1989:21).

At the time of excavation, there was no surface indication of Level 3 in this area of the dune and it was not encountered in any of the testpits, even though the Birks had previously demonstrated that it formed a continuous exposure approaching to within 22m of the high tide line just to the west

(Birks 1973: Fig. 3). By the final days of the survey, however, Level 3 had been exposed on the surface in two places above Burial Ground 2, apparently having receded considerably since the Birks' excavations in 1965/66. By the time of Hudson's excavations in 1993, sufficient sand had been eroded to expose Level 3 as a continuous palaeosol running along the dune face to the north, directly overlying Level 2 north of Burial Ground 2 (Hudson 1994:11–12, Figs. vi–vii).

Testpit Transect 1

Testpit Transect 1 is a single testpit excavated into the upper palaeosol running along the slope above a surface scatter of human bone fragments (Burial Ground 2). It overlay the lower palaeosol, separated by 52 cm of loose grey sand. They were identified as Level 2 and Level 1 respectively. Level 1 was exposed on the surface eleven metres to the southeast at an elevation of between 2.5 and 3.25 metres, i.e. approximately 2 metres below the surface level of Testpit 1. The testpit established that the surface bone almost certainly eroded from Level 2 and that the surface of Level 1 rises to the north at a gradient of 1:5. Level 1, therefore, is likely to intersect with the base of Level 2 further under the dune.

Testpit Transect 2

Testpit Transect 2 included ten testpits excavated at 2 metre intervals over a distance of 16 metres. It extended north from the storm surge line through the Level 2 exposure identified by Testpit Transect 1. The transect revealed the upper and lower surfaces of Level 2 extending level or rising slightly to the north beneath loose grey sand, at approximately 4.6 and 3.95 metres elevation respectively. At the surface, the soil layer was approximately 65 cm thick. No surface evidence of Level 1 was detected along the transect south of the Level 2

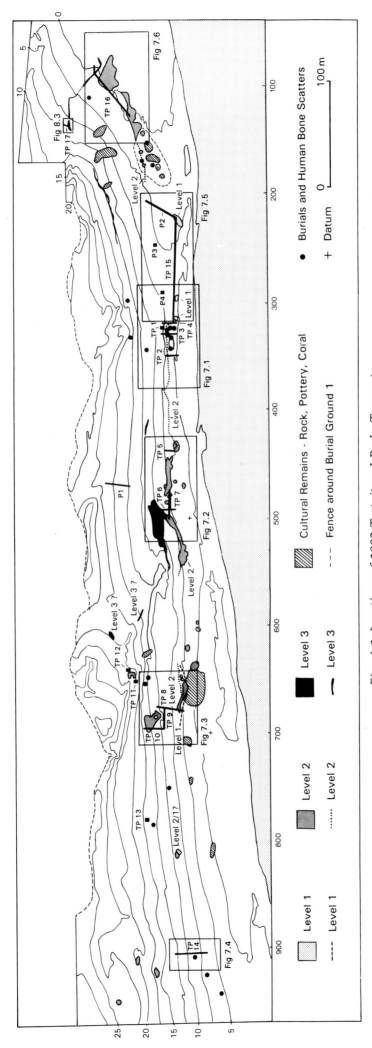

Fig. A.1 Locations of 1992 Testpit and Probe Transects.

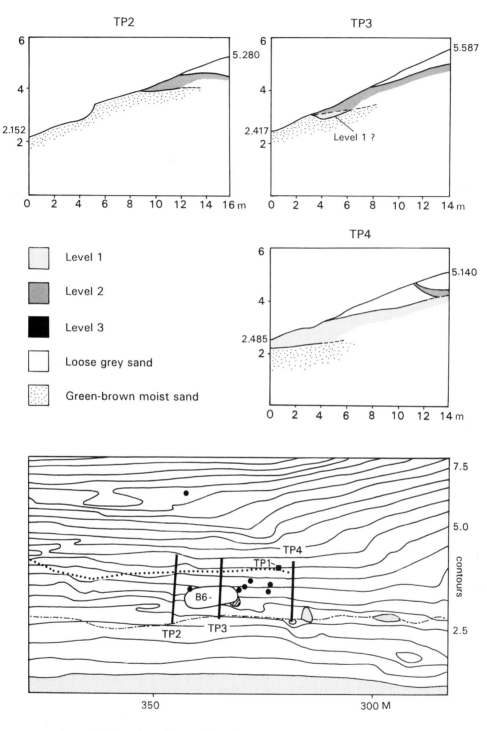

Fig. A.2 Stratigraphic profiles of 1992 Testpit Transects 2, 3, & 4.

exposure and no attempt was made to test for Level 1 by excavating below Level 2.

Testpit Transect 3

Testpit Transect 3 included nine testpits excavated at one or two metre intervals over a distance of 14 metres. It extended north from the storm surge line through the Level 2 exposure. The transect revealed the upper and lower surfaces of Level 2, the upper surface climbing evenly at a gradient of approximately 1:7.5. At the surface the soil layer was approximately 85 cm thick. To the north, it was covered in loose grey sand and overlay the moist green-brown sand that is found as a basal sand layer along the length of the site. No clear evidence was detected of Level 1, although a 30 cm deposit of dark brown sand immediately beneath Level 2 at the 4 metre mark may indicate the two levels in abutment.

Testpit Transect 4

Testpit Transect 4 included nine testpits excavated at one or two metre intervals over a distance of 14 metres. It extended north from the storm surge line through Levels 1 and 2. Level 1 was approximately 75 cm thick and rose evenly to the north at a gradient of approximately 1:9. At the surface, Level 2 had been eroded to a thin wedge and was separated from Level 1 below by loose grey sand. To the north it thickened and also rose slightly into the dune face. At approximately four metres above sea level the two palaeosols merged, Level 1 rising into the base of Level 2. They both continued rising into the dune face in abutment. The basal green-brown sand was found immediately beneath Level 1, and Level 2 was covered by loose grey sand.

Testpit Transects 5, 6, 7 and Probe Transect 1

Testpit Transects 5, 6 and 7 and Probe Transect 1 were excavated in the area 430–510M (Fig. A.1 and A.3) on a moderately sloping section of the dune face crossed by two merging exposed palaeosols and covered by scatters of pottery of Level 1 and 2 types. They identified the palaeosols as Levels 2 and 3 and indicated that Level 1 had been previously eroded or that Levels 1 and 2 were conflated. As in the area immediately east of Burial Ground 2, Level 2 survives as a roughly flat surface extending into the dune surface, but at a higher level. A slight rise in the Level 2 surface from east to west reflects the current dune form. It appears likely that, as in the area of Burial Ground 2, Level 1 previously rose into the dune face but was truncated by the deposition of Level 2 at a time when the surface was somewhat eroded and flattened. Level 1 pottery and other cultural material was consequently incorporated into the later palaeosol. A slight mound or ridge in the Level 2 surface had been used for cultural purposes, indicated by a large scatter of Level 2 type pottery.

Later erosion also caused the partial conflation of Levels 2 and 3, demonstrated by the large area of merged palaeosols on the dune surface. Level 3 here rises north into the dune face at an approximate gradient of 1:6 and would have truncated the Level 2 surface further south towards the sea, possibly explaining why the Birks did not find Level 2 on this section of the dunes (Birks 1973:Fig. 3). Further north, into the dune face, Level 3 overlies and preserves the Level 2 surface.

Testpit Transect 5

Testpit Transect 5 included eight testpits excavated at one or two metre intervals over a distance of ten metres. It extended north from a surface exposure of black/brown sandy soil associated with Level 1 and 2 type pottery including Feature 3, a late Lapita plainware pot. The transect identified the exposed palaeosol as Level 2 and indicated that it forms a relatively level surface extending north into the dune face at approximately 3.9 – 4.25 metres above sea level. It was covered by loose grey sand and overlay the green-brown base sand. The co-existence of Level 1 and Level 2 pottery on the surface indicates that conflation of Levels 1 and 2 had occurred.

Testpit Transect 6

Testpit Transect 6 included seven testpits excavated at three metre intervals over a distance of 18 metres. It extended north from an area of exposed pottery associated with Feature 5, a late Lapita plainware pot, and just west of a surface scatter of Level 2 type pottery, to a large surface exposure of black sandy soil on the dune slope above. The transect failed to give any indication of the Level 1 palaeosol with which Feature 5 is presumed to be associated, or of Level 2. The lower (southern) testpits revealed loose surface sand overlying basal green-brown or yellow/brown sand, indicating the complete erosion of all palaeosols. The surface exposure of black sandy soil further to the north proved to be Level 3. It formed a 50 cm thick layer that climbed steeply into the dune face at an approximate gradient of 1:6.

Testpit Transect 7

Testpit Transect 7 included ten testpits excavated east–west along the dune at three metre intervals for a distance of 27 metres. It crossed Testpit Transect 6 just above Feature 5 in the area of erosion indicated by that transect and demonstrated the presence of Level 2 east and west of the eroded area. Along the length of the transect Level 2 rises and falls as a slight ridge or mound, completely eroded at the centre and c.40 cm lower at the eastern end, dipping further to the east. This mound appears to have been used culturally, the remnants of pottery scatters being found in loose sand along and to the north of the transect.

To the east of the transect the Level 2 palaeosol extended as a more or less continuous surface

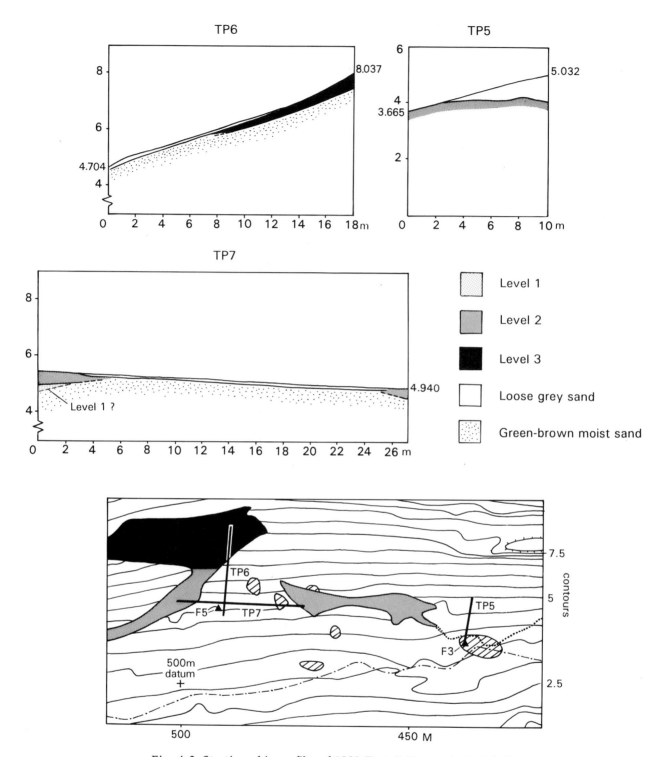

Fig. A.3 Stratigraphic profiles of 1992 Testpit Transects 5, 6 & 7.

exposure to Burial Ground 2. To the west, it formed a very large surface exposure of sandy soil grading from dark brown to black sandy soil up the dune slope. Following the test excavations, this was shown by differential drying and further erosion to be a conflation onto Level 2 of the Level 3 palaeosol encountered in Testpit Transect 6. No clear indication of Level 1 was found in the transect profile, although a deposit of moist brown sand found immediately beneath Level 2 at the western end of the transect may be a remnant of the older palaeosol.

Probe Transect 1

Probe Transect 1 included 16 probes made at two metre intervals over a distance of 30 metres from

11m to 16m elevation above the Level 2 palaeosol identified by Testpit Transects 5 and 7. The probes were made in order to locate Level 3 but failed to reach it beneath a thick deposit of striated drift sand. The transect was made before the Level 3 exposure had been revealed at the top of Testpit Transect 6 to the east, and was therefore positioned slightly too high on the dune face. By the end of the survey the wind had revealed a further surface exposure of Level 3, 50 metres to the east which, by 1993, Hudson could trace beyond Burial Ground 2 to the east (Hudson 1994:3, Fig. iii).

Testpit Transects 8–12

Testpit Transects 8–12 were excavated in the area 640–700M (Fig. A.1 and A.4), above and slightly to the west of a very large surface scatter of cultural debris containing sherds of Level 1 and 2 pottery types. The transects passed through two exposed palaeosols associated with this surface pottery and extended north to a third palaeosol exposure higher up the dune slope at c.12m elevation. The transects indicate that on this section of the dunes Levels 1 and 2 both survive as pottery bearing palaeosols rising at gradients of 1:10 and 1:6 respectively to the north, into the dune face, and a gradient of 1:10 to the west, along the dune face. There is no clear evidence on this section of the dunes of the Level 3 palaeosol, although some undiagnostic pottery and unprovenanced human bone scatters are loosely associated with a soil-less compacted grey sand layer that may be the leached remains of an occupation palaeosol post-dating Level 2.

The steep, northward-rising gradient of Level 2 contrasts with the Birks findings which show Level 2 dipping into the dune face on this section of the dunes (Birks 1973:Fig.5b). Their excavations, however, were situated at least 20 metres to the south (see Fig. 5.1) and may have been located on the back-slope of what was a low fore-dune or beach ridge in the Level 2 surface that backed onto a more steeply sloping back-dune. That Level 2 did in fact rise steeply to the north at this point is further indicated by the presence of a thick palaeosol loosely associated with Level 2 trays at 21m elevation in Testpit Transect 12. While further investigations are required to clarify the stratigraphy high on the dunes, the testpit results demonstrate the presence of Level 2 at elevations above 12 metres and suggest its presence at elevations as high as 21 metres.

Testpit Transect 8

Testpit Transect 8 included seventeen testpits excavated at one and three metre intervals over a distance of 28 metres extending north from surface scatters of pottery through two exposures of brown and black-brown sandy soil. It revealed a complex stratigraphy in which both Level 1 and Level 2 palaeosols were separated and overlain by a variety of sterile sand deposits. In the lower section of the transect Level 1 was revealed as a light brown sandy soil deposit, ranging in thickness from 20 – 30 cm, overlying the basal green-brown sand and rising unevenly to the north at an approximate gradient of 1:10. It was separated from Level 2 above by a compact grey-brown sand matrix with some soil intermixed. Level 2 was revealed as a black-brown sandy soil, 30 cm thick and rich in pottery, rising relatively evenly to the north at an approximate gradient of 1:6. Pottery recovered from the 20 metre mark at circa 8.5 metres elevation was from a single fine-walled *kuro* with asymmetrically incised decoration around the neck, an attribute characteristic of the Level 2 pottery.

The gradient differential between Levels 1 and 2 indicates a possible steepening of the seaward dune face in the intervening period and demonstrates the likelihood that pottery-bearing Level 1 deposits remain undisturbed beneath Level 2. Striated bands of wind blown sand were found overlying Level 2, separated from the palaeosol by a thin band of white sand along much of the transect. A band of dark grey iron sand with a low soil content was found above Level 2 at the top of the transect.

Testpit Transect 9

Testpit Transect 9 included ten testpits excavated at three metre intervals over a distance of 18 metres. It extended east–west from a point below the upper palaeosol exposure to join Testpit Transect 8 at the 20 metre mark. The transect identified the surface exposure as a continuation of Level 2, dipping to the east at an approximate gradient of 1:10. As with Testpit Transect 8, along the eastern half of the transect Level 2 lay beneath striated wind deposited sand and contained large numbers of sherds. Along the western half of the transect the dune surface had been eroded down to the basal layer of green/brown sand. No indication was found of Level 1.

Testpit Transect 10

Testpit Transect 10 included 8 testpits excavated at three metre intervals over a distance of 18 metres extending north from the western end of Testpit Transect 9 through an exposed palaeosol. It identified the palaeosol as Level 2, overlying green-brown basal sand and extending north into the

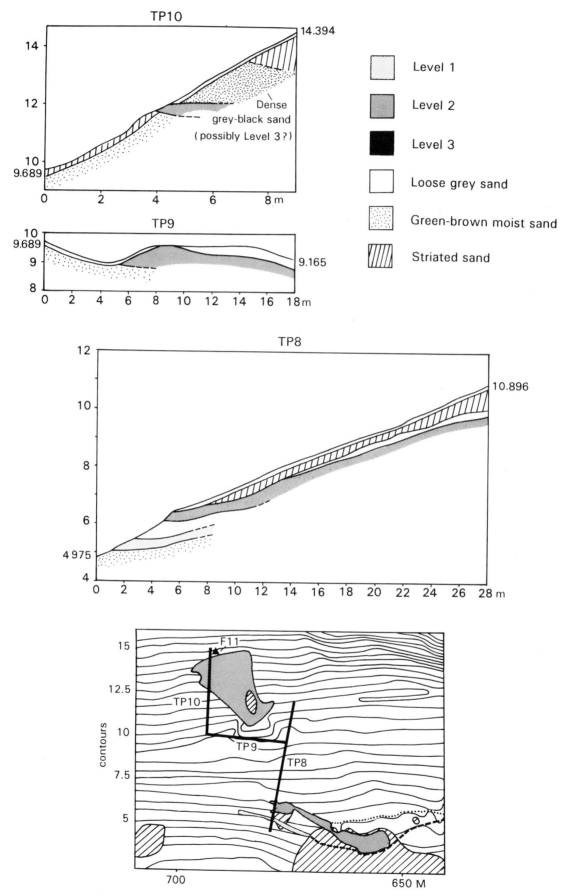

Fig. A.4 Stratigraphic profiles of 1992 Testpit Transects 8, 9 & 10.

dune relatively level at circa 12 metres elevation. This may represent a former crest or ledge in the dune surface at the time the palaeosol formed. It was overlain by deep drift sands and a dark grey, moist iron sand, easily mistaken on the surface for a palaeosol. A surface scatter of fine, plain pottery was collected near the northern end of the transect (Feature 11). It could not be positively provenanced to the exposed palaeosol, but included a number of fine-walled sherds with cross-hatch paddle impressed decoration characteristic of Level 2 pottery. Scatters of human bone located circa 40m east of the transect appeared to be associated with the compacted grey sand layer.

Testpit Transects 11 and 12

Testpit Transect 11 included two testpits excavated 1 metre apart on the south slope of an exposed palaeosol profile located high on the dunes at 650M. It identified a palaeosol containing within it a band of yellow-brown sandy clay, merging into compact dark grey sand at the base. Testpit Transect 12 included a single testpit excavated 12 metres to the north-east, on the eastern side of the same exposed profile. It identified the base of the palaeosol at 21.025m elevation, approximately 1.75 metres higher than the level recorded in Testpit Transect 11 (19.261m). This equates to a very steep gradient of 1:1.7 over 12 metres, indicating that at the time of deposition of the palaeosol this part of the dune formed a steep crest or pinnacle similar to the current configuration. Surface scatters of pottery, including fragments of Level 2 trays, were found short distances to the east and northwest of the transects demonstrating that the dunes may have been used even at this high elevation during the Level 2 occupation. An exposure of black-brown sandy soil 40 metres to the northeast could not be identified but is provisionally considered to be Level 3.

Testpit Transects 13 and 14

Testpit Transects 13 and 14 were excavated at circa 780M and 900M (Fig. A.1 and A.5), relatively high on the dunes, in order to identify and provenance isolated scatters of human bone and palaeosol outcrops located towards the western end of the surveyed area. As with the other bone scatters situated high on the dune slope, the bone at the western end could not be positively associated with a palaeosol. Testpit Transect 14, however, indicated that Burial B91/2, excavated in 1991 by Crosby and Matararaba, might be associated with the Level 2 palaeosol, which was identified rising steeply

up the dune face immediately to the east. On this section of the dunes the Level 2 surface closely resembles the current dune surface, rising sharply towards the current dune crest to the north, and climbing to the west where discontinuous outcrops of the palaeosol could be seen extending for at least a further 300 metres. No clear indication of Levels 1 or 3 were encountered in the transects.

Testpit Transect 13

Testpit Transect 13 included a single testpit located eight metres north of a surface scatter of fragmentary human bone, at approximately 780M and 13m elevation (see Fig. 6.1). The testpit failed to identify any palaeosol with which the burial might be associated.

Testpit Transect 14

Testpit Transect 14 included twelve testpits excavated at three metre intervals extending 30 metres north from a point adjacent to and below the approximate location of Burial B91/2 (Fig. A.5). It failed to identify a palaeosol with which the burial could be definitely associated. However, the transect revealed the upper surface of a black-brown sandy palaeosol commencing at the 20 metre mark and climbing to the north at an approximate gradient of 1:4.5. In 1991 this palaeosol had been momentarily exposed approximately 20 metres above the burial and contained characteristic Level 2 pottery including asymmetrically incised and finger-pinched cooking pots (Crosby, field notes and map). Given the steepness of the gradient it is possible that the skeletons of Burial B91/2 were originally deposited from or within this palaeosol. No indications of Level 1 or Level 3 were found in the transect.

Testpit Transect 15 and Probe Transects 2–4

Testpit Transect 15 and Probe Transects 2–4 were excavated in the area 200–320M (Fig. A.1 and A.6) to determine the stratigraphic relationship between the palaeosols associated with Burial Grounds 1 and 2. Best had previously noted a continuous exposure of Level 2 between the two areas (Best 1989: Fig. 2). By the time of the 1992 survey a thick deposit of drift sand had built up between the burial grounds although probe tests indicated the presence of Level 2 at circa 1m depth. Testpit Transect 15 demonstrated the survival of Level 1 as a continuous deposit running more or less along the high tide line, dipping slightly to the west from the area of

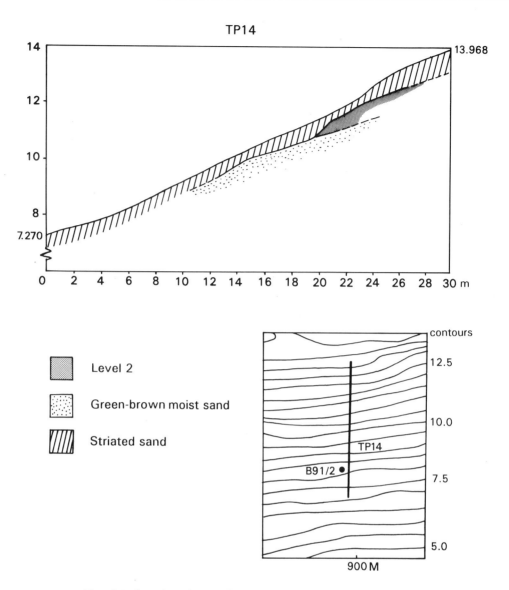

Fig. A.5 Stratigraphic profile of 1992 Testpit Transect 14.

Burial Ground 1 and then rising significantly towards Burial Ground 2. This rise of circa 2m between 250M and 300M may indicate that Level 1 overlies an extension of the old riverbank that extends beneath the dunes from the north. Further probing of the Level 1 surface just to the west of Burial Ground 1 demonstrated that it extended into the dune face more or less level or dipping slightly to the north. Significant areas of the Level 1 surface are therefore likely to survive on this section of the dunes.

Testpit Transect 15

Testpit Transect 15 included nine testpits excavated at 10 metre intervals over a distance of 100 metres extending east from the Level 1 exposure south of Burial Ground 2 to a surface exposure of

brown sandy soil approximately 50 metres south-west of Burial Ground 1 (Fig. A.6, 4.2a, b). No testpits were excavated between 40 and 80 metres where there was a deep surface deposit of loose drift sand. The transect identified the Level 1 palaeosol dipping gradually and evenly to the east at an approximate gradient of 1:20 for 40 metres before being lost beneath the deep surface sand. The palaeosol then appears to continue descending before levelling out and rising at a gradient of 1:40 towards the surface exposure at the eastern end of the transect. At various intervals the palaeosol was found beneath different deposits of loose grey sand or more compacted striated grey sands indicating several episodes of erosion and wind borne deposition of sand in this part of the dunes and accounting for the disappearance of Levels 2 and 3.

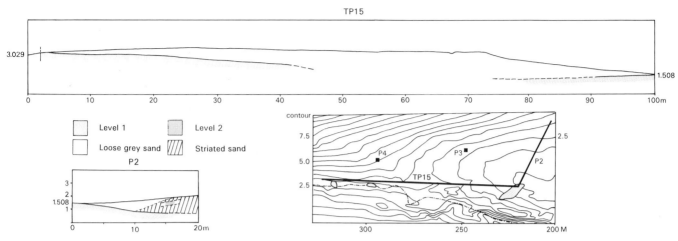

Fig. A.6 Stratigraphic profiles of 1992 Testpit Transect 15 and Probe Transect 2.

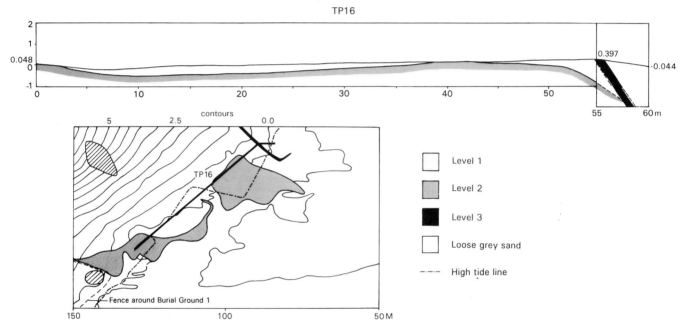

Fig. A.7 Stratigraphic profile of 1992 Testpit Transect 16.

Probe Transect 2

Probe Transect 2 included eight probes made at five metre intervals over a distance of 35 metres extending northeast from the eastern end of Testpit Transect 15 past the western end of the fenced area of Burial Ground 1 (Fig. A.6, 4.2a). The probe results are not considered accurate. The transect did however establish that Level 1 extends north into the dune face under deep surface sand, probably dipping gradually to the north at an approximate gradient of 1:20. No indication was found of Level 2.

Probe Transects 3 and 4

Probe Transects 3 and 4 were single probes made to locate the presence of Level 2 between Burial Grounds 1 and 2, north of Testpit Transect 15. The probes indicated the presence of a palaeosol at approximately 93 cm below the surface and 108 cm below the surface respectively. The probe results gave no indication of the identity of this palaeosol although it is most likely that it represents Level 2.

Testpit Transects 16 and 17

Testpit Transects 16 and 17 investigated Level 2 and Level 3 palaeosol exposures to the east and north of Burial Ground 1 in the area 80–140M (Fig. A.1, A.7, B.4). They confirmed Best's finding that Burial Ground 1 was situated on a slight rise by demonstrating that Level 2 falls away to the northeast of it. Unexpectedly, the transects also demonstrate that at the eastern edge of the surveyed area both Level 2 and Level 3 drop very sharply to the east indicating a prior edge of the dunes during both occupations. They further demonstrate that the mapped exposure of Level 3, arcing to the northwest (Plate 5), slopes down steeply to the north and northeast, representing a continuation of the dune edge around the back of the dunes during the Level 3 occupation.

Testpit Transect 16

Testpit Transect 16 included seventeen testpits excavated at 1, 2 and 5 metre intervals over a distance of 60 metres extending northeast from the large surface exposure of Level 2 in the area of Burial Ground 1 to an exposure of Level 3 which arcs up the dune slope to the northwest (Fig. A.7). The transect identified the upper surface of Level 2 dipping to the northeast from Burial Ground 1 then rising gradually before dropping very sharply away to the east

at a gradient of approximately 1:2.5. At that point Level 3, circa 1m above it, also drops sharply to the east at an even steeper gradient of 1:2. The sharp slope of both Level 2 and 3 appears to mark a significant and sustained margin at the eastern end of the dunes, possibly an old bank of the Sigatoka River.

Testpit Transect 17

Testpit Transect 17 included five testpits excavated at 1.5 and 3 metre intervals over a distance of nine metres extending northeast from the surface exposure of Level 3 investigated as Feature 6 (see Fig. B.4). It revealed the upper surface of Level 3 dropping sharply to the northeast at an approximate gradient of 1:2.5. The result indicates that the large Level 3 exposure extending southeast and west of Feature 6 represents the back edge of the dune during the formation and occupation of the Level 3 palaeosol.

Appendix B
Excavated features 1992

Details of the eleven features excavated during the 1992 survey are described below. The precise locations of these features are shown in Figs. 4.2a–d and their general locations are summarised in Fig. B.1.

Feature 1: carbonised post

Feature 1 consists of a concentration of carbonised wood. It is located within the fenced Burial Ground 1, about 10m from Burial B92/B, at 180M and an elevation of 2m. It was exposed in an eroded section of the Level 2 palaeosol. The feature is interpreted as a stump or post that had burnt in situ. It is very like the carbonised *Casuarina littoralis* features excavated in the same area during 1987–8 (Best 1989:47). At the time of the survey the feature appeared to be fully exposed on the surface and was rapidly dispersing. A sample of charcoal was collected.

Feature 2: pottery mound

A large mound covered by an exceptionally dense concentration of pottery was located in the eastern corner of the fenced area of Burial Ground 1 at 140M. A few small stones and pieces of coral were scattered amongst the pottery. This feature was in situ within the eroding Level 2 matrix. The pottery was unusual in that it consisted almost entirely of sherds with very fine to medium thickness walls which had elaborate cross-hatched paddle impressed decoration, often with rim notching. Some also had finger pinching, or finger nail impressions around the shoulder. A few sherds from trays with mat impressions were also noted but they were comparatively rare.

Because of the proximity of Feature 2 to the storm line, at less than 1m in elevation, it was in danger of being washed away at any moment. The mound was therefore excavated and all material including a very large amount of pottery was removed to the Fiji Museum.

A grid of 1m square quadrants was laid out over the feature. This grid measured 6m (N/S) by 7m (E/W) and covered the whole feature (Fig. B.2). A plan of the materials exposed on the surface was drawn up, then the surface material, most of which consisted of pottery, was collected and bagged by quadrant.

Once the surface material was removed it became clear that most of the pottery was contained within the upper 10 cm of the black-brown Level 2 palaeosol and that below this level the palaeosol became lighter in colour and contained fewer sherds to a total depth of 30 cm. The palaeosol was removed by quadrant. Each quadrant was spaded off down to the green-brown basal sand below. The material was sieved through a 5 mm mesh and all material, with the exception of some of the larger stones and pieces of coral, were bagged. Amongst the stone recovered were chert cores and flakes. The excavation established that although the upper few centimetres of Feature 2 had been eroded, and some pottery had deflated, the feature was substantially intact and was stratigraphically part of the Level 2 palaeosol. The large quantities of pottery and stone recovered during the excavation make available for analysis an unusual and unique sample of the artefacts known to be associated with the Level 2 occupation of the dunes.

Feature 3: possible Lapita pot

Part of an eroding, but still in situ pot, was recovered from the western corner of a large coral and pottery mound located at approximately 440M

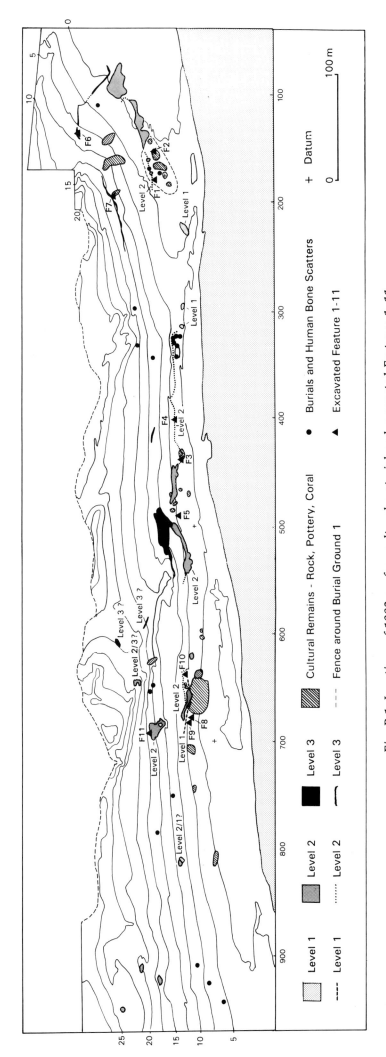

Fig. B.1 Locations of 1992 surface cultural material and excavated Features 1–11.

and elevation of 4m. This appears to be an example of late Eastern Lapita plainware. It was excavated from within an exposed dark brown, compacted sandy soil similar to the Level 2 palaeosol exposed nearby (see Testpit Transect 5).

Feature 4: *fireplace*

Feature 4 consists of a small fireplace exposed at the edge of the eroding Level 2 palaeosol. It is located around 400M, just above the storm line at an elevation of 4m.

The feature was half sectioned and one half was fully exposed. A section drawing and plan were made (Fig. B.3). The fireplace was scoop shaped. It measured 35 cm in diameter and was 8 cm deep at the centre. At the base of the feature was a layer consisting of a very dense greasy charcoal/sand matrix with large pieces of charcoal mixed through it. Over this matrix was a 2–5 cm thick layer of red,

baked clay. Samples of both the charcoal and the baked clay were collected. Sitting on the baked clay and around the lower (seaward) side were 14 red basaltic rocks and several white river rocks. Several pieces of Level 2 tray pottery were scattered on top of the feature. A sample of this pottery was collected.

The arrangement of the rocks and the layer of baked clay found in the centre of the feature suggest it may have been a fireplace used at least in part for firing pottery. If so, this feature is the first evidence recovered which suggests that the firing of pottery was among the activities carried out on the dunes. Alternatively, the presence of Level 2 trays, suggested by Birks (1973:45) to have been used for the evaporation of salt, may indicate the fireplace was a hearth used for this purpose.

Feature 5: *Lapita pot*

Fragments of an expanded rim, Late Eastern Lapita plainware pot were collected from a location just seaward of a large Level 2 exposure at around 490M and 5m elevation. The sherds were in a cluster less than 1m in diameter. They were within a matrix of loose, grey surface sand up to 20 cm deep. The deepest sherds were resting on basal green-brown sand, indicating they were not in situ

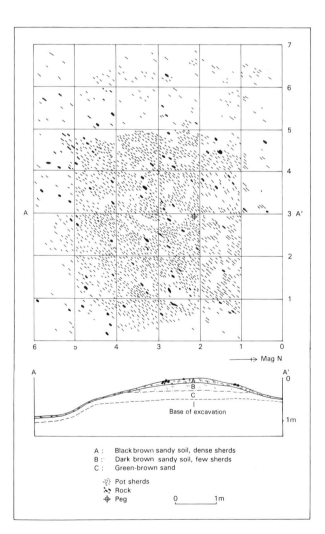

Fig. B.2 Plan and stratigraphic profile of Feature 2: Pottery mound.

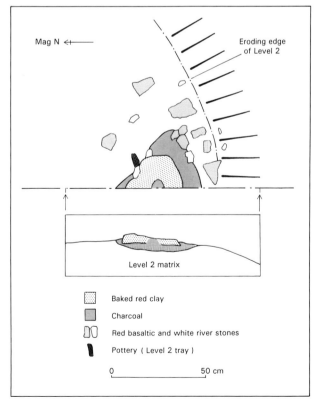

Fig. B.3 Plan and stratigraphic profile of Feature 4: Fireplace.

and had probably deflated down onto this surface (see Testpit Transects 6 and 7 for further information on stratigraphy).

Feature 6: pottery, stone and charcoal concentration

Feature 6 is located at the eastern end of the mapped area and is part of the eroding edge of Level 3 situated at 130–140M and an elevation of 5.5m. It consists of scattered pottery and stone and includes the remains of at least 5 posts, possibly more. Feature 6 is approximately 10m in diameter.

The surface of Feature 6 was cleared of loose sand and all exposed cultural material was located on a plan map (Fig. B.4). On the higher, southwestern side of the feature was a row of three, in situ, carbonised wood posts surrounded by scattered potsherds. The westernmost post was half sectioned and all the charcoal collected. It was found to be shallow suggesting that most of the Level 3 palaeosol had been eroded, leaving only a disk of carbonised wood in the base of the soil matrix. Pottery was also present down to the base of the palaeosol matrix. It seems likely that the post may have burnt above the ground and smouldered down to the base of the palaeosol. Deeper sections of post below the smoulder zone would have rotted in the underlying sand and left no trace. In line with the three posts to the east were two circular patches of red stained sand that may be burnt sand left by two further carbonised posts. A further scatter of charcoal indicated another possible post located to the north of this alignment.

The eastern half of Feature 6 was a deflated area of broken river stones, small coral rocks, dense pottery, small cores of chert and flecks of burned clay. The material lying on the higher western side appeared to be in situ in the upper surface of the Level 3 palaeosol, while on the downsloping eastern side most of the palaeosol had eroded and the cultural material was clearly deflated onto loose sand. There was little charcoal amongst the rock and pottery suggesting it was more likely a working area than a *lovo* (oven) area.

Testpit Transect 17, excavated across Feature 6, indicated that the feature lay just at the edge of where the Level 3 palaeosol dropped sharply to the northeast.

Feature 7: pottery concentration

Feature 7 consisted of a concentration of pottery eroding from the base of the exposed edge of Level 3 located at around 200M and 10m in elevation. The

sherds were eroding from the Level 3 exposure then gradually scattering downslope. Four small coral rocks were also noted amongst the sherds. The area of scattered pottery measured approximately 3.5m across the slope and 10m downslope. Although the area of scattered pottery was quite large, the sherds appeared to have all come from only one or two pots. For this reason it was decided to collect the sherds.

The sherds were collected in two parts. The upper part of the feature, from the Level 3 exposure to 2m downslope, was surface collected

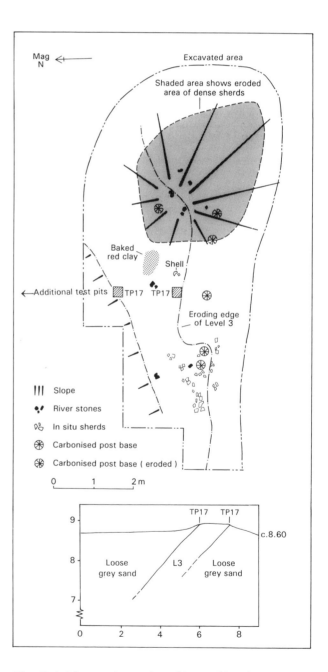

Fig. B.4 Plan and stratigraphic profile of Feature 6: Pottery and rock concentration.

then trowelled. Most sherds were collected in situ from within the upper part of the eroding edge of the Level 3 palaeosol. The lower 8m of the feature were simply surface collected as all sherds in this area were in loose shifting sand and had clearly been displaced downhill. A further cluster of sherds within the uneroded section of the Level 3 matrix was not excavated, although this cluster appeared to be the original source of the collected sherds.

Feature 8: pottery concentration

Feature 8 consisted of a concentration of broken scattered sherds measuring about 2m by 1.4m in area. It was located on the western side of a large Level 2 pottery blow-out, and just downslope of the eroding Level 1 palaeosol, at approximately 680M and an elevation of 5.5m. Only unprovenanced sherds present in the upper 2 cm of loose grey surface sand were collected, however the presence of Late Eastern Lapita expanded rim forms amongst the sherds indicate they probably originate from Level 1.

Feature 9: pottery concentration

Feature 9 consisted of a concentration of broken potsherds measuring about 1m in diameter. It was located at approximately 680M, just uphill and west of Feature 8 at an elevation of 6m. A small exposure of the Level 1 palaeosol was present 2m above Feature 9 and 5m further uphill the Level 2 palaeosol was exposed (see Testpit Transect 8 for details of stratigraphy in this area).

Initially, a 1m by 1m square was surface collected and 3 cm of loose grey sand was removed. Beneath the loose sand was a moist, black to brown soil containing further sherds. The soil was removed to a depth of 20 cm. Pottery was recovered from throughout this layer. The soil was then removed to a depth of 30 cm. Between 20 cm and 30 cm pottery was only present in the northeastern corner of the square. This pottery included rim sherds with the characteristically expanded and notched rims of Late Eastern Lapita plainware. The square was then extended approximately 50 cm to the north and east and two further clusters of sherds were recovered at around 30 cm below the surface. Excavation continued to a depth of 45 cm where a green-

brown basal sand was found. No sherds were recovered below 30 cm in depth.

Sherds recovered from Feature 9 included forms characteristic of both Level 1 and Level 2 pottery. However, only one soil layer was excavated. Two explanations are possible. The Level 2 sherds could have deflated down onto the Level 1 surface below. Alternatively, at this location Levels 1 and 2 may consist of a single soil layer with Level 2 sherds present in the upper part and Level 1 sherds present in the lower part.

Feature 10: Lapita pots

The remains of two eroded Late Eastern Lapita plainware pots were collected from the eastern corner of a large Level 2 pottery blow-out located at around 640M and an elevation of 5.5m. Both pots were lying at or close to the interface of the Level 1/2 palaeosol and the green-brown basal sand. It was unclear whether the pots were in situ or whether erosion and deflation had served to mix them with a Level 2 deposit. Further details of the stratigraphy in this area can be found in the discussion of Testpit Transect 8. The excavated area was less than 50 cm in diameter and the maximum depth of the removed sherds was 20 cm.

The two pots were quite different. One was a completely plain, coarse, thick walled pot with a strongly carinated shoulder and an everted rim – somewhat similar to Vessel 23, Type 1D illustrated in Birks (1973:99). The second was a very fine, thin walled pot with a notched rim similar to Vessel 26, Type 1C illustrated in Birks (1973:95).

Feature 11: Level 2 pot

Feature 11 consisted of a group of sherds resting as a cluster on and in loose sand. It was located on the northern side of a large Level 2 exposure at approximately 690M and an elevation of 15m. The sherds were recovered from an area measuring about 75 cm in diameter. They were all from a fine walled *kuro*, some with cross-hatch paddle impressed decoration. Although the sherds all appeared to be from a single pot broken in situ they were not directly associated with any of the three palaeosols. It is thought likely that the sherds originate from Level 2. For details of the stratigraphy in this area see discussion of Testpit Transect 10.

Appendix C
Excavated burials 1991 and 1992

Detailed descriptions of the burials excavated in 1991 by Crosby and Matararaba and those excavated during the 1992 survey are given below. The precise locations of the burials are shown in Figs. 4.2a–d and they are summarised in Fig. 6.1. Details of the excavation methods and conservation treatments are given in Chapter 3.

Burial B91/1

Burial B91/1 was excavated by Crosby and Matararaba in July/August 1991. In December 1990, Mr. David Clotworthy of Club Masa Resort had brought to the attention of the Fiji Museum an exposed cranium. He placed the burial under a temporary cover of driftwood and sand. The burial was located on what was then a moderately sloping section of the dunes, some 30–40 metres north of the storm surge line, in what appeared to be a recently exposed section of a black-brown sandy palaeosol. Spade testing at the time of excavation, confirmed by testpitting during the 1992 survey, identified this palaeosol as Level 2. There was only a small amount of fragmentary human bone found on the surface in association with the burial and no pottery or other artefacts.

The burial comprised a group of four adult skeletons positioned together in the upper surface of the palaeosol (Fig. C.1). The crania were found resting on the highly moist Level 2 surface while post cranial material was found bedded a up to 10–15 cm into the soil layer, suggesting they had been buried by the excavation of shallow scoops into the soil towards the end of the Level 2 occupation period. Spade testing indicated that the Level 2 surface at the time of burial sloped down slightly to the north at an approximate gradient of 1:20 but remained level in an east–west direction.

There was no evidence of any surface covering placed over the skeletons other than the thin deposit of Level 2 matrix covered by moist grey wind deposited sand. The excavation recovered no fragments of coral or basaltic stones similar to those used to cover burials in the area of Burial Ground 1. Bone degradation was severe. The most severely damaged bones were those raised above the surface of Level 2 (crania and knees). Preservation increased from south to north, individuals at the southern margin of the burial being the most prone to erosion and suffering the highest degree of exposure and drying. Excavation proved difficult due to the moist sand conditions, poor degree of preservation and squally weather conditions at the time.

The four skeletons were found in flexed positions, positioned on their backs, crania slightly elevated, with legs drawn up. The feet were positioned below the pelvis and the arms were placed variously down the side of the body, drawn up across the chest, or placed across the lap. All four individuals were placed in parallel alignment with their heads to the west and feet to the east. All four individuals appear to have been buried as a single event having been carefully arranged with no evidence of disturbance or redeposition of any bones.

The four individuals may have been buried as two discrete pairs. The left forearm of Individual A directly overlay the right arm (flexed) of Individual B. The left humerus and wrist of Individual C directly overlay the right shoulder and forearm respectively of Individual D. Individuals B and C were placed at the same level, apparently laid side by side, the right hand of Individual C very partially overlying the left hand of Individual B.

The grouped burial arrangement of flexed individuals oriented facing to the east or northeast is clearly similar in every respect to those excavated in Burial Ground 1 by Best (Best 1989; Visser 1994). If Best's findings on the reservation of coral mounds

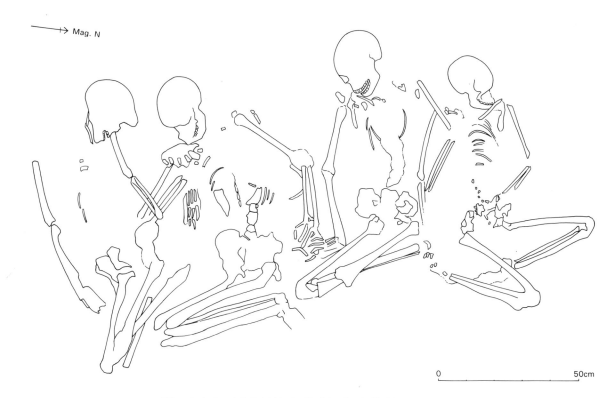

Fig. C.1 Burial B91/1, Individuals A (left) to D (right).

for individuals of presumed higher status are correct, the absence of any coral or stone covering associated with this burial may be significant.

Burial B91/2

Burial B91/2 was excavated by Crosby and Matararaba in August 1991, having been identified by them during an earlier reconnaissance survey (Crosby 1991b). It was located at c.900M on a steeply sloping section of dune face circa 75m north of the high tide line, well to the west of any previously reported burials. It was not marked in any way and no cultural debris was found in close association, although further scatters of badly eroded human bone were noticed to the west and southwest. At the time of the excavation, however, an eroding edge of the Level 2 palaeosol was exposed running across the dune face circa 20m to the north at an elevation of circa 2.5m above the burial. The palaeosol was spilling characteristic Level 2 pottery, including fragments of leaf impressed trays and sherds from pots decorated by finger pinching, fingernail gouging, asymmetric incision and rim notching, all of which have been identified by Best (1984) as distinctive markers of ceramic changes occurring in Fiji during the 3rd century AD.

The burial included three individuals, two of which (A and B) had been exposed earlier in the year and were re-covered in order to protect them for excavation (Fig. C.2). The third individual (C) was found circa 1m west of Individual B and only a bundle of disarticulated leg bones were uncovered (not illustrated).

When first discovered, Individual A was complete and included a largely intact cranium positioned more or less vertically, facing slightly south of west. Individual B had apparently been exposed for some period, the skull was badly smashed, the post-cranial skeleton above the pelvis had been badly eroded, and the legs above the lower shins had been smashed or removed. By the time they were excavated, the driftwood pile placed to protect the skeletons had been interfered with, the skull of Individual A had also been smashed and there was no trace of the legs of Individual C.

The excavations revealed that the two individuals had been buried together in a fully articulated condition. Individual A lay on its back in a flat position, with the arms laid down the sides and the legs drawn up with the knees together and the feet positioned slightly underneath the pelvis on either side. The unnatural positioning of the feet as such indicates that the body had at least partially decomposed prior to burial. Individual B also lay on its back and had been positioned beside Individual A to the south and slight-

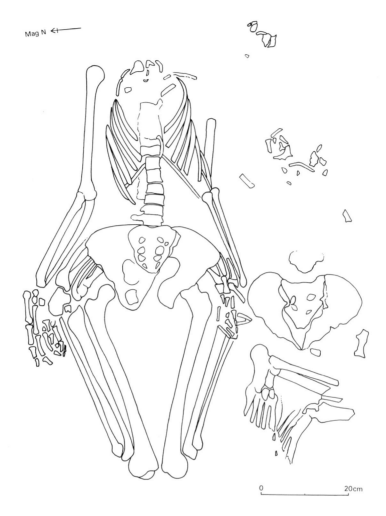

Mag N

0   20cm

Fig. C.2 Burial B91/2, Individuals A (left) and B (right).

ly to the west, so that its head would have rested at the level of Individual A's shoulder. Its arms had also been laid down the sides of the body, its right hand slightly underlying the left hand of Individual A. The legs had been drawn up with the knees pointing to the south and the feet placed together in a more natural position at the base of the pelvis.

The excavations did not recover any cultural material and established that the skeletons were not positioned within a cultural palaeosol, but lay in loose drift sand. It is tempting by association to provenance them to the eroding Level 2 palaeosol to the north, perhaps having been buried in a pit excavated into underlying loose sand. The configuration of the group compares well with the Level 2 burials of Burial Ground 1 and of Burials B91/1 discussed above. It is also tempting to suggest that the positioning of the individuals indicates the burial of a partially decomposed large, presumably male individual, with a smaller, presumably female, undecomposed individual placed in a subordinate position at its side. The relatively good condition of the bone recovered, however, and the west-facing orientation of this group suggest they may have a different, somewhat later provenance than those recovered further to the east.

The subsequent excavation by Burley of two superimposed burials in loose sand approximately one kilometre further to the west (Burley 1997:36–39, West Sigatoka Dune Burial 1a,b), may support the later date. Burley thought those burials to be associated with a nearby hearth dated at c.230 BP. Numerous surface scatters of relatively "fresh" looking human bone found immediately west of B91/2 during the 1992 survey and during Hudson's 1993 excavations may also indicate that the burials on this part of the dunes are relatively recent.

Burial B92/A

Burial B92/A was first identified by Sepeti Matararaba during a routine inspection of the dunes in July 1992. The burial was located at the extreme eastern end of the visible in-situ cultural deposit on the dunes, directly on the line of access onto the dunes from Club Masa. At the time of Matararaba's visit, the upper surface of a cranium and the knees of a set of legs, apparently drawn up in a flexed position, were visible above loose surface sand. Matararaba covered the bones to protect them until they were fully excavated during the 1992 survey.

The burial was excavated from a mixed matrix of loose and dry surface sand overlying a slightly consolidated matrix of moister sand. It was not associated with any of the visible palaeosols. Level 2 could be seen as an exposed soil layer and pottery scatter 15 metres to the southeast and approximately 1.5 metres lower in elevation. Level 3 could be seen 10 metres to the northwest running as an exposed edge of an eroding palaeosol running from high on the dunes to the northeast, north and east of the burial.

Test excavations from Level 3 (Testpit Transect 17, Feature 6) indicate that, on this part of the dunes, Level 3 sloped down from west to east. That is, Level 3 has been eroded from the area of the Burial B92/A and would previously have overlain the burial, perhaps by a metre or more. Conversely, Best's excavations, and Testpit Transect 16 show that Level 2 in the vicinity remained relatively level in an east–west direction and probably dipped slightly from south to north. That is, Level 2 could be expected to be found intact underlying Burial B92/A by approximately 1.5–2 metres. The burial is therefore thought likely to post-date the Level 2 occupation.

A large number of fragments of cranial and leg bones were found in the upper 5 cm of loose surface sand covering the burial. These bones were collected and bagged without conservation treatment. They represent bone damaged during the brief exposure of cranium and knees prior to Matararaba's discovery of the skeleton.

The upper part of the cranium and knees had been severely damaged by exposure and were in poor condition. The rest of the skeleton, including maxillary structure and mandible was complete and was found in fair condition. All teeth were present. The bones, however, were extremely fragile and, despite consolidation, commonly fractured or disintegrated when lifted.

The skeleton appeared to represent a small but developmentally mature individual. There was no sign of incomplete epiphyseal fusion. The teeth were badly worn. There was no apparent sign of trauma.

The skeleton had been placed in a semi-flexed position lying along the dune with the head to the east and the feet to the west (Fig. C.3). The upper body had been placed lying flat with the head slightly raised and the legs drawn up. Both cranium and legs had fallen to the south. The arms had been placed with the right forearm laid across the lower chest and the left hand drawn up to the left shoulder.

There were no artefacts of any kind found with the skeleton. Nor was there any surface pottery or other cultural material apparent within 10 metres of the burial. The burial had not been covered by stones or coral boulders.

The absence of stratigraphic context precludes an interpretation of how or when the individual was buried on the dunes. While the burial resembles the Level 2 skeletons excavated by Best, both in the

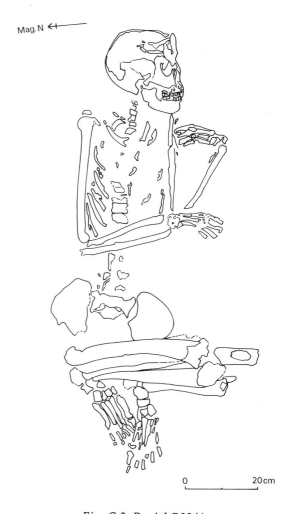

Mag. N

0   20cm

Fig. C.3 Burial B92/A.

degree of bone preservation and the burial position, it could only have originated from the Level 2 occupation if it had been positioned on or over a metre of loose sand overlying the Level 2 palaeosol. It is more likely, stratigraphically, that the burial was positioned in a deep pit excavated from Level 3. A third option, that the burial post-dates Level 3 and was placed in loose sand after the Level 3 palaeosol had already eroded from this section of the dune face is unlikely given the relatively poor preservation and apparent antiquity of the bone and the close proximity of the eroding edge of the still intact palaeosol.

Burial B92/B

This burial was discovered by Crosby during a routine inspection of the dunes in May 1992, and was recovered during the 1992 survey. It consisted of a scatter of fragmentary surface bone located at the northern margin of the burial ground area excavated by Best along the current line of the eroding edge of Level 2. The bone was found in loose association with surface scatters of Level 2 pottery, stone and charcoal. It lay just beyond the margins of Best's excavations as reconstructed from his datum. Best had to stop his excavations in this area in 1988 due to the great depth of loose surface sand (see Plate 12).

The burial was in extremely poor condition, apparently having been exposed to the surface for some time prior to its discovery. Loose fragments of bone in the surface sand, including fragments of cranium, were bagged without conservation treatment.

Following the removal of a 5 cm layer of surface sand, fragments of in situ bone were found embedded in the black-brown consolidated matrix of Level 2. In situ bones included fragments of cranium and mandible, left and right humerus, clavicle, ribs, pelvis, left and right femora and foot (Fig. C.4). The lower limbs were missing having been destroyed by erosion and exposure.

The skeleton appeared to have been positioned similarly to those excavated by Best. It lay in a semi-flexed position on its back, its head slightly raised and facing to the east. Its arms had been placed with the left forearm positioned across the stomach and its right hand raised towards the left shoulder, crossing the chest. Leg position could not be precisely determined, although a fragment of foot immediately beneath the pelvis indicated that the body had been positioned with the legs drawn up

No coral or other stones were found associated with the burial, as was the case with most of the skeletons located at the outer margins of the burial ground excavated by Best. This accounts for the skeleton's poor preservation. The burial appears certain to be contemporary with those excavated by Best, representing an individual buried at the edge of the burial ground.

Burial B92/C

This burial was almost completely eroded. A scatter of teeth was collected from an area measuring approximately one metre in diameter. These remains were removed to the Fiji Museum. The teeth were not examined in detail but a brief examination suggested more than one individual was probably represented.

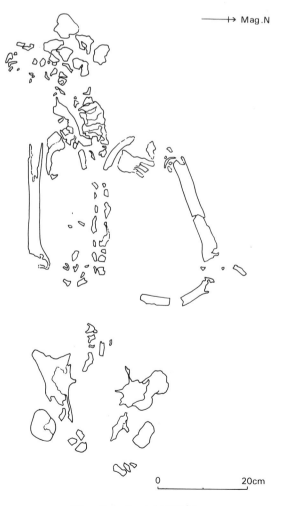

Fig. C.4 Burial B92/B.

Appendix D
Investigations behind the dunes 1992 and 1993

In the course of mapping the main dunes, it was noticed that pottery was eroding out of the exposed black soil in the cut bank along the side of the road to Club Masa. Sherds were surface collected in three locations (Fig. D.1). The majority of these sherds came from Beach Ridges 1 and 3 with only a small number recovered from Beach Ridge 2. A preliminary analysis of these sherds suggested a long span of occupation. Late Lapita Plainware rims, paddle impressed decoration and vessel forms characteristic of Level 3 pottery were all present suggesting the full time span of occupation found

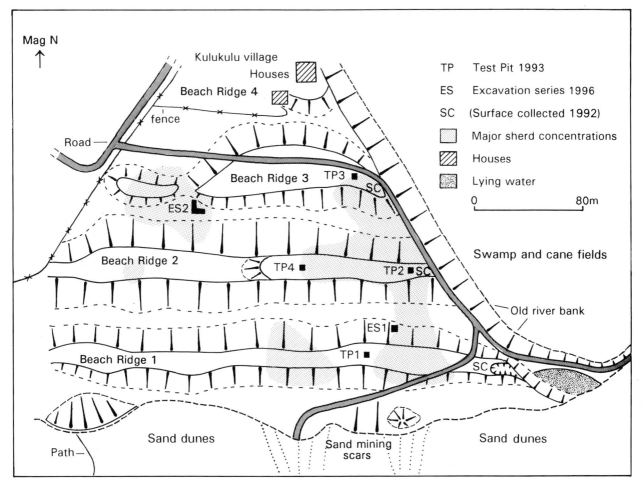

Fig. D.1 Survey map of the beach ridges at the back of dunes showing the locations of the 1992 surface collections and the four 1993 testpit excavations.

on the main dunes was also present on these ridges. If this proved to be the case it opened the possibility that the structural remains of settlements which were so ephemeral on the dunes might be better preserved in this more protected location. Similarly, faunal remains and other quickly eroded materials might survive here when they would not on the dunes. Returning to the dunes to conduct test excavations in this area was therefore considered a high priority.

Funding from the Green Foundation and the University of Auckland Research Committee enabled Yvonne Marshall to return to Sigatoka in April 1993. At this time the beach ridges behind the dune were mapped and four testpits excavated (Fig. D.1). This work was carried out with the assistance of Sepeti Matararaba, Field Officer with the Fiji Museum, and Joji Chongsu of Kulukulu village. Vicky Luker and Farhaz Khan also volunteered their time to help.

In the course of mapping, four beach ridges running parallel to the back of the dunes were identified. Beach Ridge 1 runs along the foot of the dunes (Plate 17). Beach Ridge 2, alongside it, is the highest and most prominent of the ridges and has a small knoll near its midpoint. Beach Ridge 3 is low, wide and quite flat. Its northern side has been disturbed by the Club Masa road which also cuts across the eastern ends of all three ridges. Eroded pottery and black cultural soil were associated with all three cuts (Plate 16). The most southerly house of Kulukulu village is built on the eastern end of Beach Ridge 4. Scatters of pottery were identified in disturbed soil around this house. A fifth beach ridge, shown on old aerial photographs to the south of Beach Ridge 1, has now become buried beneath the advancing backslope of the dunes.

The distribution of surface and eroding cultural material behind the dunes suggested two possible patterns. Firstly, occupation may be associated with

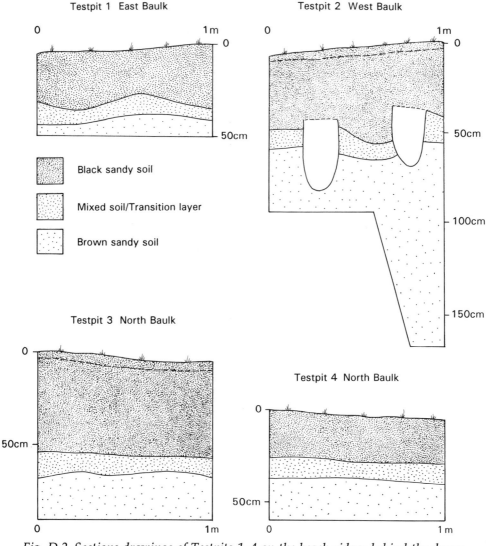

Fig. D.2 Sections drawings of Testpits 1–4 on the beach ridges behind the dunes.

high points and, therefore, cultural remains would be present along the tops of each of the ridges. Secondly, occupation may have been restricted to the eastern ends of all four ridges and associated with the steep paleo-cut bank along the eastern margin which falls away into a wide flat area of swamps and cane fields (Plates 17 and 18). This bank is the western edge of an old river channel. Despite being disturbed by the building of the Club Masa road it is clear that the southern end of this bank extends beneath the advancing north face of the dunes.

The four testpits were positioned in order to establish whether cultural deposits were distributed along the crests of the ridges or whether they were restricted to the eastern ends of each ridge, along the bank of the old river channel. The stratigraphy in all four testpits was very similar (Fig. D.2). Beneath the turf was a black sandy soil which varied in depth from 25–60 cm. Cultural remains were found only in this layer. Below the black soil was a transitional layer approximately 10 cm deep which graded into a natural brown sandy soil.

The results were conclusive. Testpits 1 and 4 were largely sterile. This was surprising given that Testpit 4 had been placed in the small knoll on Ridge 2, the highest point along the four ridges. In contrast, significant cultural remains consisting of pottery and charcoal were found in Testpits 2 and 3, indicating that the preferred occupation sites were located at the eastern ends of the ridges, along the riverbank. In these two testpits the black sandy soil in which the cultural remains were found was both deeper and darker than in Testpits 1 and 4. In Testpit 2 posthole features were also identified (Fig. D.2).

While surface or excavated pottery deposits were recovered from the eastern ends of all four beach ridges, no significant deposits were recovered from Testpits 1 and 4 and no surface pottery was found elsewhere on the ridges or in the valleys between. This pattern points strongly to settlement along the bank of the old river channel. The result suggests that the river itself was a focus for settlement and that the river course passed along the paleo-cut bank during the occupation of the beach ridges.

The pottery recovered during surface collections in 1992 and from the 1993 testpits is summarised by main form and decorative diagnostic categories in Tables 3 and 4 and is listed by surface and excavated contexts in Table 5. Despite plough disturbance of the upper 45 cm, each of the collections are stylistically homogenous, indicating a single period of occupation on each of the beach ridges.

A total of 137 sherds were surface collected from Beach Ridge 1. This pottery came from a large depression cut into the ridge to allow truck access to a sand mining cut (Fig. D.1, Plate 11). It includes rim and neck forms of *kuro* (narrow mouthed cooking pots), oil lamps, *dari* (open, flared rim bowls) and a low incidence of decoration by paddle impressed rib and spot relief, indicating a date of occupation between AD 1000 and AD 1500.

A total of 384 and 370 sherds were recovered from Testpits 2 and 3 respectively. A further 336 sherds were surface collected from the eastern end of Beach Ridge 3. All three collections indicate that the eastern ends of Beach Ridges 2 and 3 were occupied almost exclusively during or shortly after the Level 1 occupation on the front of the dunes.

Ridge	Context	Carin. bowl	Flat bowl	Globular bowl	Globular pot	Early kuro	Kuro	Dari	Oil lamp
1	Surface	0	0	0	0	0	7	1	1
	TP1/0-40cm	0	0	0	0	0	2	0	0
2	TP2/0-30cm	0	0	1	7	0	2	0	0
	TP2/30-45cm	0	1	0	8	0	0	0	0
	TP2/45-50cm	0	1	0	8	0	0	0	0
	TP2/50-60cm	0	0	0	5	0	0	0	0
	TP2/60-70cm	0	0	1	5	0	0	0	0
3	Surface	0	1	3	41	0	0	0	0
	TP3/0-45cm	0	1	0	14	4	0	0	0
	TP3/45-50cm	0	0	0	1	0	0	0	0
	TP3/50-60cm	1	0	0	1	1	0	0	0
	TP3/60-70cm	2	0	0	22	0	0	0	0
	TP3/70-80cm	1	2	1	6	0	0	0	0

Table 3 Numbers of sherds in main vessel form categories.

All are dominated by Late Lapita Plainware rim and neck forms, many of which are finished by wiping and scraping of the exterior surface. They include expanded and/or bevelled rims of globular pots and inturned rims of globular or dish-like bowls similar to those described from Level 1 by Birks (1973:75–113).

The sherds from Beach Ridges 2 and 3, however, are generally less expanded, more rounded and lack the distinctive rim-notching prevalent on the Level 1 sherds from the front of the dunes. This difference, along with a low incidence of dentate shell arc stamping, probably indicates a later occupation, around 300 BC. The presence of the rounded expanded rims together with a sherd of heavy rib relief in Testpit 3 has been described by Crosby as indicative of a transitional potting technology between late Eastern Lapita plainware and later paddle impressed styles (Crosby 1988:215). The additional presence of some early paddle impressed decorative elements (rib, irregular hatching and some wavy or chevron relief) and early *kuro* rim forms suggests that occupation of both beach ridges may have continued from circa 400 BC to AD 200, spanning the period of interruption between Levels 1 and 2 on the front of the dunes.

In 1996 the Simon Fraser University Fieldschool followed up on this preliminary work. They dug a grid of 73 shovel test holes covering the area between the Club Masa Road and the base of the dunes (Burley 1996:23). On the basis of the pottery recovered in these shovel tests they defined the main areas of pottery concentration. As anticipated, the greatest concentrations of pottery were found along the ridge tops at their eastern ends (Fig. D.1).

The comparative lack of cultural remains in the valleys between the ridges was confirmed by an excavation, ES1, located by Burley just north of and at the base of Beach Ridge 1 (see Fig. D.1). A 3 x 3 metre area was excavated revealing a stratigraphy identical to that found in 1993 (Burley 1996:26–30). A total of only 280 sherds was recovered, a relatively small number for such a large area. Of these, 10% were decorated. They included paddle impressed pottery with cross hatched, squared and parallel rib designs, paddled spot relief, (unspecified) incised sherds and "one rim sherd with side-tool indentations on the lip". This pottery is thought by Burley to be consistent with a date after 900 BP (Burley 1996:29), although the undistinguished nature of the stratigraphy, excavation by arbitrary spits, and the presence of "Lapitoid" rims in his nearby shovel unit 1 would seem to indicate the likelihood of a mixed ceramic assemblage.

Burley's shovel test survey turned up one unexpected feature; a large concentration of dense pottery at the western end of Ridge 3. A second series of 11 one metre square excavations, ES2, were put in to investigate this feature (see Fig. D.1). The same basic stratigraphy was again present (Burley 1996:28–34). A large number of sherds (1691) were recovered, of which 5% were decorated.

Burley asserts that this pottery, which included parallel rib paddle impressed designs, paddled spot relief, incising, wiping, scratching, and tool impression, is consistent with a later prehistoric occupation. Such a date is supported by a radiocarbon date of 510 ± 60 BP which he obtained from a charcoal sample associated with a hearth feature. Once again, however, the relatively mixed nature

Ridge	Context	Dentate:shell	Red slipped	Wiped	Scraped	PI:heavy rib	PI:irregular	PI:rib	PI:spot
1	Surface	0	0	0	0	0	0	2	2
2	TP2/0-30cm	0	0	14	0	0	0	0	0
	TP2/30-45cm	0	1	4	4	0	0	1	0
	TP2/45-50cm	0	0	10	3	0	0	1	0
	TP2/50-60cm	1	0	7	0	0	0	0	0
	TP2/60-70cm	0	0	1	0	0	0	0	0
3	Surface	0	0	22	4	0	0	0	0
	TP3/0-45cm	0	0	3	1	0	0	1	0
	TP3/45-50cm	0	0	1	0	0	0	0	0
	TP3/50-60cm	0	0	2	1	0	3	0	0
	TP3/60-70cm	0	0	16	1	0	0	0	0
	TP3/70-80cm	0	0	5	0	1	0	0	0

Table 4 Number of sherds in main decorative/surface finish categories.

Ridge	Context	Number	Category*	Form**	Vessel type	Decn./surface finish***
1	Surface	2	C43/B60	Rim, kuro, normal	Kuro	
1	Surface	1	C87/B142	Rim, bowl, inturned, flared	Dari	
1	Surface	1	B91	Rim, oil lamp, rounded, flared	Oil lamp	
1	Surface	1	C69/B117	Rim, bowl, rounded	Open bowl	Pl:rib
1	Surface	1	C54	Rim, kuro, pointed, inclined in	Kuro	
1	Surface	4	C122/B162	Neck, sharp	Kuro	
1	Surface	2	C196/B226	DBS		Pl:spot
1	Surface	1	C190/B223	DBS		Pl:rib
1	Surface	124	C167-71/B214	PBS		
1	TP1/0-40cm	2	C49	Rim, kuro, rounded	Kuro	
1	TP1/0-40cm	12	C167-71/B214	PBS		
2	TP2/0-30cm	1	C58/B84	Rim, bowl, inturned, rounded	Globular bowl	
2	TP2/0-30cm	1	C52	Rim, kuro, rounded-pointed	Kuro	
2	TP2/0-30cm	1	C56	Rim, kuro, rounded, raised edges	Kuro	
2	TP2/0-30cm	1	C27/B45	Rim, pot, concave, normal	Globular pot	
2	TP2/0-30cm	1	C21/B34	Rim, pot, expanded, concave, bevelled	Globular pot	Wiped
2	TP2/0-30cm	1	C22/B37	Rim, pot, expanded, bevelled (rounded)	Globular pot	Wiped
2	TP2/0-30cm	1	C122/B162	Neck, not measurable		
2	TP2/0-30cm	4	C135/B181	Neck, rounded	Globular pot	Wiped
2	TP2/0-30cm	8	C177	DBS		Wiped
2	TP2/0-30cm	1	C178/B215	DBS		Dentate (complex)
2	TP2/0-30cm	72	C167-71/B214	PBS		
2	TP2/30-45cm	1	B102	Rim, bowl, pointed, inturned	Subglobular bowl	Red slipped
2	TP2/30-45cm	1	C21/B34	Rim, pot, expanded, concave, bevelled	Globular pot	Wiped
2	TP2/30-45cm	1	C27/B45	Rim, pot, expanded, concave, normal	Globular pot	Wiped
2	TP2/30-45cm	3	C21/B34	Rim, pot, concave, bevelled	Globular pot	Scraped
2	TP2/30-45cm	1	C27/B45	Rim, pot, concave, normal	Globular pot	Scraped
2	TP2/30-45cm	1	C135/B181	Neck, rounded	Globular pot	Wiped
2	TP2/30-45cm	1	C135/B181	Neck, rounded	Globular pot	
2	TP2/30-45cm	1	C177	DBS		Wiped
2	TP2/30-45cm	1	C190/B223	DBS		Pl:rib
2	TP2/30-45cm	51	C167-71/B214	PBS		
2	TP2/45-50cm	1	C27/B45	Rim, pot, bevelled	Globular pot	
2	TP2/45-50cm	2	C27/B45	Rim, pot, concave, bevelled	Globular pot	Wiped
2	TP2/45-50cm	1	C23/B38	Rim, pot, expanded, concave, flat	Globular pot	Wiped
2	TP2/45-50cm	2	C22/B37	Rim, pot, expanded, bevelled (rounded)	Globular pot	
2	TP2/45-50cm	1	C61/B100	Rim, bowl, rounded, inturned	Subglobular bowl	
2	TP2/45-50cm	2	C135/B181	Neck, rounded	Globular pot	
2	TP2/45-50cm	7	C177	DBS		Wiped
2	TP2/45-50cm	1	C190/B223	DBS		Pl:rib
2	TP2/45-50cm	3	new	DBS		Scraped
2	TP2/45-50cm	150	C167-71/B214	PBS		
2	TP2/50-60cm	1	C22/B37	Rim, pot, expanded, bevelled (rounded)	Globular pot	Dentate (shell)
2	TP2/50-60cm	2	C22/B37	Rim, pot, bevelled (rounded)	Globular pot	Wiped
2	TP2/50-60cm	2	C135/B181	Neck, rounded	Globular pot	Wiped
2	TP2/50-60cm	3	C177	DBS		Wiped
2	TP2/50-60cm	31	C167-71/B214	PBS		
2	TP2/60-70cm	1	C27/B45	Rim, pot, bevelled	Globular pot	
2	TP2/60-70cm	1	C27/B45	Rim, pot, expanded, concave, normal	Globular pot	
2	TP2/60-70cm	1	B86	Rim, bowl, flat, inturned	Globular bowl	
2	TP2/60-70cm	3	C135/B181	Neck, rounded	Globular pot	
2	TP2/60-70cm	1	C177	DBS		Wiped
2	TP2/60-70cm	14	C167-71/B214	PBS		
3	Surface	2	C58/B84	Rim, bowl, rounded, inturned	Globular bowl	
3	Surface	3	C27/B45	Rim, pot, bevelled	Globular pot	
3	Surface	1	C27/B45	Rim, pot, concave, bevelled	Globular pot	Scraped
3	Surface	3	C40	Rim, pot, expanded, concave, bevelled	Globular pot	
3	Surface	1	C40	Rim, pot, expanded, concave, bevelled	Globular pot	Scraped
3	Surface	5	C27/B45	Rim, pot, concave, bevelled	Globular pot	
3	Surface	5	C27/B45	Rim, pot, concave, bevelled	Globular pot	Wiped
3	Surface	2	C27/B45	Rim, pot, concave, normal	Globular pot	Wiped
3	Surface	1	C40	Rim, pot, expanded, concave, bevelled	Globular pot	Wiped
3	Surface	1	C40	Rim, pot, expanded, concave, normal	Globular pot	Scraped
3	Surface	1	B82	Rim, bowl, rounded (flared), inturned	Globular bowl	
3	Surface	1	C62/B101	Rim, bowl, rounded-pointed, inturned	Subglobular bowl	
3	Surface	6	C135/B181	Neck, rounded	Globular pot	
3	Surface	9	C135/B181	Neck, rounded	Globular pot	Wiped
3	Surface	2	C138/B184	Neck, sharp-rounded	Globular pot	
3	Surface	2	C138/B184	Neck, sharp-rounded	Globular pot	Wiped
3	Surface	3	C177	DBS		Wiped
3	Surface	1	new	DBS		Scraped
3	Surface	1	C176	DBS		Burnished
3	Surface	1	C203	DBS		Pl:large diamond

Table 5 List of all pottery by collection contexts and ceramic categories.

3	Surface	1	C192/B223	DBS		Pl:wavy
3	Surface	284	C167-71/B214	PBS		
3	TP3/0-45cm	3	C45/B62	Rim, kuro, straight, bevelled	Early kuro	
3	TP3/0-45cm	1	C30/B48	Rim, pot, concave, rounded	Globular pot	Wiped
3	TP3/0-45cm	2	C30/B48	Rim, pot, concave, rounded	Globular pot	
3	TP3/0-45cm	1	B104	Rim, bowl, flat, inturned	Subglobular bowl	
3	TP3/0-45cm	1	C22/B37	Rim, pot, bevelled (rounded)	Globular pot	Wiped
3	TP3/0-45cm	1	C39	Rim, kuro, straight, flat/normal	Early kuro	Pl:rib
3	TP3/0-45cm	1	C22/B37	Rim, pot, bevelled (rounded)	Globular pot	
3	TP3/0-45cm	5	C135/B181	Neck, rounded	Globular pot	
3	TP3/0-45cm	1	C135/B181	Neck, rounded	Globular pot	Scraped
3	TP3/0-45cm	1	C135/B181	Neck, rounded	Globular pot	Wiped
3	TP3/0-45cm	2	C138/B184	Neck, sharp-rounded	Globular pot	
3	TP3/0-45cm	151	C167-71/B214	PBS		
3	TP3/45-50cm	1	C22/B37	Rim, pot, expanded, bevelled (rounded)	Globular pot	
3	TP3/45-50cm	1	C177	DBS		Wiped
3	TP3/45-50cm	9	C167-71/B214	PBS		
3	TP3/50-60cm	1	B95	Rim, bowl, carinated	Carinated bowl	
3	TP3/50-60cm	1	C40	Rim, pot, expanded, concave, bevelled	Globular pot	Wiped
3	TP3/50-60cm	1	C43/B60	Rim, kuro, straight, flat/normal	Early kuro	Scraped
3	TP3/50-60cm	1	C177	DBS		Wiped
3	TP3/50-60cm	3	C183/B222	DBS		Pl:irregular cross
3	TP3/50-60cm	16	C167-71/B214	PBS		
3	TP3/60-70cm	4	C27/B45	Rim, pot, concave, bevelled	Globular pot	Wiped
3	TP3/60-70cm	1	C21/B34	Rim, pot, expanded, concave, bevelled	Globular pot	
3	TP3/60-70cm	1	C27/B45	Rim, pot, bevelled	Globular pot	Scraped
3	TP3/60-70cm	1	B95	Rim, bowl, carinated	Carinated bowl	
3	TP3/60-70cm	1	C62/B101	Rim, flat dish	Carinated bowl	
3'	TP3/60-70cm	4	C135/B181	Neck, rounded	Globular pot	
3	TP3/60-70cm	9	C135/B181	Neck, rounded	Globular pot	Wiped
3	TP3/60-70cm	2	C138/B184	Neck, sharp-rounded	Globular pot	
3	TP3/60-70cm	1	C138/B184	Neck, sharp-rounded	Globular pot	Wiped
3	TP3/60-70cm	2	C177	DBS		Wiped
3	TP3/60-70cm	95	C167-71/B214	PBS		
3	TP3/70-80cm	1	C22/B37	Rim, pot, expanded, concave, bevelled (round	Globular pot	
3	TP3/70-80cm	1	C22/B37	Rim, pot, expanded, concave, bevelled (round	Globular pot	Wiped
3	TP3/70-80cm	1	C27/B45	Rim, pot, concave, bevelled	Globular pot	Wiped
3	TP3/70-80cm	1	C58/B84	Rim, bowl, rounded	Globular bowl	
3	TP3/70-80cm	2	B105	Rim, bowl, flat	Subglobular bowl	
3	TP3/70-80cm	3	C135/B181	Neck, rounded	Globular pot	Wiped
3	TP3/70-80cm	1	C142/B190	Carination, sharp	Carinated bowl	
3	TP3/70-80cm	1	C202	DBS		Pl:heavy rib
3	TP3/70-80cm	34	C167-71/B214	PBS		

*Categories are those defined by Crosby (1988:91-95) and/or Best (1985:Appendix A1)

**DBS = Decorated body sherd; PBS = Plain body sherd

***Pl = Paddle impressed

Table 5 continued.

of the pottery, including wiped sherds usually associated with Level 1 pottery, and at least one sherd each with leaf impressions and rim notching, usually considered characteristic of the Level 2 occupation, indicate that pottery of several periods may be represented.

The presence of this relatively large area of cultural material situated well back from the old riverbank demonstrates the need for further archaeological testing of the beach ridge area. While the distribution of cultural material clearly identifies the ridge tops along the old riverbank as the primary early occupation areas, it also seems likely that more extensive occupation, unassociated with the riverbank occurred later.

The Club Masa road clearly had a significant impact on the archaeological sites distributed along the eastern ends of the beach ridges. Not only did it destroy the eastern ends of the ridges it also opened them up to erosion. When Marshall and Crosby revisited the area in November 1997 they found the area around Testpit 3 had been completely destroyed by erosion and the eastern ends of Ridges 1 and 2 had also eroded badly (Plate 18). It therefore seems unlikely that much remains of the archaeological sites located along the eastern ends of Ridges 1–3. Intact sites may, however, still be present on Beach Ridge 4 at the corner of the Kulukulu settlement and they almost certainly remain on beach ridges south of Beach Ridge 1. Unfortunately, these ridges now lie beneath the advancing north face of the dunes.

References

Allen, J. C. 1984. Pots and Poor Princes: A multidimensional approach to the role of pottery trading in coastal Papua. In S. E. van der Leeuw and A. Pritchard, eds, *The Many Dimensions of Pottery: Ceramics in Archaeology and Anthropology*, pp. 407–463. Instituut voor Praeen Protohistorie, University of Amsterdam.

Allen, J. C. 1985. Comments on Complexity and Trade: A view from Melanesia. *Archaeology in Oceania* 20:49–57.

Allen, J. C., Gosden, C. and White, J. P. 1989. Human Pleistocene Adaptations in the Tropical Island Pacific: Recent evidence from New Ireland, a Greater Australian outlier. *Antiquity* 63:548–561.

Anderson, A., Burke, C. and Clark, G. 1996. Prehistoric Colonisation and Settlement of Fiji: An initial report to the Fiji Museum. Unpublished report held at the Fiji Museum, Suva, Fiji.

Babcock, T. F. 1976. An Analysis and Reanalysis of Taveuni Pottery. Unpublished MA thesis, Eastern New Mexico University.

Babcock, T. F. 1977. A Re-analysis of pottery from fortified sites on Taveuni, Fiji. *Archaeology and Physical Anthropology in Oceania* 7:112–134.

Bellwood, P. S. 1975. The Prehistory of Oceania. *Current Anthropology* 16:1–26.

Bellwood, P. S. 1989. The Colonization of the Pacific: Some current hypotheses. In A. V. S. Hill and S. W. Serjeantson, eds, *The Colonisation of the Pacific: A genetic trail*, 1–59. Clarendon Press, Oxford.

Best, S. B. 1981. Excavations at Site VL 21/5, Naigani Island, Fiji. A preliminary report. Unpublished report held at the Department of Anthropology, University of Auckland.

Best, S. B. 1984. Lakeba: The Prehistory of a Fijian Island. Ph.D. dissertation, Department of Anthropology, University of Auckland.

Best, S. B. 1987a. A Preliminary Report on the Sigatoka Burials. *Domodomo* 3:2–15.

Best, S. B. 1987b. Sigatoka Dune Burials (Site VL 16/1). A Preliminary Report. Unpublished report, University of Auckland.

Best, S. B. 1989. The Sigatoka Dune Burials (Site VL 16/1). Unpublished report, University of Auckland.

Best, S. B. 1993. At the Halls of the Mountain Kings: Fijian and Samoan fortifications: Comparison and Analysis. *Journal of the Polynesian Society* 102:385–447.

Best, S. B., Sheppard, P., Green, R. C. and Parker, R. 1992. Necromancing the Stone: Archaeologists and adzes in Samoa. *Journal of the Polynesian Society* 101:45–85.

Birks, L., 1973. *Archaeological Excavations at Sigatoka Dune Site, Fiji*. Bulletin of the Fiji Museum, No 1. Fiji Times and Herald, Suva.

Birks, L. and Birks, H. 1966. Archaeological Investigations at Sigatoka, Fiji. Unpublished report to the Fiji Museum, Fiji Museum, Suva.

Bott, E. 1982. *Tongan Society at the Time of Captain Cook's Visits: Discussions with Her Majesty Queen Salote Tupou*. The Polynesian Society, Wellington.

de Brisay, K.W. and Evans, K.A. (eds.) 1975. *Salt, The Study of an Ancient Industry*. Colchester Archaeological Group, Colchester.

Burke, C. 1995a. Archaeologist's Report. *Fiji Museum Archaeology Newsletter*. Fiji Museum, Suva.

Burke, C. 1995b. Fieldnotes of 1995 Fiji Museum Excavations at Sigatoka. Manuscript at Fiji Museum, Suva.

Burley, D. V. 1997. Archaeological Research, Sigatoka Dune National Park June 1996. Unpublished report. Department of Archaeology, Simon Fraser University.

Burley, D. V. and Shortland, R. 1999. Report on 1998 Field Work Activities Sigatoka Dunes National Park Viti Levu, Fiji. Unpublished report. Department of Archaeology, Simon Fraser University.

Cabaniuk, S., Tamani, A., Vula, E. and Ratabula, A. 1986. A Draft Advisory Plan for the Conservation and Development of the Sigatoka Sand Dunes for National Park and Reserve Purposes. Unpublished plan, Department of Town and Country Planning, Suva.

Campbell, I. C. 1992. *Island Kingdom: Tonga Ancient & Modern*. Canterbury University Press, Christchurch.

Clark, R. 1979. Language. In J. D. Jennings, ed., *The Prehistory of Polynesia*, pp. 249–270. Australian National University Press, Canberra.

Clark, G. 1997. Preliminary Report on Excavations on Ugaga Island, Beqa, Fiji. Unpublished report held at the Fiji Museum, Suva, Fiji.

Clark, G. n.d. Preliminary Report on Excavations at Navatu (Site 17a), Ra, Viti Levu. Unpublished report held at the Fiji Museum, Suva, Fiji.

Clark, J. T. and Terrell, J. 1978. Archaeology in Oceania. *Annual Review of Anthropology* 7:293–319.

Clunie, F. 1977. *Fijian Weapons and Warfare*. Bulletin of the Fiji Museum No. 2, Fiji Museum, Suva.

Clunie, F. 1986. *Yalo i Viti*. Fiji Museum, Suva.

Crosby, A. D. 1988. Beqa: Archaeology, Structure and History in Fiji. Unpublished MA thesis, University of Auckland.

Crosby, A. D. 1991a. Proposal for Archaeological Survey of Sigatoka Sand Dunes. Unpublished proposal prepared for the Fiji Museum and Department of Town and Country Planning, Suva.

Crosby, A. D. 1991b. Further Burials at the Sigatoka Sand Dunes

(Site VL 16/1). Unpublished report prepared for the Fiji Museum, Suva.

Crosby, A. D. 1991c. Map of archaeological deposits on the Sigatoka Sand Dunes (VL 16/1). Unpublished map held by the author.

Crosby, A. D. 1992. Archaeological Sites at the Sigatoka Sand Dunes: A Preliminary Assessment and Recommendations. Unpublished report prepared for the Fiji Museum, Suva.

Crosby, A. D. and Marshall, Y. M. 1998. Pots and People in Fiji and Western Polynesia. Paper presented to the "Objects and Persons in Western Polynesia Symposium", Sainsbury Centre for the Visual Arts, University of East Anglia, 12–13 November 1998.

Davidson, J. 1977. Western Polynesia and Fiji: prehistoric contact, diffusion and differentiation in adjacent archipelagos. *World Archaeology* 9(1):82–94.

Davidson, J., Hinds, E., Holdaway S. and Leach, F. 1990. The Lapita site of Natunuku, Fiji. *New Zealand Journal of Archaeology* 12:121–155.

Dickinson, W. R. 1968. Singatoka Dune Sands, Viti Levu (Fiji). *Sedimentary Geology* 2:115–124.

Dickinson, W. R. 1980. Foreign Temper at Yanutha on Viti Levu (Petrographic Report WRD-73). Appendix B in T. L. Hunt *Towards Fiji's Past: Archaeological research on southwestern Viti Levu*, pp. 215–217.

Dickinson, W. R., Burley, D. V., Nunn, P. D., Anderson, A., Hope, G., de Biran, A., Burke, C. and Matararaba S. 1998. Geomorphic and Archaeological Landscapes of the Sigatoka Dune Site, Viti Levu, Fiji: Interdisciplinary Investigations. *Asian Perspectives* 37(1):1–31

France, P. 1969. *The Charter of the Land*. Oxford University Press, Melbourne.

Friedman, J. 1981. Notes on Structure and History in Oceania. *Folk* 23:275–295.

Friedman, J. 1982. Catastrophe and Continuity in Social Evolution. In C. Renfrew, M. Rowlands, B. Seagraves, eds, *Theory and Explanation in Archaeology*, pp. 175–196. Academic Press, New York.

Frost, E. L. 1974. *Archaeological Excavations of Fortified Sites on Taveuni, Fiji*. Asian and Pacific Archaeology Series No. 6, University of Hawaii, Honolulu.

Frost, E. L. 1979. Fiji. In J. D. Jennings, ed., *The Prehistory of Polynesia*, pp. 61–81. Australian National University Press, Canberra.

Gallipaud, J. C. 1990. The Physico-chemical Analysis of Ancient Pottery from New Caledonia. In M. Spriggs, ed., *Lapita Design, Form and Composition*, pp. 134–142. *Occasional Papers in Prehistory No. 19*. Department of Prehistory, Australian National University, Canberra.

Garanger, J. 1971. Incised and Applied-relief pottery, its chronology and development in southeastern Melanesia, and extra areal comparisons. *Pacific Anthropological Records* 12:53–66.

Geraghty, P. 1981. Qoma Pottery: A preliminary report. Unpublished report held at the Fiji Museum, Suva.

Geraghty, P. 1993. Pulotu, Polynesian Homeland. *Journal of the Polynesian Society* 104:343–384.

Gifford, E. W. 1949. Excavations in Viti Levu. *Journal of the Polynesian Society* 58:83–90.

Gifford, E. W. 1951 Archaeological Excavations in Fiji. *Anthropological Records* 13 (3) 189–288.

Golson, J. 1961. Report on New Zealand, Western Polynesia, New Caledonia and Fiji. *Asian Perspectives* 5:166–180.

Gosden, C. Towards an understanding of the Regional Archaeological Record from the Arawe Islands, West New Britain, Papua New Guinea. In J. Allen and C. Gosden, eds, *Report of the Lapita Homeland Project*, pp. 205–216. Occasional Papers in Prehistory 20, Research School of Pacific Studies, Australian National University.

Gosden, C. 1992. Production Systems and the Colonization of the Western Pacific. *World Archaeology* 24:55–69.

Gosden, C. 1993. Understanding the Settlement of Pacific Islands in the Pleistocene. In M. A. Smith, M. Spriggs and B. Fankhauser, eds, *Sahul in Review: Pleistocene Archaeology in Australia, New Guinea, and Island Melanesia*, pp. 131–136. Occasional Papers in Prehistory 24, Research School of Pacific Studies, Australian National University.

Gosden, C. and Robertson, N. 1991. Models for Matenkupkum: Interpreting a late Pleistocene site from southern New Ireland, Papua New Guinea. In J. Allen and C. Gosden, eds, *Report of the Lapita Homeland Project*, pp. 20–45. Occasional Papers in Prehistory 20, Research School of Pacific Studies, Australian National University.

Gosden, C. and Specht, J. 1991. Diversity, Continuity and Change in Bismarck Archipelago, Papua New Guinea. In P. S. Bellwood, ed., *Indo-Pacific Prehistory 1990*, Vol. 2, pp. 276–280. Bulletin of the Indo-Pacific Prehistory Association 11, IPPA and Asosiasi Prehistorisi Indonesia, Canberra and Jakarta.

Graves, M. and Green, R. C. (eds) 1993. *The Evolution and Organisation of Prehistoric Society in Polynesia*. New Zealand Archaeological Association Monograph 19, New Zealand Archaeological Association, Auckland.

Green, R. C. 1963a. A Suggested Revision of the Fiji Sequence. *Journal of the Polynesian Society* 72:235–253.

Green, R. C. 1963b . Two Collections of Pottery from Sigatoka, Fiji. *Journal of the Polynesian Society* 72:261–64.

Green, R. C. 1967. The Immediate Origins of the Polynesians. In G. A. Highland, R. W. Force, A. Howard, M. Kelly and Y. H. Sinoto, eds, *Polynesian Culture History, Essays in Honor of Kenneth P. Emory*, pp.215–240. B. P. Bishop Museum Press, Honolulu.

Green, R. C. 1974 . A Review of Portable Artifacts from Western Samoa. In R. C. Green and J. M. Davidson, eds, *Archaeology in Western Samoa*, Vol. 2. pp. 245–275. Auckland Institute and Museum Bulletin 7, Auckland Institute and Museum, Auckland.

Green, R. C. 1976. Lapita Sites in the Santa Cruz Group. In R. C. Green and M. M. Cresswell, eds, *Southeast Solomon Islands Cultural History: A preliminary survey*, pp. 245–265. Bulletin 11, The Royal Society of New Zealand.

Green, R. C. 1979. Lapita. In J. D. Jennings, ed., *The Prehistory of Polynesia*, pp. 27–60. Australian National University Press, Canberra.

Green, R. C. 1981. Location of the Polynesian homeland: A continuing problem. In J. Hollyman and A. Pawley, eds, *Studies in Pacific Languages and Cultures in Honor of Bruce Biggs*, pp. 133–158. Linguistic Society of New Zealand, Auckland.

Green, R. C. and Palmer, J. B. 1964. Fiji Sequence: Corrections and Additional Notes for Sigatoka Sites. *Journal of the Polynesian Society* 73:328–333.

Groube, L. M. 1971. Tonga, Lapita pottery, and Polynesian origins. *Journal of the Polynesian Society* 80:278–316.

Gould, S. J. 1989 . *Wonderful Life: The Burgess Shale and the Nature of History*. Norton, New York.

Hale, H. 1846. *Narrative of the United States Exploring Expedition, during the years 1838, 1839, 1840, 1841, 1842, under the command of Charles Wilkes, U.S.N.* Vol. 6, Ethnography and Philology. C. Sherman, Philadelphia.

Herdrich, D. J. and Clark, J. T. 1993. Samoan *Tia 'ave* and Social Structure: Methodological and theoretical considerations. In M. W. Graves and R. C. Green, eds, *The Evolution and Organisation of Prehistoric Society in Polynesia*, pp. 52–63. New Zealand Archaeological Association Monograph 19, New Zealand Archaeological Association, Auckland.

Hirst, J. A. and Kennedy, E. M. 1962. Singatoka Iron Sands.

Economic Investigations No 1, Geological Survey Department, Suva, Fiji.

Hocart, A. M. 1929. *Lau Islands, Fiji*. Bernice P. Bishop Museum Bulletin No. 62, Bernice P. Bishop Museum, Honolulu.

Hocart, A. M. 1952. *The Northern States of Fiji*. Royal Anthropological Institute of Great Britain and Ireland Occasional Publication 11, The Institute, London.

Hocart, A. M. 1970. *Kings and Councillors*. University of Chicago Press, Chicago.

Howells, W. W. 1973. *The Pacific Islanders*. Scribner, New York.

Hudson, E. 1994. Sigatoka Dune Site Archaeological Rescue Project 1993. Unpublished report prepared for Fiji Museum, Suva. Auckland Uniservices Limited, Auckland, New Zealand.

Hughes, P. J., Hope, G. S., Latham, M. and Brookfield, H. G. 1979. Prehistoric Man-induced Degradation of the Lakeba Landscape: Evidence from two inland swamps. In H. G. Brookfield, ed., *Lakeba: Environmental Change, Population, and Resource Use*, pp. 93–111. UNESCO/UNFPA Island Reports 5, UNESCO/UNFPA, New York.

Hunt, T. L. 1980. Toward Fiji's Past: Archaeological research on southwestern Viti Levu. Unpublished MA thesis, University of Auckland.

Hunt, T. L. 1986. Conceptual and Substantive Issues in Fijian Prehistory. In P. V. Kirch, ed., *Island Societies: Archaeological approaches to evolution and transformation*, pp. 20–32. Cambridge University Press, Cambridge.

Hunt, T. L. 1987. Patterns of Human Interaction and Evolutionary Divergence in the Fiji Islands. *Journal of the Polynesian Society* 96:299–334.

Irwin, G.J. 1992. *The Prehistoric Exploration and Colonisation of the Pacific*. Cambridge University Press, Cambridge.

Irwin, G.J. 1993. Voyaging. In M. Spriggs, D. E. Yen, W. Ambrose, R. Jones, A. Thorne, and A. Andrews, eds, *A Community of Culture*, pp. 73–87. Occasional Papers in Prehistory 21, Research School of Pacific Studies, Australian National University, Canberra.

Kaeppler, A. 1978. Exchange Patterns in Goods and Spouses: Fiji, Tonga and Samoa. *Mankind* 11:246–252.

Kay, R. 1984. Analysis of Archaeological Material from Naigani. Unpublished MA thesis, University of Auckland.

Kirch, P. V. 1978 . The Lapitoid period in West Polynesia: Excavations and survey in Niuatoputapu, Tonga. *Journal of Field Archaeology* 5:1–13.

Kirch, P. V. 1984. *The Evolution of the Polynesian Chiefdoms*. Cambridge University Press, Cambridge.

Kirch, P. V. 1986. Rethinking East Polynesian prehistory. *Journal of the Polynesian Society* 95:9–40.

Kirch, P. V. 1988. *Niuatoputapu: The prehistory of a Polynesian chiefdom*. Thomas Burke Memorial Washington State Museum Monograph No. 5, The Burke Museum, Seattle.

Kirch, P. V. 1997. *The Lapita Peoples: Ancestors of the Oceanic world*. Blackwell, Cambridge, Mass.

Kirch, P. V. and Green, R. C. 1987. History, phylogeny, and evolution in Polynesia. *Current Anthropology* 28:431–456.

Kirch, P. V. and Hunt, T. L. 1988. The Spatial and Temporal Boundaries of Lapita. In P. V. Kirch and T. L. Hunt, eds, *The Archaeology of the Lapita Cultural Complex: A critical review*, pp. 9–31. Thomas Burke Memorial Washington State Museum Research Report 5, Thomas Burke Memorial Washington State Museum, Seattle.

Kuhlken, R. and Crosby, A. D. 1999. Agricultural Terracing at Nakauvadra, Viti Levu: A late prehistoric irrigated agrosystem in Fiji. *Asian Perspectives* 38:62–89.

Lambert, R. 1971. Botanical identification of impressions on archaeological potsherds from Sigatoka. *Records of the Fiji Museum* 1(5):123–148.

Lawlor, I. 1981. Report on an Archaeological Survey of Northern Lau, Fiji. Working Paper No. 60, Department of Anthropology, University of Auckland.

Leach, H. M. 1993. The Role of Major Quarries in Polynesian Prehistory. In M. W. Graves and R. C. Green, eds, *The Evolution an Organisation of Prehistoric Society in Polynesia*, pp. 33–42. New Zealand Archaeological Association Monograph 19, New Zealand Archaeological Association, Auckland.

Linton, R. 1955. *The Tree of Culture*. A. A. Knopf, New York.

Marshall, Y. M. 1985. Who Made the Lapita Pots? A case study in gender archaeology. *Journal of the Polynesian Society* 94:205–234.

Moser, S. 1998. *Ancestral Images: The iconography of human origins*. Sutton, Phoenix Mill, Gloucestershire.

Nunn, P. D. 1990. Coastal Processes and Landforms of Fiji: Their Bearing on Holocene Sea Level Changes in the South and West Pacific. *Journal of Coastal Research* 6: 279–310.

Nunn, P. D. 1994. *Environmental Change and the Early Settlement of Pacific Islands*. East–West Center Environment Series Working Paper 39.

Nunn, P. D. 1997. *Pacific Island Landscapes*. Institute of Pacific Studies, University of the South Pacific, Suva, Fiji.

Palmer, J. B. 1967. Archaeological sites of Wakaya Island. *Records of the Fiji Museum* Vol. 1, No. 2. Fiji Times Press, Suva.

Parry, J. B. 1969. Ring-Ditch Fortifications on Windward Viti Levu, Fiji. *Archaeology and Physical Anthropology in Oceania* 4:181–197.

Palmer, J. B., Shaw, E. Dickinson, P. and Sykes, M. 1968. Pottery-Making in Sigatoka, Fiji. *Records of the Fiji Museum*, Vol. 1, No. 3. Fiji Times Press, Suva.

Parry, J. T. 1977. *Ring-Ditch Fortifications. Ring-ditch fortifications in the Rewa Delta Fiji: Air photo interpretation and analysis*. Bulletin of the Fiji Museum 3, Fiji Museum, Suva.

Parry, J. T. 1982. *Ring-Ditch Fortifications. Ring-ditch fortifications in the Navua Delta Fiji: Air photo interpretation and analysis*. Bulletin of the Fiji Museum 7, Fiji Museum, Suva.

Parry, J. T. 1987. *The Sigatoka Valley: Pathway into Prehistory*. Bulletin of the Fiji Museum 9. Fiji Museum, Suva.

Pavlides, C. and Gosden, C. 1994. 35,000-year sites in the rainforests of West New Britain, Papua New Guinea. *Antiquity* 68:604–10.

Pawley, A. 1972. On the internal relationships of Eastern Oceanic languages. *Pacific Anthropological Records* 13:1–142.

Pawley, A. 1981. Melanesian Diversity and Polynesian Homogeneity: A unified explanation for language. In J. Hollyman and A. Pawley, eds, *Studies in Pacific Languages and Cultures in Honour of Bruce Biggs*, pp. 269–309. Linguistic Society of New Zealand, Auckland.

Petchey, F. 1994. Pottery and Stone Analysis. In E. Hudson Sigatoka Dune Site Archaeological Rescue Project 1993. Pp. 28–39.

Petchey, F. 1995 The Archaeology of Kudon: Archaeological Analysis of Lapita Ceramics from Mulifanua and Sigatoka, Fiji. MA Thesis, Department of Anthropology, University of Auckland.

Poulsen, J. 1967. A Contribution to the Prehistory of the Tongan Islands. Ph.D. dissertation, Australian National University.

Ravuvu, A. D. 1987. *The Fijian Ethos*. Institute of Pacific Studies, University of the South Pacific, Suva.

Rechtman, R. B. 1992. The Evolution of Sociopolitical Complexity in the Fiji Islands. Unpublished Ph.D. dissertation, University of California, Los Angeles.

Rosenthal, M. E. 1991. Realms and Ritual: The form and rise of *civitas* and *urbs* in southeastern Fiji. Unpublished Ph.D. dissertation, The University of Chicago.

Rossitto, R. 1987. Terrecotte Figine. Unpublished Ph.D. dissertation, Universita' Degli Studi di Urbino.

Rossitto, R. 1992. Fijian Pottery in a Changing World. *Journal of the Polynesian Society* 101:169–190.

Routledge, D. 1985. *Matanitu: The struggle for power in early Fiji.* Institute of Pacific Studies, University of the South Pacific, Suva.

Sahlins, M. D. 1958. *Social Stratification in Polynesia.* University of Washington Press, Seattle.

Sahlins, M. D. 1962. *Moala.* University of Michigan Press, Ann Arbor.

Sahlins, M. D. 1985. *Islands of History.* University of Chicago Press, Chicago.

Sahlins, M. D. 1990. The Return of the Event, Again. In A. Biersack, ed., *Clio in Oceania*, pp. 37–99. Smithsonian Institution Press, Washington D.C.

Sand, C. 1993. A Preliminary Study of the Impact of the Tongan Maritime Chiefdom on the Late Prehistoric Society of 'Uvea, Western Polynesia. In M.W. Graves and R.C. Green, eds, *The Evolution and Organisation of Prehistoric Society in Polynesia*, pp. 43–51. New Zealand Archaeological Association Monograph 19, New Zealand Archaeological Association, Auckland.

Serjeantson, S. W. and Hill, A. V. S. 1989. The Colonization of the Pacific: The genetic evidence. In A. V. S. Hill and S. W. Serjeantson, eds, *The Colonization of the Pacific: A Genetic Trail*, pp. 286–294. Clarendon Press, Oxford.

Shaw, E. 1967. A Reanalysis of Pottery from Navatu and Vuda, Fiji. Unpublished MA thesis, University of Auckland.

Shaw, E. n.d.. Prehistoric Sites of Taveuni. A preliminary survey. Unpublished typescript held by the Fiji Museum, Suva, Fiji.

Shepherd, M. J. 1988. The Higher-Energy Coasts of Southern Viti Levu, Fiji with Particular Reference to the Deuba Coast. *Journal of Pacific Studies* 14:1–19.

Shepherd, M. J. 1990. The Evolution of a Moderate Energy Coast in Holocene Time, Pacific Harbour, Viti Levu, Fiji. *New Zealand Journal of Geology and Geophysics* 33:547–566.

Sheppard, P. J. and Green, R. C. 1991. Spatial Analysis of the Nenumbo (SE-RF-2) Lapita Site, Solomon Islands. *Archaeology in Oceania* 29:53–68.

Smart, C. D. 1965. Preliminary Report on Archaeological Fieldwork in Kabara, Southern Lau Islands, Fiji. Unpublished report held at the Fiji Museum, Suva.

Smith, A. 1995. The Need for Lapita: Explaining change in the Late Holocene Pacific archaeological record. *World Archaeology* 26:366–379.

Spriggs, M. 1992. What Happens to Lapita in Melanesia? In J.C. Galipaud, ed., *Poterie Lapita et Peuplement*, pp.219–230. Actes du Colloque LAPITA, ORSTOM, Noumea.

Spriggs, M. 1997. *The Island Melanesians.* Blackwell, Oxford.

Terrell, J. E. 1997. The postponed agenda: archaeology and human biogeography in the twenty-first century. *Human Ecology* 25:419–436.

Terrell, J. E., Hunt, T. L. and Gosden, C. 1997. The Dimensions of Social Life in the Pacific: Human diversity and the myth of the primitive isolate. *Current Anthropology* 38:155–195.

Thompson, L. 1938. The Pottery of the Lau Group, Fiji. *Journal of the Polynesian Society* 47:109–112.

Vayda, A. P. and Rappaport, R. A. 1963. Island Cultures. In F. R. Fosberg, ed., *Man's Place in the Island Ecosystem*, pp. 133–144. Bishop Museum Press, Honolulu.

Visser, E. P. 1988. Hotel Masa Survey – Sigatoka. Unpublished report, Fiji Museum, Suva.

Visser, E. P. 1994. The Prehistoric People from Sigatoka: An Analysis of Skeletal and Dental Traits as Evidence of Adaptation. Ph.D. Dissertation, University of Otago, Dunedin.

Waterman, D. 1995 Saving the Sand Dunes of Sigatoka. Time Connections: A Quarterly Newsletter from the Friends of the Fiji Museum. Summer 1994–5, pp.2–3

Weisler, M., ed. 1997. *Prehistoric Long-Distance Interaction in Oceania: An interdisciplinary approach.* New Zealand Archaeological Association Monograph 21, New Zealand Archaeological Association, Auckland.

Wood, S., Marshall, Y. and Crosby, A. 1998. Mapping Sigatoka, Site VL 16/1: The 1992 field season and its implications. Unpublished report prepared for the Fiji Museum and the New Zealand High Commission, Suva.

Plate 1 Sigatoka Sand Dunes, August 1992. General view of the surveyed area. The view looks east from the high ridge which marks the western extent of the 1992 investigations, across to the Sigatoka River which exits just beyond the dunes. The high ridge can be seen in the background of Plate 2. The photograph shows the wedge shaped profile of the dunes, climbing steadily from east to west. An exposed palaeosol is visible as a dark outcrop high on the dunes to the left (left arrow). This is the Level 2 exposure located at approximately 1150M and 31 metres elevation. A low foredune covered in vegetation, runs along much of the seaward edge of the dunes (far right). Just to the left of this foredune, directly below the small vegetated knoll, a brown area indicates the location of the cultural remains shown in Plate 2 (right arrow).

Plate 2 Sigatoka Sand Dunes, August 1992. Exposed cultural remains. The photograph was taken at 630M and 2.5 metres elevation. It looks west to the high ridge from which Plate 1 was taken. In the foreground pottery and other cultural remains can be seen spilling from the eroding edges of the Level 1 and Level 2 palaeosols (right middle). This was the largest concentration of cultural material identified during the 1992 survey. The low foredune visible to the left lies along the high tide line and is the same dune visible on the far right of Plate 1.

Plate 3 Sigatoka Sand Dunes, August 1992. Surveying in the upper baseline. Shannon Wood, Sepeti Matararaba and Yvonne Marshall survey in the upper baseline (Baseline 2) which ran along the steep upper slopes of the dunes. The station is set up over the 300M point. Shannon Wood looks west along the 100 metre tape, past Sepeti Matararaba who is steadying the tape against the wind. The theodolite is set up over a plywood base to prevent it sinking into the loose sands.

Plate 4 Sigatoka Sand Dunes, August 1992. Checking the accuracy of the baselines. View of Vasiti Ritova and Sepeti Matararaba running a perpendicular transect between the lower and upper baselines at the 600M point. Because the surface of the dunes consists of endlessly shifting sand, survey station points were constantly checked by chaining and plumbing in multiple steps down the steep dune slopes between the baselines. This was only possible during rare, wind free periods. The dune visible in the background is the same foredune that runs along the high tide line in Plates 1, 2 and 3.

Plate 5 Sigatoka Sand Dunes, August 1992. The eroding edge of the Level 3 palaeosol. The photograph is taken from the eastern end of the eroding Level 3 palaeosol, located at the high tide line at 80M (see Fig. 4.2a). The driftwood in the foreground marks the storm surge line. The view looks north and west along the dune where the exposed Level 3 palaeosol can be seen curving high onto the dunes. The palaeosol slopes down steeply from west to east (left to right) and from north to south. Feature 6, an eroding area of pottery, stone and carbonised wooden posts lies just below the saddle in the dune crest (arrow). A large eroding lovo (oven) lies high on the dunes to the left. It is located at 200M. The logs in the middle foreground mark the approximate position of Burial B92 A. The photograph reproduced in Burley 1997: Fig. 23 shows the same scene in 1996, but taken from slightly higher on the dune.

Plate 6 Sigatoka Sand Dunes, September 1992. Sea erosion at the eastern end of the surveyed area. General view from the east of the eastern section of the dunes showing the area 0–200M. Waves have broken through the foredune and formed a lagoon, which extends up to 200 metres inland of the foredune. The Level 3 palaeosol shown in Plate 5 extends up the dune slope from the lagoon edge, curves through the dark exposure of Feature 6 situated in front of the high dune crest (right arrow), and passes above the lovo visible as a small crest on the skyline above Sepeti Matararaba's head. The fenced area of Burial Ground 1 lies beside the lagoon in the middle background (left arrow). By August 1993 the area of the lagoon and most of Burial Ground 1 had been washed away.

Plate 7 Sigatoka Sand Dunes, August 1992. General view of the surveyed area of the dunes from the east. The view looks west from a remnant of foredune located at 250M and 3.9 metres elevation (see Fig. 4.2b). The green/brown basal sand shows in the centre foreground. The bamboo post on the far right marks burial B91/1. The driftwood to the left of this post protects exposed bone associated with Burial Ground 2. The eroding edge of the Level 2 palaeosol (not visible) extends from the post and passes beneath the dune crest in the middle of the photograph (located at approximately 550M). It then climbs high up the dune slopes to the right of the high dune crest in the background. Although storm waves had washed away part of the foredune when this photograph was taken, the dune slope below Burial Ground 2 remained relatively gentle. The foredune further west remained intact and is the same foredune that can also be seen in Plates 1–4.

Plate 8 Sigatoka Sand Dunes, 1965 or 1966, showing Helen and Lawrence Birks' excavations in progress. The excavators are working north into the steep dune face and throwing their spoil behind them. The darker sand of what is probably Level 1 is visible at the bottom of the west baulk. Photo courtesy of the University of Auckland Photo Archive.

0 2 4 6 8 10 12
Inches

Plate 9 Flat bottomed dish or tray from Level 2 at Sigatoka. Photo originally published by R. C. Green 1963, Journal of the Polynesian Society, Volume 72, p.260 Plate 1.

Plate 10 Sigatoka Sand Dunes, 1988. The photograph looks west across the excavation of Burial Ground 1. The coral mounds overlying Burial Groups B15, 16 and 17 are to the right, and Groups 18 and 19 are to the left. In the background, the western baulk shows the steeply angled laminations of a striated, wind-deposited (eolian) sand layer, which overlies Level 2.

Plate 11 Sigatoka Sand Dunes, 1988. General view of the excavation of Burial Ground 1, taken from high on the dunes and looking south. Burial Groups B15–19, shown in Plate 10, can be seen exposed between the blue and white tarpaulins. In the left background is the tea shelter. Behind the excavations, the exposed surface of Level 2 shows up as a compact brown sand dotted with eroded cultural remains. In the foreground is loose grey sand. As shown in Plates 6 and 7, the substantial foredune visible in the background of this photo had almost completely disappeared by 1992.

Plate 12 Sigatoka Sand Dunes, 1988. General view of the excavation of Burial Ground 1 looking southwest. The brown sand around the tarpaulin is the exposed surface of Level 2. Only a few metres from this exposed surface, Simon Best and Sepeti Matararaba use a soil probe to search for the continuation Level 2 beneath deep deposits of loose wind blown sand.

Plate 13 Sigatoka Sand Dunes, December 1993. General view looking east along the dunes of the rescue excavations directed by Elisabeth Hudson. The excavation in progress is of Trench 1. The lower cliff layer (Level 2) is exposed just beneath the excavators and the upper cliff layer (Level 3) can be seen in the foreground just above the excavations. Photo by Hamish Macdonald.

Plate 14 Sigatoka Sand Dunes, May 1994. General view of the surveyed area of the dunes from the east. The photograph looks west from a position at approximately 300M and 12 metres

elevation. When this photograph was taken, following Cyclone Kina, storm waves had stripped away the lower slopes of the dunes in the eastern half of the surveyed area. The location of B91/1, marked by a bamboo pole in Plate 7, is now immediately seaward of the Level 2 palaeosol "cliff face" seen exposed on the far left (see arrow). Hudson excavated this vertical "cliff face" in December 1993. Early and late Lapita pottery was found eroding along with Level 2 pottery from this cliff face exposure indicating that Level 2 and Level 1 were conflated on this section of the dunes. In the middle foreground the newly exposed Level 3 curves down towards and then away from the Level 1/2 exposure. The western section of the surveyed area remained largely unaffected although the foredune visible in Plates 1–4 and 7 had been removed along the full length of the seaward edge. By the time of Burley's survey in 1996, however, the lower dune slopes had also been washed away to the west, up to the base of the low dune crest in the middle of the photograph.

Plate 15 Sigatoka Sand Dunes, November 1997. General view of the surveyed area of the dunes from the east. The photograph looks west from approximately 250M. It shows how in the interval between 1994 and 1997 the sand has begun to accumulate again. The bamboo pole in Plate 7, the arrow in Plate 14 and the arrow in Plate 15 all indicate approximately the same location. The arrow in Plate 15 indicates the eroding edge of the Level 2 palaeosol. All evidence of the eroding Level 3 palaeosol visible in Plate 14 has disappeared beneath drift sand. As shown in Plate 14, in 1994 the high tide line came right up to the eroding face of the Level 2 palaeosol. However, by 1997, as can be seen in this photograph sand and driftwood have built up the area between the eroding palaeosol and the sea.

Plate 16 Sigatoka Sand Dunes, August 1992. View of exposed soil profile and eroding pottery behind the dunes on Beach Ridge 3. The photograph looks due south from the Club Masa road to the back of the dunes. It shows the approximate location of Testpit 3 on Beach Ridge 3. The top of Beach Ridge 2 cuts off the view of the lower part of the sand dunes. Sand mining has caused the vertical cuts into the steep back of the dunes, visible in the background. Sand lorries using the road shown in the foreground and driving across the beach ridges have now destroyed the site on Beach Ridge 3.

Plate 17 Sigatoka Sand Dunes, August 1992. View to the east along the series of beach ridges located on farm land behind the dunes. Three beach ridges running parallel to the dunes are visible between the back of the dunes and the house to the left. Beach Ridge 1 lies along the base of the dunes with Beach Ridges 2 and 3 to the left. Testpits were excavated on these ridges as indicated by the arrows. The house marks the edge of Kulukulu village and lies on a fourth ridge. A further ridge, located to the right of Beach Ridge 1, has now been buried beneath the advancing back-slope of the dunes. As can be seen in the photograph, ploughing has disturbed the beach ridges. A paleo-cut bank, marking an old bank of the Sigatoka River, crosses the photograph just above the arrows marking the Testpits. It extends from Kulukulu village, passing beneath the dunes to the right and is visible as a change in vegetation colour from light to dark green. Plate 18, which shows this old riverbank, was taken from just in front of the trees at the corner of Kulukulu village. Club Masa is located in the background.

Plate 18 Sigatoka Sand Dunes, November 1997. View of the old riverbank behind the dunes. The photograph looks due south to the steeply sloping back of the sand dunes. The old riverbank runs down the centre of the photograph. It slopes from the brown, higher and dryer ground of the beach ridges down to the to the green vegetation the lower flood plain. The old Club Masa road, now eroded and disused, runs along the upper edge. Arrows mark the approximate locations of Testpit 2 on Beach Ridge 2, and Testpit 3 on Beach Ridge 3. The precise location of Testpit 3 has been completely eroded.